Praise for *Calling the Rain*

"From its preface to the conclusion, *Calling the Rain: Memoir of an American Woman in Africa,* by Sandra Mahaniah, is an important account of one person's engagement with one African country. The Democratic Republic of the Congo, also known as the Belgian Congo and Zaire, coveted for its mineral wealth by both the US and the USSR, the fourth most populous country in Africa and the most populous French-speaking country in existence, endured a long history of colonial and Cold War intervention, the impact of which continues to manifest itself. Set in a country struggling to emerge as a truly independent nation, Sandra Mahaniah's memoir of her life and nation-building work there from the late 1960s to the early 1990s is truly riveting, absorbing reading."

David L. Easterbrook, Curator Emeritus, Herskovits Library of African Studies, Northwestern University

"In *Calling the Rain, A Memoir of an American Woman's Life in Congo*, Sandra Mahaniah evokes the lost idealism of an era. Eschewing her sheltered midwestern upbringing and its immutable racism, she marries an African from Zaire (now Congo) and they travel to his homeland to start a new life and change the world. Armed with passionate determination, Mahaniah learns to survive with limited resources in the bush, teach in missionary systems rife with post-colonial favoritism, and embrace a communal culture rich in natural beauty, ritual, and ceremony. Delicately weaving the personal and the political, we feel the pain of her growing, inter-cultural family's plight–whether by malarial scares or political unrest–along with the destabilizing chaos of both the Mobutu regime and her own marriage. Powerful, impassioned, and inspiring, this is a gorgeously written memoir for anyone who has ever attempted to make a difference or is seeking wisdom from someone who has. Highly recommend!"

Lissa Franz, author and memoir workshop teacher

"One always wonders: a young woman takes a chance on a new life and love in a dangerous place and bets on the odds of her own fate. The decades pass, the improbable marriage is tested, and somehow, when the world falls apart, the wisdom remains. So Sandra Mahaniah traveled from Minnesota to Kinshasa, to Democratic Republic of Congo, to marry and raise a family. In this riveting account, she gives us a tale of tempestuous days and personal triumphs, and finds redemption in her survival."

Jacki Lyden, author of the memoir ***Daughter of the Queen of Sheva,***
former NPR host

"*Calling the Rain* is a brave, searching memoir—one that resists tidy answers to a life lived against expectation. With clarity and candor, Mahaniah traces the convergence of love, rebellion, political awakening, and motherhood that shaped her decisions. This is a compelling portrait of intimacy across cultures and generations, and a powerful meditation on choice, consequence, and the lifelong work of understanding one's own story."

Kristian Bair, author of ***Clementine Crane Prefers Not To***

CALLING THE RAIN

Minneapolis, Minnesota

FIRST EDITION 2026

Calling the Rain: Memoir of an American Woman in Congo.

ISBN: 978-1-962834-75-9
10 9 8 7 6 5 4 3 2 1

Cover artwork Adam Cohn
Book cover and book design Gary Lindberg

CALLING THE RAIN

MEMOIR OF AN AMERICAN WOMAN IN CONGO

SANDRA MAHANIAH

Minneapolis, Minnesota

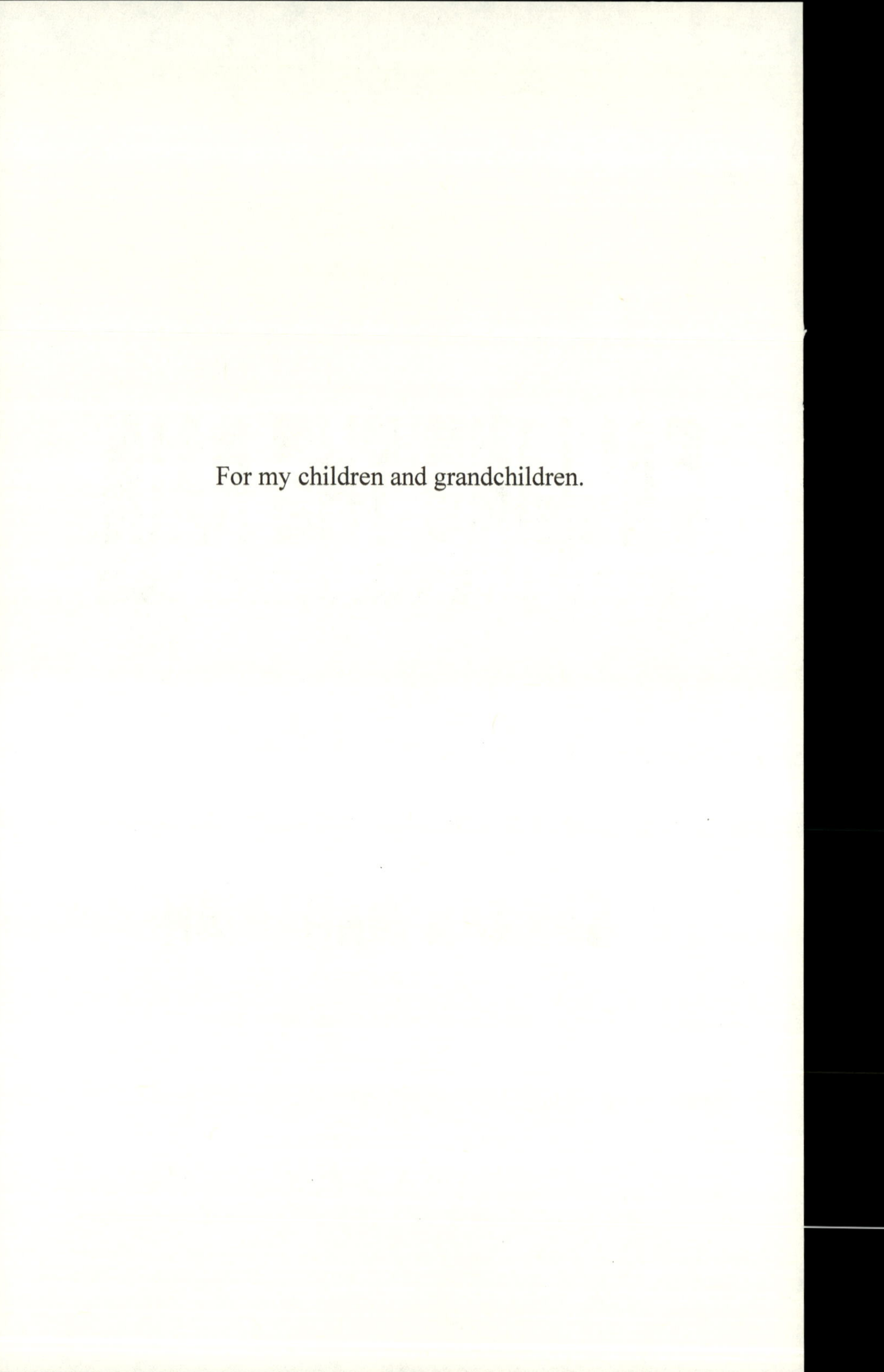

For my children and grandchildren.

Vo tumisi mvula, mankondo sikila.

If you've called the rain to come, tie up your banana trees.

(Prepare for the consequences of your actions.)

—Kongo proverb

Table of Contents

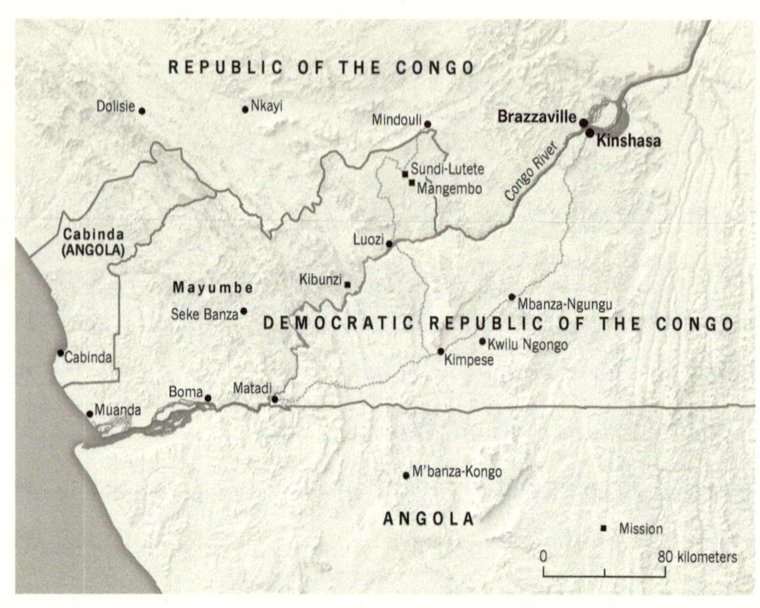
REPUBLIC OF THE CONGO
Dolisie
Nkayi
Mindouli
Brazzaville
Kinshasa
Sundi-Lutete
Mangembo
Congo River
Cabinda
(ANGOLA)
Luozi
Kibunzi
Mayumbe
Seke Banza
Mbanza-Ngungu
DEMOCRATIC REPUBLIC OF THE CONGO
Kwilu Ngongo
Kimpese
Cabinda
Boma
Matadi
Muanda
M'banza-Kongo
ANGOLA
Mission
0
80 kilometers

Preface

What would cause a sheltered young woman from a Midwestern suburb to marry an African student and move to Africa? I never developed a satisfying response to that question, no matter how many times I heard it over the nearly sixty years since my marriage in 1968. I often asked myself the same question. Searching for the answer provided the principal motivation for writing this memoir. "I fell in love" is a small part of the story. "I wanted to save the world" is another part, but the rest is far more complicated, involving the spirit of rebellion that infused young people of that era, forging ethics outside a religion that I rejected, and a need to wrest control of my life away from parents determined to keep it. I want my children to know what led their father and me to the decisions that shaped their unusual childhood. Documenting the history of those years was a secondary but equally compelling reason. Few books about daily life in Zaire during the 1960s and 1970s have been written in English, and not many more in French. I want to describe what life was like for me in an African family, not in an expatriate bubble. Americans hear about Zaire only when violence breaks out, or when an epidemic or a natural disaster occurs.

Congo (called Zaire from 1971 to 1998) certainly has seen more than its share of wars, rebellions and epidemics. Yet during much of the time I lived there, I felt safer than I did in an average American city. My husband's clan welcomed me, and I came to love them and the rich culture of the Kongo, an ethnic group that populates the western region of the Democratic Republic of Congo, the Republic of Congo to the north and Angola to the south. The strong bonds of the extended family, the pop music all of Africa dances to, the painting and sculpture that can take your breath away—none of that shows up in news reports, academic studies or diplomatic dispatches. I miss it still.

I lived and traveled only in Kinshasa and the region west of it, and even that small area is full of scenic wonders: the Congo River, Zongo Falls, Kisantu's Botanical Gardens, the Crystal Mountains, the beach at Moanda, and even in the cities, a wealth of exotic plants. For American readers, the setting of the story is dramatic, even exotic. Still, my story is intensely personal, with a marriage, children, obstacles, triumphs and the consequences of decisions made in my twenties. My children, my parents and my sisters have had to face those consequences as much as I have. We are all still living it. A Kikongo proverb says, "A marriage may end, but the in-law relationship never dies."

The Democratic Republic of Congo has a complicated history. At the end of this book is a short summary of that history. You may want to refer to it if you find the chronology confusing.

Note on Names

The Democratic Republic of Congo has had several names in its modern history. Some major cities and regions changed names in 1966. In this memoir, I use the name in use during the relevant time period.

Country

Date Span	Country Name
1908–1960	Belgian Congo
1960–1971	Democratic Republic of Congo (or Congo)
1971–1997	Republic of Zaire (or Zaire)
1977–Present	Democratic Republic of Congo (or Congo)

Cities

Before 1966	After 1966
Leopoldville	Kinshasa
Stanleyville	Kisangani
Elisabethville	Lubumbashi

Regions

1908–1971	1971–2013
Katanga	Shaba
Bas-Congo	Bas-Zaire
Kivu	Kivu

Chapter 1
Dangerous Places

In December of 1967, I walked across the hot tarmac to the metal staircase fifty feet away and boarded the Air Congo flight to Kinshasa, the only flight operating between Uganda and the capital of Congo. The last to board, I found my seat near the front, behind a White couple with their teenage son—Americans. I knew from a look at their clothes and shoes. I sat as far away as possible from the noisy group of young African men in the back, who had clearly indulged themselves at the airport bar. I'd been in Africa three months—long enough to know not to smile. They stared at me curiously for a moment before resuming their conversation.

When the American woman saw me, she tried to hide her surprise.

"I'm Cathy Anderson," she said, "and this is my husband Bart and my son Jason. We're Baptist missionaries going back to our post. Why are you going to Kinshasa?"

A burst of laughter caused us both to turn around. The men were talking loudly with the Zairian flight attendant. She too was alone.

"We're musicians," one of the men said in French. "We're going back home after playing for a week here." At least I thought that was what he said.

Cathy, the Missionary, frowned in disapproval.

"You'd best steer clear of that group," Cathy said. "Is someone meeting you in Kinshasa?"

"My fiancé," I said. "He's Zairian, a teacher in the countryside."

She nodded, her expression carefully neutral, and glanced again at the musicians. "The airport can be... well... difficult sometimes. We'll try to watch out for you after we land in case you run into any trouble."

"Thank you," I said. Jackson had not written anything about the airport, so I had no idea what she was talking about, except that I already knew how unpredictable African airports could be. I had faked imminent fainting to get through Customs when I first arrived in Nairobi. I had more immediate concerns about the dance band ten rows behind us.

After we took off and the flight attendant served the musicians a second round of drinks, she stopped by my seat and asked, "*Vous parlez français?* (Do you speak French?)"

"*Oui.*" A slight exaggeration.

"*Voulez-vous voir la cabine? Suivez-moi.*"

I asked her to repeat the question, unsure that I had understood her correctly, but yes, she had indeed asked me if I wanted to see the cockpit. She led the way, while Cathy's stare bored into my back.

The young flight crew—pilot, co-pilot and navigator—greeted me as I came through the door.

"Hallo, hallo, welcome! Look at this view!" said the co-pilot, gesturing to the large windscreen in front of us. Below, an expanse of dense forest extended to the horizon, with mountains poking up in the distance.

"It's spectacular. But am I really supposed to be here?"

"No, but not to worry," said the slim blond navigator cheerfully. He looked younger than the others. They all had British accents. "We had to ask you what on earth you are doing on this flight. We couldn't believe it when we saw you board."

"I'm meeting my fiancé for Christmas vacation. I'm a student at University College in Nairobi."

The co-pilot nodded. "Ah, I see. You look younger, actually." He thought for a moment.

"Listen," he said, "the airport in Kinshasa can be really rough—soldiers confiscating luggage, demanding bribes, arresting people, harassing women, that kind of thing. Does your guy have any political connections?"

"Not that I know of," I said.

"You're sure he'll be there?"

"Yes, he wrote that he would."

"Even so… we can't just leave you on your own," he said. "Tell you what. We get through passport control and customs really fast, so we'll wait to make sure you've found your guy. If we don't see you come out, we'll come in looking for you."

"That's very kind of you."

Before boarding the plane, I wasn't afraid; now I began to wonder why the Kinshasa airport had everyone so concerned.

West of the Virunga mountains, the wide, greenish-brown Congo River appeared below, snaking in wide curves through the rain forest, then through the savannah. The flight attendant took me back to my seat for the landing.

"Good luck!" the pilot called.

Walking out of the plane felt like getting into a warm bath. No signs guided passengers to Arrivals—I just followed everyone else across the tarmac, dodging baggage carts and other airport vehicles. Scattered across the airfield in the near distance stood small private planes and military aircraft.

The immigration agent barely glanced at me, flipped through my passport, and stamped it with an officious flourish before handing it back. I joined the other passengers in the small baggage area. At least a dozen armed soldiers stood around in small groups. I heard them muttering *mwana missionnaire* (missionary child) as I passed. Would the missionaries have lied to them? Certainly the British flight crew would have. Possibly the soldiers simply assumed it—few young women, White or Black, traveled alone to Kinshasa. It was hardly a tourist attraction, and not a transport hub either. Their assumption made for a convenient fiction. Later, I learned that missionaries had a reputation for not paying bribes and haggling so much that it wasn't worth the soldiers' time. Arresting missionaries also brought unwanted attention from foreign diplomats and high-level politicians, so masquerading as a missionary child carried protection I didn't even know I needed.

I picked up my small suitcase from the single, short conveyor belt. In Customs, which I dreaded most, soldiers assessed informal customs duties on the musicians' flashy clothes, big new cameras and designer watches. They focused on a band member with a large camera around his neck, who argued with them volubly in Lingala. I didn't see the missionary family. One of the soldiers waved me through with a flick of his AK–47. Just outside the exit, I saw Jackson. In the throng of dark faces jostling around the exit, he stood out as if lit by a spotlight. I felt a surge of relief and elation as feelings and memories sprang to life from my subconscious, where I had pushed them while I dealt with the purely practical effort required just to get this far. He was the reason I had come. I waved to the flight crew, who waited nearby as promised. They waved back and left.

In Congo, as in Kenya, men and women did not show affection in public, so we shared only a quick embrace.

"We need to get a taxi," Jackson said. A dozen drivers swarmed around us, trying to grab my suitcase. Jackson fended them off and started to bargain. In Kenya, the taxis—all the same color, by law—had meters, although people joked about how well they worked. I watched him carefully.

"You bargain for a taxi?" I asked.

"We bargain for everything here," he said, and pointed to the chosen driver. The taximan he selected led us a hundred feet away to a dusty parking lot. Armed soldiers prevented cars from parking any closer. Once in the taxi, we held hands, strangely subdued, constrained by the taximan and by that speechlessness that comes over lovers who have lived apart too long—since July, when Jackson graduated from Kalamazoo and came back to Congo.

Crowds of people walked briskly on the shoulders of the two-lane road—there were no sidewalks. Most of the women and some men carried baskets, bags, beer crates and occasionally single bottles balanced on their heads. Often a woman also had a child on her back, secured by a piece of cloth knotted over her chest. Trucks, buses, taxi-buses and a few private cars competed for road space with *pousse-pousseurs* pulling metal hand carts as big as a car. Occasional clusters of small shops, markets and roadside stands lined the road, selling everything from onions to tennis shoes. Murals in a unique pop-art style adorned many walls, and everywhere Congolese pop music blared from radios and loudspeakers. Behind the shops, vast residential neighborhoods of single-story houses and shacks stretched farther than I could see.

"My sister lives near here," Jackson said. "Another day we'll visit her."

We drove for half an hour before reaching a major cross street. Traffic grew heavier, and even more pedestrians thronged the roads. Gendarmes in small metal towers directed traffic at major intersections. We passed dingy colonial buildings and a few new ones, mostly under construction. Downtown Kinshasa had few modern buildings, and, like Nairobi, still looked much as it had during the not-so-distant colonial past. The taxi stopped in front of the Memling Hotel, a musty colonial landmark on the Boulevard du Trente Juin, the main thoroughfare of downtown Kinshasa, named for the date of the country's independence, June 30, 1960. The sallow-faced Belgian hotel clerk asked for my passport and studied it carefully before handing it back with a contemptuous look. We walked across a hotel courtyard filled with tropical plants to our room. An ancient air conditioner whirred in the corner, but the late-afternoon air remained hot and stuffy. Jackson tried to adjust it and gave up. It didn't occur to either of us to complain to the Front Desk, certain as we were of a shrug in response.

At last we could embrace for real. We made love until darkness fell and hunger pulled us across the street to an outdoor café.

Jackson gestured to the waiter as he asked, "How was the flight? You never know with Air Congo."

"Fine. A little odd." I told him about my would-be protectors, and asked, "Why were they so concerned?"

"Soldiers always want money, and foreign embassies have complained. The Government is trying to improve the situation, but there are still problems."

"What about harassing women?"

"I never heard anything like that. But I wouldn't be surprised."

"You didn't write me about that," I said.

"Sometimes it's better not to know ahead of time. You know how to protect yourself."

"I'm not as sure of that as you are."

"If you didn't come out with the rest of the passengers, I would have found you."

My sandwich order came with mayonnaise instead of ketchup for the accompanying French fries. I made a face.

Jackson smiled. "Belgian taste. They always eat mayonnaise with French fries."

After we ate, I ordered a beer, Jackson a Coke.

"Coke? Really?" He drank plenty of beer in college.

"I don't drink alcohol anymore," he said. "In the countryside, there is a lot of jealousy, and when people drink alcohol, they don't pay attention if someone tries to put something in their drink."

"You really think someone would want to poison you?"

"I am the first Congolese teacher with a university degree at Sundi. Many people are envious. Did you have a problem getting a visa?"

"With the Congolese Consulate? Yes. I liked Kampala though."

I explained that the only Congolese Consulate in East Africa was in Kampala. None of my Ugandan friends lived in the city, so they advised me to stay at a mission hostel. All eight hostel residents shared two bathrooms. We had family style meals in a common dining hall. In the evenings I could hear a children's choir down the hill in the chapel. The only lock on my room was a hook-and-eye closure on a screen door. Although the Mission had guards, it was scary compared to Nairobi where all the doors and windows were barred and locked. Early each morning, a waiter in a long Sudanese robe brought tea to my room. Everyone else left their doors open so that the waiter could bring tea to their bedsides, but I put on a bathrobe and took it from him at the door. The differences between Kampala and Nairobi surprised me. Every morning I took an hour-long bus ride to the Congolese Consulate. Hardly anyone came in or out of the Consul's office except his Asian secretary, but he said he was "too busy" to see me. Another woman, a European with heavy makeup, sat at her desk and read the paper all day long. I guessed she was probably the Consul's mistress. The only other person who came into the office during that week was a young man who had left Zaire the year before and wanted to go back. The Consul probably suspected, as I did, that he had been fighting in one of the guerilla groups in Eastern Congo. After six days, the Consul's secretary felt sorry for me and called me in to the Consul's office. The Consul told me to come back the next day for my visa. When I thanked him, he said, "Do you have something to give me?" I pretended innocence and confusion, and he gave up. I knew what he wanted, but I didn't have much money and didn't like to give bribes unless I had no choice. He gave me my multiple entry visa the next day.

"I can't believe you got it without paying anything," Jackson said. "You *do* know how to take care of yourself."

* * *

The next morning we went grocery shopping with a Dutch teacher, Jaap, and his wife Grete, who were staying at the Mission Hostel nearby. As we entered the small grocery store, I saw two young men walking by, watching a third man on the other side of the street.

"Hey, aren't those your pants?" one of the two said in French.

They turned around and walked toward the third man, who took off running.

The shop had many shelves of canned peas and little else, but Grete managed to fill half a grocery cart. As we left the store, I saw the same two young men walking back, one of them now holding a pair of pants and a belt.

"Did those two just steal the pants off the other guy?" I asked Jackson.

"Maybe they're taking back what was stolen from them," he said.

Nothing there was what it seemed. Where else, I wondered, would I see two men steal the pants off someone in broad daylight, with no one intervening? I should have taken that as a warning.

The next day we went to stay with Jackson's uncle, an educated man and pastor of a large Protestant church, in the family's comfortable bungalow. Uncle Biandudi had spent time in the US and spoke very good English. He introduced me to his oldest daughter, a merchant. The family was very welcoming, but Uncle's wife didn't speak French or English, so we couldn't talk. In the evening, we all sat outside on the open veranda. Crowds of young men walked by, arguing fiercely.

"Are they coming from a political meeting?" I asked.

Everyone laughed. "A soccer match," Jackson said. "People get emotional about their teams."

We planned to take a train the next day to Kimpese, where Jackson had attended the region's most prestigious Protestant high school, run by a coalition of American and European missionaries. At the ticket window, a crowd of Congolese clamored for the clerk's attention, no foreigners among them. There was no queue—it was every man for himself shoving to get to the window. I waited in the back of the room, and eventually Jackson emerged from the fray with two first-class tickets.

The train dated from the 1950s. Each European-style compartment opened off an aisle and could seat six people. Our compartment was half-empty, and no one spoke to us. Jackson lifted a young woman's suitcase onto the overhead rack. She glanced at it without comment.

"No manners," he murmured. Everyone sweated in the heat. Even though I was the only White person on the train, nobody paid any attention to me.

The train moved at little more than walking speed through the hilly savannah. At one point, hundreds of people waited at a junction. I could see a large open-air market atop a nearby hill and heard its surprisingly loud roar. Women in colorful traditional clothes with baskets on their heads and babies on their backs waited for the train to pass. I felt as though I were looking through a window into African life of the 19th century.

"What is that?" I asked, pointing to men carrying glass jugs of milky liquid on their heads.

"*Lungwila.* Moonshine, made from sugar cane."

When we got off the train six hours later, we saw no one at the Kimpese station. Jackson managed to find a man with a hand cart—a *pousse-pousseur*—who agreed to take our suitcases to the nearby Protestant mission.

"I want you to meet another American who married a Mukongo," Jackson said as we walked. "He's the pastor at the Kimpese church and used to be my teacher here. His first wife died in childbirth. When he went to the States with his daughter, he married Janet."

Most of the mission houses were built in the 1950s and resembled simple American ranch houses, made of red brick with tile floors. The missionary builders used as little wood as possible because of the prevalence of termites and other wood-boring insects.

"These houses were reserved for missionaries until a few years ago," Jackson said. "Even now, I had to fight to get a missionary house where I'm teaching."

"Where did they expect you to live?"

"Housing for African teachers," he said. "Those houses are much smaller and closer together, half a mile away, with no indoor plumbing."

"Segregation here too," I said.

"Did you expect anything else? Americans, British and Swedes ran these missions. But here it's changing faster than in America."

At the pastor's house, we shook hands with everyone, including the children and a woman nursing a baby.

"Janet is in the hospital. She'll be back tomorrow," Pastor Jean Massamba said. "She had a minor medical procedure and has a little malaria." He spoke of malaria as if it were a common cold. When she returned the next day, Janet and I walked around the mission, and she described her life in it. I couldn't figure her out—she didn't seem unhappy, but she wasn't particularly enthusiastic about anything either. By this time the entire trip seemed like a weird dream: the warm-bath atmosphere, myriad languages swirling around me with only the occasional French word, the strange, colorful clothes, the hypnotic music that blared from every radio. And yet I felt completely comfortable and assured of Jackson's ability to navigate it all.

He found us a ride back to Kinshasa with a missionary family—two and a half hours in a car instead of six on the train, even with all the roadblocks. In late 1967, there was fighting in much of Eastern Congo, some of it involving South African mercenaries. That was the excuse, anyway—the real reason for the roadblocks was probably to keep the army busy and allow them to solicit bribes from drivers to supplement their meager income. We saw other drivers arguing with the soldiers, but they didn't try to shake down the missionaries. From the Protestant Mission Hostel, we took a taxi to Jackson's sister's house near the airport, about forty minutes from downtown Kinshasa. Jackson directed the taxi onto a dirt road and through a maze of unpaved streets to a neighborhood of small houses, mostly made of handmade clay bricks. We saw no other cars, moving or parked. It was early afternoon on Sunday, and the family was still at church when we arrived. Friendly neighbors brought out chairs for us, but there was no shade. Under our feet, the soil was almost pure sand. A few scraggly trees marked the corners of the property, and I could see the yard was large by Zairian standards, probably twenty-five meters square and utterly barren, like all the other, smaller yards in the neighborhood. Boys played with balls of string instead of soccer balls. Girls played a clapping and jumping game that resembled Paper, Stone or Scissors.

"They'll be back soon," called a neighbor. She bantered with Jackson for a while and then gestured to me.

"She wants to know what you'll do if I marry a second wife," he said, translating.

"As long as I am the head wife, that would be all right," I lied.

She laughed. Back in Nairobi, when I thought about her comment later, I realized she wasn't just engaging in pleasant banter. She was giving me a warning of what might happen. I had yet to learn how few men in Congo remained with one woman.

"My brother-in-law is the head of an independent church," Jackson said, "in the tradition of the prophet Kimbangu. He has maybe two hundred followers."

I read about Kimbangu, founder of an independent church in the 1920s. During his short preaching career, thousands of people in the Kongo Central province left their villages and their work with the colonial administration to follow him. Recognizing the political implications of any mass movement, the Belgians arrested him, convicted him of sedition, and sent him to prison, first in the northeast. And when he converted not only prisoners but guards to his beliefs, they sent him to the south, near the Zambian border. He converted prisoners and guards there too. A Belgian guard snapped the only known photograph of him there before he died in 1951. In 1959, the colonial government officially recognized the church. After Independence, the church grew to nearly a million members. By 1967 it had over five million.

Kimbangu was the most successful of many religious leaders generally called "prophets"—so called not because they foretold the future but because they awakened the consciousness of people to their true spiritual nature and the obligation to lead a moral life. Tata Pascal, Jackson's brother-in-law, was one of these leaders, although during the week he worked as a foreman for a construction company.

Eventually Jackson's sister Suzanne arrived with the children and unlocked the door to the house, but we stayed outside. She didn't look like her brother at all. She had fine, small features and a slim, delicate build. Tata Pascal arrived a little later, resplendent in a white cap and robes. Curious neighbors came to greet Tata Pascal and his unusual visitors. Some men wore the traditional *pagne* cloth wrapped in a kind of pantaloon. The house was so tiny I wondered where they all slept. The place had all the trappings of poverty, from an American point of view. Yet Tata Pascal was a wealthy man by local standards. He owned his house and several other plots of land and had a good job. Even in the relatively good economic times of the late '60s, not many men could make those claims. He followed his own teachings: monogamy, abstinence from alcohol, and strict adherence to the Ten Commandments. He clearly enjoyed great respect in his neighborhood.

We had soft drinks, and Jackson conversed with Tata Pascal and his neighbors for a couple of hours. I couldn't follow the conversation in Kikongo and spent the time observing the neighborhood. On the surface, it was unprepossessing: sand, dust, simple cinderblock buildings with corrugated metal roofs, and little vegetation. All the neighbors knew each other. Children roamed freely, unhindered by traffic or fear of crime. Boys played soccer in streets marked only by the residents' makeshift borders of bushes and rocks. Mothers often interrupted the girls' games so that they could help run errands or do housework.

Two days later, I boarded an Air Congo flight back to Nairobi.

* * *

Jackson showed me life in Congo exactly the way it would be if I married him, and on the surface it was not an attractive picture. Yet the warmth and energy of the people, the sense of common culture, the potential of the country, and even the music, drew me in. I admired Jackson's own commitment to his people. On this visit I saw for the first time how different his behavior was from other Congolese—more restrained, more thoughtful. He said and did exactly what he said he would do, everything pointing toward his most important goals. I asked myself: Was I so in love that I would go anywhere with Jackson? Or was my need to escape America's racism and my inability to change it so great that I ignored common sense? Was I so fearful of succumbing to my parents' control that I was running irrationally in the opposite direction? Or was marrying Jackson the gateway to an original and fulfilling life? All of this ran through my mind. I didn't fool myself that I had done anything to ensure the safety of my journey so far. I knew I'd just been lucky, but still I felt no fear. People who live in dangerous places seem to just get tired of being afraid all the time. They still take precautions to protect themselves, but they don't worry constantly about every possible danger.

Had I been a member of the high school elite—a cheerleader, or a swimming champion—maybe I would have followed the prescribed path for an upper-middle-class girl. Or if Mom and Dad had allowed me to take a few risks early on, maybe I wouldn't have felt the need to break through the constraints so dramatically. Instead, like many foreigners before me, I became addicted to the excitement of Africa. I don't know exactly what transformed me from an overprotected suburban teenager into an international risk-taker. Certainly, my love for Jackson and my rebellion against my parents determined my final decision. I had been moving toward an unconventional life for years. Still, had I known all of what lay ahead, I might have made a different choice.

Chapter 2
Forging a Path

Nothing in my cloistered Midwestern childhood pointed toward an interest in foreign countries and cultures, except for my fascination with National Geographic, one of our family's few magazine subscriptions. In the far west Chicago suburbs, closer to farms and prairies than to the city, National Geographic provided the only window to the world beyond for me and my two younger sisters. Although my mother and probably many of our neighbors were second-generation immigrants, only our next-door neighbor showed any attachment to the Old World. He signed the family Christmas card "Chez deRosset," which I found wonderfully exotic. A French immigrant could trumpet his French heritage. Anyone with German ancestry kept it quiet in the 1950s, even if it was three generations back, like my father's. My parents' generation, forced to fight in Europe during the war, now turned inward, relieved to return to their insular American life.

When I was ten or eleven, as I flipped through the latest issue of the magazine, I said, "I want to go to South Africa. It looks so beautiful."

"Oh, but they have terrible racial problems there," my mother said, and showed me a newspaper article about the Sharpeville massacre, when police killed more than fifty people who were protesting peacefully against apartheid. My mother had never shown me a report about such violence, although she had never censored my reading. Although I concluded that South Africa could wait, I didn't stop dreaming.

Mom and Dad were eager to escape from the small farms and hardscrabble towns of their childhood. Now I longed to escape from the suburban house they worked so hard to get. I dreamed of other places, most of them imaginary. I loved fairy tales, the more unusual the better. As my reading progressed, I added stories about the past to my reading list: biographies of famous people, the Little House on the Prairie books about the Midwest in the 1870s, and later still, 19th century Russian novels.

As a child often sidelined by illness, I learned at an early age that I couldn't trust adults. At three, I had an operation for strabismus (crossed eyes). A year later a kidney infection put me in the hospital again, where my parents could visit me only a few minutes a day. After the eye operation, the nurses put me in a straitjacket to keep me from tearing off my bandages, and I blamed Mom and Dad for letting it happen. I never forgot that feeling of abandonment. I remember calling for them to come back as they walked away from me down the hallway. They didn't even turn around. My vivid memory of that experience fueled a mistrust of adults that stayed with me through my childhood and adolescence.

At five, I contracted mononucleosis and had to stay in bed all summer. I wore thick glasses and came in last in every race I was forced to enter. I couldn't throw a ball, or catch one. I realized even then that I disappointed my mother. Athletic and intensely religious, she must have wondered why God had cursed her with this weak and sickly daughter who had no interest in outdoor play. During my many illnesses, Mom gave me books, puzzles and crayons, but she didn't go out of her way to distract or reassure me. Probably desperate to get me involved in any kind of physical activity, she enrolled me in a kindergarten ballet class. I dreamed of becoming a ballerina, and of course read everything I could about ballet. I still remember my first recital, and my costume—dark-green and yellow satin, with little sprays of gold flowers on the shoulders. I kept it in my closet for years.

I had one other obsession—the piano. An old upright came with the house, and it called to me from the minute I saw it. I couldn't stay away from it. I plinked away, begging my mother to teach me more. She knew only enough to haltingly bang out a few hymns, but no teacher would take me until I learned to read letters. When the day finally came, Mom (probably by chance) happened to choose an excellent teacher who had studied in Europe and married an opera singer. I adored Mrs. Russell as much as I feared her.

"You must practice an hour a day," she demanded. "Nothing less."

Often I played for two hours, although some of it didn't constitute "practice" by Mrs. Russell's standards. By the time I was twelve, I had a solo recital and prepared for it as diligently as a pre-adolescent could. Much as I enjoyed the piano, ballet remained my first love. As I leaped and twirled, I imagined myself beautiful, talented and free. Then, in fifth grade, came a shock.

"Your sisters need lessons too. We can't afford both ballet and piano for you," Mom said. "You have to choose."

"Ballet," I said at once.

Her mouth compressed into a straight line of disapproval. “We think piano would be a better choice.”

Why did she pretend to give me a choice? She understood me so poorly that she expected me to choose piano. I knew I couldn’t argue. I couldn’t even show my resentment without risking punishment. My sister Beth, two years younger, took ballet, and Jo, six years younger, wouldn’t be far behind. I understood that. Still, I immediately began to doubt my talent for dance. I had often begged my father to take pictures of my ballet poses, while Beth and Jo made fun of my pitiful arabesques. I was devastated. My vision was poor, but I wasn’t blind. Apparently, no one believed I had any talent for dance, and I felt humiliated.

* * *

One day in the fall of 1956, when I was nine, Mom and I were alone when she took a phone call. I hated having to be quiet when she was on the phone, so I remember it was a long call, although she listened more than she spoke. When she hung up, she said, “Your grandfather died. We have to go to Minnesota.” She sounded more angry than sad and remained dry-eyed as she carried on with the housework. Grandpa had suffered a stroke the previous summer, so it wasn’t entirely a surprise. He was always kind to me, and I knew I would miss him. I started to cry. Mom did not, nor did she offer me any consolation, not even a brief hug. When I kept crying, Mom said sharply, “Sandie, stop it.” Even at that age, this struck me as unduly harsh. Once again I felt abandoned. That was the last time I expected any comfort from her. It was a lonely feeling.

Many years later, a cousin told me that my grandfather did not die of a stroke. He locked himself in the garage, started the car and died of carbon monoxide poisoning. My grandmother found him when she came home from church. Mom and Dad kept the secret their entire lives. Mom never had a good relationship with her father, and I can imagine his suicide made her furious. It puts her coldness in a different light. I wish I had known sooner.

* * *

At thirteen, I signed up to learn Spanish, offered for the first time at my school as an alternative to Home Economics (for girls) or Shop (for boys). I loved it and quickly became interested in Spain and Mexico. My other grades were good, but I really excelled in Spanish. When I was sixteen, a charismatic teacher created a special summer Spanish course that concluded with a week in Saltillo, Mexico. Mom and Dad considered the course "frivolous," so I paid for it myself with the money I earned from playing piano for dance classes. I had the highest grade in the class, and the Mexico trip was a fantasy fulfilled. Along with two other girls from my class, I lived with a local family and made nightly chaperoned excursions to a dance club called the Picnic, where I met my first-ever boyfriend—eighteen, tall and attractive. He and his friends serenaded me and my roommates one night in the traditional style, and I floated back to Chicago on a cloud.

At home, my new enthusiasm appalled my parents, even though I told them nothing about Luis Alfonso. They treated my interest in Mexico like a drug addiction, refusing to let me go again the following year, even if I paid for it myself. What were they so afraid of? I felt betrayed. Up to then, I'd done everything they expected of me. Had I been so obedient that they didn't believe I could think for myself? The seeds of rebellion took root. From that moment on, Mom and Dad were enemies.

I knew then, at sixteen, that I didn't want the life my parents had, the one they wanted for me. They believed their actions stemmed from love for me. I didn't see it that way. Even in the Bible they claimed to revere, the well-known verses about love (Corinthians 13) says that love "…does not insist on its own way." In limiting my choices, trying to control every detail of my life, my parents had tried to make me into a replica of themselves. That is not love—it's a compulsion to control. And despite their professions of faith, supposedly with disdain for worldly concerns, they cared far more about money and the opinions of their friends and neighbors than they would ever have admitted.

In my junior year, I applied to be a foreign exchange student with the American Field Service, certain no one could beat my language skills. A committee of teachers and administrators chose only one candidate from each school, and to my disbelief they chose another girl. I was crushed. By my senior year, I had the highest Spanish grades in the school and earned a perfect score on the Spanish SAT Achievement Test. Once again, that achievement drew more anxiety than appreciation from Mom and Dad. Foreign languages didn't fit into the plan they had mapped out for my life. No matter how high my grades, they kept building barriers to what I wanted to do with my life, trying to force me into following the path they chose.

"Teaching is the best profession for a woman," my mother kept insisting. "She can work and still be home at the same time as her children."

Who said I wanted to have children? I didn't ask that out loud, of course, because Mom brooked no opposition from me and my sisters to any of her ideas. Children or no children, I knew I did not want to teach. That became even more problematic when it came to music. Beginning in seventh grade, I played piano for dance classes, for the choruses and choirs, and later for singers and solo instrumentalists. I played for the annual high school musical and for Community Theater in the summers. I still played classical music but did not aim for a concert career. I had no idea that "accompanist" could be a career, if not a well-paid one. I would have jumped at that, had I known it existed, but I did not enjoy solo performance. Adulation and applause could not compensate for the hours of practice and pressure of performing onstage, all endured alone. Maybe I didn't have a big enough ego, but I did not want a concert career. That meant that the only musical profession open to me would be teaching piano to children, or music to junior high students. And, of course, that's what Mom and Dad expected me to do. Both prospects made me shudder.

I gravitated naturally to music, dance and books, but not to religion. The Lutheran faith dominated our family life, whether my sisters and I wanted it or not. Dad was an Elder in the Church, which meant we spent our entire Sunday mornings there and had to wait for an hour or more after the last service while he and the other Elders counted the offering. Mom was active in all the women's groups and taught Old Testament in the church's rigorous confirmation classes. We went to church meetings, potluck dinners, rummage sales, choir practice, confirmation classes and youth groups, all obligatory for me and my sisters. It wasn't that I especially disliked religion, and I liked Sunday School well enough until my teenage years, but I was a nervous, restless child, and church was mostly just boring. Still, I read the New Testament, the psalms and the liturgies in the Lutheran Hymnal, just because I read anything I could get my hands on. When Mom forbade reading at meals, even if I was alone at the table, I read the backs of cereal boxes. Mom and Dad didn't censor my reading at all, so I read the Chicago newspaper that came to the house, and from the age of seven learned about the evils that lurked in the outside world. Sometimes those stories gave me nightmares, but I would never have admitted it.

The Church had explanations of why God allowed evil to exist and sometimes flourish, but I never found them convincing. I started reading about other religions, then about the Holocaust (still before I turned twelve), and my wondering grew into serious doubts. In the end, though, it wasn't a book that finished off my religious beliefs. It was a Disney show about evolution that I watched in seventh grade. The science made sense to me, where the Biblical Creation story didn't. So God didn't create the world, at least not in the way I'd been taught? And if the Creation story was a myth, I concluded that the rest could not be true either. As I started reading about other religions and their history, I threw out the idea that Jewish people, even those murdered in the Holocaust, were doomed to Hell because they didn't believe in Jesus. After reading James Michener's *Hawaii*, I couldn't accept that the Polynesians, who didn't learn about Jesus until the missionaries arrived, were damned. How could Christians be right and everyone else wrong? So, despite lifelong indoctrination in the Lutheran Church, I no longer believed in God by the time I turned sixteen. I believed in the need for ethical behavior, I saw that religion provided a moral framework and a kind of armor against life's burdens and misfortunes, but I couldn't make myself believe—and I tried hard. I voiced my doubts to no one—not my sisters, not my friends. It never occurred to me to seek guidance from the pastor of my church, even though I knew him well and liked him. I read books I thought might inspire me and threw myself into the few ecumenical activities my church offered. Sometimes my quest led to wonderful discoveries, like Khalil Gibran's *The Prophet*, and *The God That Failed*, a book of essays critical of Communism, by Arthur Koestler. I read *Siddhartha* and other popular books about spiritual quests. Most of my reading was way over my head. My emotional understanding lagged far behind my vocabulary.

I could not imagine telling Mom I no longer believed in God. I knew she would pack me off to the pastor to straighten me out and would make me go to church even more often. She and Dad would probably make me pray with them for my salvation. I couldn't bear that, so I struggled on my own to work out what I believed and how it would determine the rest of my life. The summer after my junior year, in return for parental permission to drop out of the church youth group, I agreed to go to a week-long Lutheran work camp at the newly formed Ecumenical Institute on Chicago's West Side, one of the poorest and most troubled neighborhoods in the city. The idea came from Mom and Dad, quiet supporters of the Civil Rights movement. They admired Dr. King, although they doubted he could reach his goals.

"That man isn't long for this world," Mom would say as we watched the news.

"Don't say that!" I objected each time, as if voicing the idea made it more likely to happen.

At the Ecumenical Institute, we had classes every morning in liberation theology and the role of religious faith in protest movements based on moral principles. We started with the opposition forces during the Spanish Civil War, then went on to study the life of Dietrich Bonhoeffer, a German theologian critical of

Hitler who died in a concentration camp. From there, we learned about the Civil Rights movement—sophisticated material for a bunch of high school students, but exactly what I needed. I still believed in the need for moral action, and the teachers at the Ecumenical Institute gave me a framework for my convictions, as well as an example of what to do with them. In the afternoons, we did maintenance on a newly acquired building and built a set of primitive storage lockers in the basement. We went on heavily chaperoned field trips, mostly to churches, sometimes handing out leaflets advertising upcoming events at the Institute. The program gave us a glimpse of urban poverty that none of us had seen firsthand. After that, I knew I couldn't go back to Clarendon Hills and carry on with the plan Mom and Dad had laid out for me, even though I still didn't know exactly where my convictions would lead.

* * *

Before my senior year, I'd only gone on two or three dates, all with boys my own age. Through a friend, I met a boy who graduated from high school a couple of years earlier, a Cuban immigrant, and dated him for a few months, until he started pressuring me for sex. He lost that battle, because I had no intention of jeopardizing my escape from the suburbs by getting pregnant. He knew how to charm my mother, and I think she was a little disappointed when I broke up with him. She didn't know why, of course. I knew I had to go to a college that had a strong Junior Year Abroad program, and I still loved Mexico, so I researched which colleges had the best Latin American studies programs.

"I'm applying to the University of Arizona," I announced one night at the dinner table.

Mom and Dad exchanged glances.

"It's too far away," Mom said. I longed for Dad to contradict her, but he never did. She was the Enforcer, and he rarely disagreed.

"How about Middlebury College?" I asked. "It has a really good language program."

"Also too far away. There are so many good schools right around here. You could even live at home."

"No way."

"We'd buy you your own car," Dad said.

"No thanks." I didn't care about cars.

"Apply to Valparaiso," Mom said. It was a Lutheran college in the Indiana boondocks, known as a party school. I would have been embarrassed to tell anyone I was going there.

"It has nothing I'm interested in."

"How about DePauw? Or somewhere in Illinois?" Mom countered.

I felt like screaming, *Don't you get it? I have to get out of here! I can't stay in Illinois!* That wouldn't get me anywhere, I knew, so I said, "Maybe I won't go to college at all, then. I'll stay here and work, maybe go to nursing school."

"No. Find a school somewhere in the Midwest," Mom said.

Silence fell over the dinner table. Beth and Jo looked at me as though I'd committed a sacrilege.

Finally, we compromised on Kalamazoo College, halfway between Chicago and Detroit ("And too far from both," my fellow students later joked.) "K College" had an innovative four-year program that included an internship and Foreign Study for all students. I wouldn't get left out this time. I was accepted on Early Decision. I decided not to spend the summer working at a meaningless retail job. The pastor of my church helped arrange a project for me with an inner-city Lutheran congregation that had two pastors for their parallel English and Spanish-speaking congregations. Mom couldn't object, given the backing of three Lutheran pastors, but she wasn't pleased that I didn't make any money that summer. The religious training I had received at church and at home constantly told me that the love of money was the root of all evil, so I could not understand why suddenly she thought it was so important. The neighborhood at Roosevelt and Ashland Avenue was poor, but not dangerous in 1965, at least during the day. I drove around the neighborhood visiting families from the congregation and never felt unsafe. The pastors suggested I get a group of girls together from a big apartment building near the church. I could use the church basement for a kind of informal Girls' Club for girls from ages nine to twelve. The Spanish-speaking pastor introduced me to the parents, and to my surprise, they trusted me with their daughters—I suppose it was better than letting them play in the street. I also tutored a very sweet boy in English in the mornings, but he appeared incapable of learning to read. I had never heard of dyslexia, a learning disability I learned about years later. With the girls, I taught cooking, sewing and art projects, and they must have enjoyed it because they kept coming back, and I enjoyed them too. At the end of the summer, I piled them all into my parents' VW bus and took them to Clarendon Hills for the day. My sisters and I gave them all our outgrown dolls. We had a great time.

On weekends, I dated a college senior, an engineering major who worked at the Community Theater. He didn't have much more experience with dating than I did. I should have wondered why he bothered with a high school girl instead of someone his own age. I knew nothing then about male insecurities. Had I been more perceptive, I would have realized he was looking for a wife, while I just wanted a little fun on weekends.

Suddenly summer was over. I remember standing at the ironing board in the kitchen, looking out at the little plum tree in the backyard, its coin-shaped golden leaves sparkling in the sun, and thinking… *This is how I want to remember this place. And I am leaving it for good.*

Chapter 3

All You Need Is Love

September, 1965

For Move-in Day at Kalamazoo College, I wore my favorite outfit, a mohair A-line dress in a red paisley print. Mom and Dad helped me carry my two suitcases, my portable typewriter (their graduation gift) and my precious hi-fi up to my tiny dorm room. Nobody had a mini fridge in the 1960s. The dorm's ancient electrical system probably couldn't have handled it, and there was no space for it, anyway. I could barely squeeze in the hi-fi.

"Should we stay for lunch?" Mom asked. She glanced around at the parent–student groups pulling luggage out of their cars and heading for the dormitories.

"You don't have to. I'm not hungry, anyway," I said. I wanted them to leave as soon as possible.

Mom and Dad looked at each other. "Well then, we'll be on our way," Mom said. She pulled me in for a quick hug—for her, a sign of deep emotion. Norwegians don't hug. I'm sure she was as relieved to drive away as I was to see her go.

* * *

At Thanksgiving, I broke up with the mechanical engineer. I knew when I left for college that I had outgrown him—I just didn't have the courage then. Back at Kalamazoo I had one date—and only one—with the captain of the college football team, a good-looking senior. He talked about his ideal life: a white picket fence and a colonial house in the suburbs with a stay-at-home wife. I told him about my social justice activities, my hunger for foreign study, and my relief at escaping the confines of my religious family. We could hardly have been less compatible. I felt claustrophobic just listening to him. He gave me a chaste good night kiss, and I could tell it would be the last. Years later I saw his name in an alumni magazine—a lawyer, still single, in California. Maybe he never found a woman who met his standards.

A friend arranged a date for me with the leading campus radical, a skinny guy with long hair, of the scruffy type common at the time. Politically, we agreed on everything: opposition to the Vietnam War, solidarity with civil rights, power to the people, and hey, hey, ho, ho—LBJ has got to go.

"We're completely compatible," he said. "But there's no chemistry, is there?"

"None. It's too bad—we'd be perfect for each other."

We looked at each other, completely baffled. He shrugged and laughed. "We'll be friends. Can't have enough of those these days."

Couples at Kalamazoo College didn't exactly "go out." They took meals together in the cafeteria, studied together at the library or the Student Center, or went to college events—films, plays, concerts. The hardy few ventured across town to Western Michigan University. They had better parties, but it was a couple of miles away. There was no bus service, and it's cold in Michigan. Student etiquette discouraged begging a ride from one of the few students who had a car unless you had to go to the Emergency Room. Not that there was much to do anyway in Kalamazoo, a sprawling, poorly planned city of 100,000 with one movie theater, little public transportation, and three nightclubs, all far away—one all White, one mixed, one all Black. Bars, liquor stores and nightclubs carded aggressively, and a fake ID only worked if you really *looked* twenty-one to a suspicious bartender, and I didn't. Our campus, true to its waning Baptist heritage, did not allow alcohol.

Then I met Jackson Mahania.

I met him only because he was dating an acquaintance of mine named Maya, a striking woman from Detroit who wore big dangly earrings and talked freely about other men she was dating. I wished I could be as freewheeling as Maya. I thought maybe I could learn something from her. When Jackson joined Maya's lunch group, I was immediately attracted to him and flirted with him to the best of my ability, but I couldn't compete with Maya. The three of us ate lunch and dinner together in the cafeteria with other friends, and I nursed my seemingly hopeless crush. Then one weekend Maya found love in Detroit and transferred to another school. Jackson didn't seem especially broken up. A junior from the Democratic Republic of Congo (its name changed later), Jackson was twenty-five. His posture and slim, muscular build made him look taller than he really was, and he had a beautiful smile. He always wore what we called the "African uniform"—white dress shirt and sport coat with dress pants, no tie, and dress shoes. This strange formality added to his exotic appeal, although looks weren't important, I told myself. It was his mind that attracted me, a half-truth I told myself. He'd come to the US in 1961, an especially turbulent time in Congo.

Then twenty years old, he had spent a year at a New Jersey high school learning English, a year at Montclair State, and two years at Virginia Union in Richmond. His sponsors, the International Christian Youth Exchange, made him transfer to Kalamazoo.

"It will be better for you academically," they said, but he suspected the real reason was his civil rights work in the South. The sponsors wanted him on an academic track, not dead or in a Mississippi jail. Jackson had no interest in small talk or campus gossip, and I didn't miss it. I loved the intensity of his conversations about African and world politics. I hadn't thought much about Africa since my early National Geographic days, and in my first semester I was still a Spanish major, although I was disillusioned with the Spanish department. I thought about switching to French in the second semester.

Previous boyfriends complained, justifiably, about my intensity and constantly shifting interests, but Jackson ignored all that. What I did when I wasn't with him didn't concern him. He wanted to talk, and I wanted to listen. He wrote articles for the school paper about African nationalism. The city newspaper published a full-page feature on him, the idealistic Congolese student eager to return to work for his country. His sense of commitment mesmerized me. Less clear is what he saw in me. Other women chased him, and I was just an averagely pretty, intensely political White girl from the suburbs, naïve and immature, with annoying aspirations. What appealed to him, I imagine now, was my uncritical appreciation of him and his ideas. An admirer of Patrice Lumumba, a Congolese leader murdered in 1961, he supported a strong central government for a Congo shaken by repeated secessions and rebellions. I signed up for an African History class and Introductory French in the spring quarter.

We took all our meals together, often sitting with the other few African students. On weekends we went to parties near the Western Michigan campus, at a ramshackle wood frame house rented by Nigerian students. In a living room devoid of furniture, we drank beer and danced to Nigerian High Life tunes of musicians like King Sunny Adé and the hypnotic rhythms of OK Jazz, a famous Congolese band. Couples regularly disappeared upstairs, sometimes briefly, sometimes for the night. After a couple of months, we arranged to spend the night together.

Middle-class American society had a vague expectation in 1966 that female college students would meet their future husbands in college. I did not imagine Jackson as a future husband. I didn't think about marriage at all. I loved him and would be with him until he went back to his country. And now I needed birth control. The price of free love in the 1960s was the risk of getting pregnant. That would mean either an illegal abortion, consenting to adoption or dropping out of school and a shotgun wedding, all out of the question for me. I didn't know how to get an abortion, I knew I could never give up a baby, and I shuddered at the thought of single motherhood. Shotgun weddings were common among my friends, even the political radicals. Supposedly a woman could get a relatively safe illegal abortion in Chicago, with a few hundred dollars and some connections. I didn't have any, and no one performed abortions in Kalamazoo, as far I knew. A friend gave me the name of the only doctor in town willing to prescribe birth control pills to students. We passed around a wedding ring that we wore to our appointments. That spring my love affair with Jackson intensified. At Easter, I brought him to my parents' house for a visit. I introduced him just as someone I was dating. He joked easily with my sisters, then sixteen and twelve. He talked to my parents with formal respect and emphasized his Protestant faith. Mom and Dad made no comments about the visit afterward, and I did not ask what they thought.

Jackson and a friend, a Congolese math major, moved off campus, and I spent more and more time at their basement apartment. Jackson and I were both involved in civil rights and anti-war activities, but rarely together. Mixed couples couldn't safely walk around town together, so I always came to his apartment alone. Both he and his roommate were under intermittent police surveillance, for no reason that we could figure out, except that they were Black in a mostly White neighborhood. His roommate was a total nerd who left the apartment only to go to class or the library.

Only a year before, I thought I was in love with my high school boyfriend. What I felt for Jackson was far more intense. When still in high school, I couldn't think beyond getting to college and getting away from home. Now my life seemed to speed up, heading in a direction I hadn't expected. At least once a week, Jackson would say, "You must understand. I am going back to my country when I graduate."

"And I want you to understand I'm not going to marry you," I said. "I'm going to finish college."

I appreciated his honesty. As far as I knew, he never lied to me, and while we were dating, never went out with any other women, unlike other men I knew at Kalamazoo, including my friends' boyfriends. Neither of us tried to change the other's mind about the impermanence of our relationship—not then. I thought as little as possible about the day he would go back to Congo.

* * *

The college expected freshmen to go home for the summer, and I couldn't find a job in Kalamazoo, anyway. I couldn't stay with Jackson and didn't know anyone else with an apartment there, so I returned to my parents' house. I couldn't find a full-time job at home in Clarendon Hills, either, competing with the largest cohort of nineteen-year-olds in American history, so I tried to go back to the unpaid social work I'd done the summer before.

"That was a one-time learning experience," Mom said. "Now you have to earn some money."

Money? It was ridiculous. I applied for a summer job at a mental health clinic but didn't get the job, so I turned to retail. Working part time at minimum wage, I would make only $250 for the entire summer, before expenses, and I had to use my parents' car to drive to work. The only purpose of my job at the mall was to confirm to Mom that she still controlled me. I already resented it, and I soon found out that wasn't enough for her. One night after dinner, my parents sat me down on the back porch, where Beth and Jo presumably couldn't hear (though of course they maneuvered to do exactly that). We had never had a family conference before. Mom looked pale and uncomfortable. As usual, I couldn't read Dad's expression. In the near distance, I could hear the neighborhood children shouting, "Allee allee in free!" just as I had done a few years before.

"I've read your diary, Sandie," Mom said.

"You—what?"

I'd kept a diary since junior high. I'd never bothered to hide it—I didn't think anyone would be interested in it, least of all Mom. I felt my insides turn to ice.

"I know what you did. If you want to go back to Kalamazoo, you have to agree not to continue your... um... physical relationship with Jackson."

My mind raced. I knew I hadn't written anything explicit. What exactly did she read that gave it away? I wanted to say, "Just a minute," and run upstairs to check. Instead, I said, "You read my diary?"

"It's my duty to protect you."

"How could you read my diary? I'm nineteen, not twelve!"

"Then act like it. Why did you do it? Did you think we don't love you?" Her voice carried a mixture of anguish and exasperation. Clearly, she did not consider me an adult. To Mom and Dad, I was still a child not entitled to make her own decisions. I struggled through my rage to answer her. I wondered with bitterness how she reconciled reading my diary with her supposedly strict moral code.

"That has nothing to do with it! And it's none of your business!" I said.

"Having sex before marriage is against God's commandments. We can't allow you to do that."

"I could leave home right now, and you couldn't stop me."

"Then it would be your responsibility," said Dad. "As long as we're paying your expenses, you'll live by our rules."

I didn't want to drop out of college. I'd wanted a college degree ever since I could remember, and I knew what my job prospects would be without it. But I couldn't imagine living by my parents' rules. I left the table without answering and went upstairs to the room I shared with Beth. I flipped through my diary to find the offending passage. I had written: "So that's the much-vaunted loss of innocence. It is seriously over-rated. So much for that."

Damn. Had I known that before the confrontation, I could have weaseled my way into an acceptable explanation, though it wouldn't have been easy. Then again, maybe they would have tried to find another way to separate me from Jackson. I didn't believe my parents were racists. They might have done the same thing if it involved any boyfriend. They certainly gave the mechanical engineer the cold shoulder. On the other hand, they may have been afraid of me marrying Jackson and going to Congo, even though Mom wouldn't have found that idea in my diary.

"If you want to run away, I'll give you my money," said Beth. "I have five hundred dollars saved."

Beth hated to spend money, so I found this gesture very touching.

"Thanks for the offer," I said. "But there's no use both of us being in trouble with the parents. And I haven't decided yet if I'll leave."

If I didn't leave home, I would have to lie, because I knew I wouldn't change my relationship with Jackson. But I was too insecure and immature to strike out on my own without financial support. And I could not imagine dropping out of college. In the end I rationalized my dishonesty. They had been deceptive, and wrong to violate my privacy, and therefore I could justify being as deceptive as they were. I saw my lie as an unfortunate necessity and found the whole situation demeaning. I saw no good reason why they should interfere in my love life, and my mother's deception horrified me.

"All right," I told them the next day. "I won't have sex with Jackson."

I had no intention of complying. Instead, I stopped writing in my diary.

Chapter 4
Resistance

At the end of the summer, I flew to Washington, DC, to spend a week with Jackson. Mom couldn't object, since we were staying with families he had lived with in his first few years in the US.

"Don't do anything more foolish than you already have," Mom said just before I boarded the plane.

Give it a rest! I thought. I pretended not to hear her.

After visiting one family in DC (the father was a Baptist minister), Jackson and I took separate buses to Richmond to visit Yvonne, who had rented a room to Jackson during the two years he spent at Virginia Union. Yvonne owned a successful beauty salon. I think she rented rooms to African students more for the company than for the money.

In 1966, interracial couples could not safely travel together, especially in the South. I found a cab outside the bus station in Richmond and gave the White cab driver the address. After about fifteen minutes, he looked around and said, "This is a *Black* neighborhood."

"Yes, I know," I said, trying to see the addresses obscured by ivy and big shade trees along the wide street lined with single-family brick houses.

"I hope you know what you're doing. That's the house right there."

* * *

At the beginning of my sophomore year, student protests escalated—against the Vietnam War, segregation and school policies. On a wall above the entrance to our dormitory, an inscription chiseled in cement read, "The End of Learning Is Gracious Living." Students suspended a banner over it that read, "The End of Learning Is Gracious LOVING." We protested the college's doctrine of *in loco parentis* (in place of the parents) that dictated curfews for women students but not for men, mandatory chapel attendance, and a dress code that required women to wear skirts to classes and meals. National news outlets reported student takeovers at Berkeley and Duke, and protests at Columbia. With demonstrations and student takeovers at schools like that, ours often didn't even make the local news. In September of 1966, Martin Luther King led a march in all-White Cicero, where my father worked, protesting segregated housing. Despite heavy National Guard and police presence, a large hostile crowd threw bricks, bottles and other missiles during the march. King was hit in the head. He told reporters, "I have never seen, even in Mississippi and Alabama, mobs as hateful as I've seen here in Chicago," a pronouncement still quoted fifty years later.

I knew the situation in Kalamazoo and elsewhere in the Midwest was much the same. Integrated housing didn't exist. I saw civil rights as the most important social issue in the country, but I didn't know what I could do about it. In addition to the protests, I joined a group of students who tutored children in Kalamazoo's Black elementary school on the other side of town. I remember being surprised that such a small city could be so segregated, conveniently forgetting that no people of color at all lived in the Chicago suburb where I grew up.

The tutoring program required a permission slip from the parents of the boy I was tutoring. He told me that his father worked long hours and was only home on weekends, so I trekked the forty-five minutes to their house on a Saturday. As in most old Midwest houses, the living room was at the front, with windows opening onto a wide front porch. I sat on a worn sofa while the boy's father took the paper I gave him and sat down at the dining room table. The house had only minimal furnishings: the ancient sofa, two mismatched armchairs, a small television set. A bare bulb dangled from the ceiling. No lamps, no rugs, no decorations on the walls.

What was taking him so long? I thought, irritated. All he had to do was sign at the bottom of the paper. The man stood up and went into the kitchen a couple of times, came back, and studied the paper again. Then he stood up again, disappeared somewhere else in the house, and came back a few minutes later. This went on for more than an hour. Finally, he called the boy over. They had a whispered conversation, and the father brought me the permission slip. At the bottom was a large black X, in pencil.

I tried to conceal my shock, thanked him, and folded the paper. We shook hands, and I left. I felt ashamed of my impatience and failure to understand his hesitation. The man couldn't have been older than thirty. I wouldn't have been surprised if someone had told me there were still many illiterate sharecroppers in Mississippi. But here in Michigan? In high school history we never learned about the Great Migration from the South that was still going on all around us. I was only beginning to appreciate the reasons for it.

I felt helpless. All I could do was go to marches and tutor children, but I was looking for something more. I had stopped believing in God years before, but I still held to the basic moral principles instilled during all those hours in church and Sunday School, fortified by my reading and my experience at the Ecumenical Institute. Surely I'd had time enough to think about what direction I wanted my life to take. To me, leading a moral life was more important than making money, or even finding personal happiness. I just didn't know yet exactly how I would put that belief into practice. I began to think about social work.

In April I began an internship at the Chicago State Mental Hospital. I changed my major from Sociology to Psychology to make myself eligible for it. My parents wouldn't agree to a faraway location, so Chicago was the best I could do. Jackson wanted me to take an internship in Kalamazoo, but nothing interesting surfaced there. I hated the town, anyway, and I wasn't going to let our relationship keep me from doing what I wanted. After all, I wasn't going to marry him.

With Dad's help, I found a furnished apartment near the hospital, in Oak Park, then an all-White suburb. I shared the apartment with Lynn, another psychology intern from Kalamazoo.

Chicago State Hospital occupied an entire city block, with six thousand patients and dozens of old red brick buildings, all enclosed by a high iron fence. On most wards, patients could leave their designated space and wander the extensive grounds. A few of the wards for violent and severely ill patients were locked, as were the two children's wards. Near the middle of the block, a large building had been turned into a workshop where patients could work five hours a day. The idea was to help patients get used to working, have them interact with staff and other patients, and earn a little money. There were two sections, one for simple assembly operations that required no skill and minimal interaction with other workers, and another section with a slightly more complex assembly line. The hospital had subcontracts with companies that sold the products produced there. A gruff middle-aged woman, Jane, handled overall management of the workshop. She reminded me a little of my mother.

Most patients were heavily medicated, mainly with Thorazine, a powerful anti-psychotic rarely used today. That was what enabled staff to let patients wander the grounds so freely, although the idea of freeing mental patients from confinement was still controversial. Part of the supervisors' job, and ours as interns, was to wake up patients who nodded off while working. I talked to the few patients who were capable of conversation. One of them was Eric, a middle-aged former music professor with severe depression, for which he had undergone many shock treatments before coming to Chicago State. He described them as unbearably painful. He told me about some of the other treatments and drugs he had tried. "None of them help much," he said.

Since the workshop operated only five hours a day, the staff spent the other three hours together in the cramped office next door, mostly playing gin rummy and occasionally squabbling. After a week of card-playing, I decided to make better use of my time and asked to tour other sections of the hospital. Jane, Dan and Lurleen, who'd all worked in the wards and knew everybody, made sure I was able to see everything other than the most violent men's ward and the so-called "Hydro" ward that housed new admissions. One men's ward housed some of the sickest non-violent men, and I wanted to see how the hospital handled them.

"You don't want to see that," one of the aides said. "It's pretty upsetting."

I kept insisting, and finally the aides let me walk through alone.

In several large rooms, dozens of men sat, stood or lay on the floor, completely out of contact with our world, all of them either hallucinating or catatonic. They weren't isolated from each other or the staff because they rarely caused harm to anyone. Workers and aides didn't intervene except to clean them up when they soiled themselves. The aides were clearly disappointed that I didn't run out crying.

"Don't they get treatment?" I asked one of the aides.

"Drugs. What kind of treatment can you give when the patient can't even hear you?"

I had no answer—only a sense that there must be a better solution.

I spent many lunch hours in the art department, a big sunny room with art materials and a full-time art therapist, where about twenty people could work. Patients from the violent wards came in small groups, under guard. Non-violent patients could drop in any time. Those from the violent wards were by far the most interesting because they were generally "in contact," meaning they responded to others. They often produced good work, but the alcoholics, both men and women, created the best art. I wondered if some of them had been artists before their hospitalization. One man came in every few days and made the same pencil drawing each time, a plane flying high over the hospital, dropping a bomb on it. He wouldn't talk about his drawings.

I visited the two children's wards, which were locked and heavily staffed. The larger one held the more tractable children.

"Lots of these kids are like Jonah," Lurleen warned me, referring to a developmentally disabled patient we worked with. "You're not going to see anything wrong with them. Families abandon them, or just can't afford to take care of them. A lot of people end up here just because they're poor."

The second ward held the genuinely ill children. Although some of them appeared heavily medicated, the place did its best work with the children. The ratio of staff to patient appeared to be about two to one, and the staff seemed dedicated and protective. Whenever possible, children received treatment beyond drugs, including group therapy.

After a month in Chicago, I went back to Kalamazoo to visit Jackson. We went to a party, where someone asked him if Africans lived in trees.

"Yes," Jackson said, deadpan. "Each of us in the family has his own tree."

I didn't know anyone at the party, and after that exchange, I wanted to leave. We argued on the way back to his apartment. He was still angry that I didn't stay in Kalamazoo for my internship and kept harping on it. What did he expect me to do, abandon my internship? I felt him trying to control me just as my parents had, and I couldn't stand it. At the end of the weekend, I told him I didn't want to see him for a while. I didn't tell him that I thought it might be forever.

A few days after I went back to Chicago, an aide at the hospital named Joe stopped by to chat at the workshop. Lynn, my roommate, was with me. Joe had met a previous K-College intern whom I knew slightly. Jane, the workshop manager, gave him a hostile glance, but didn't say anything. When she left the room, Joe asked, "She make a pass at one of you yet?"

"What are you talking about?" Lynn said. "She's always professional."

"Huh," he grunted. "She's a dyke, you know."

"She lives with her girlfriend," I said.

"Better watch out. Hey, I have a friend I'd like you to meet. He knew Shelley too. OK if I bring him by?"

I shrugged. "After four o'clock, maybe."

Jane bustled over. "Time to get back to work, Joe."

He withdrew with a slight bow.

Joe brought two friends to the workshop: Jude, who was Jewish, and Bill, who was Black. Jude started dating Lynn. He had long, wild hair and dressed like a hippie when he wasn't working at Chicago State. I went out with Bill, who worked as an aide in an acute hospital. Bill had short-cropped hair and nearly always wore a suit and tie.

"I dated Shelley when she interned here last year," Bill said. "She dumped me for some guy at college. Were you dating anyone in Kalamazoo?"

"I just broke up with my boyfriend."

Once we established our rebound status, we went out as often as his work schedule allowed. He often worked nights, or so he said. Mostly we'd hang out in Old Town, an entertainment district on the Near North Side, more racially integrated than downtown. Some weekends we camped at Joe's apartment on the South Side. Bill lived with an elderly aunt whom I never met. We never stayed at my apartment for more than five minutes.

One evening when I was out with Bill, two plainclothes policemen came to the apartment. Lynn let them in.

"I probably wouldn't have," I said, when she told me about them later.

"I checked their ID. They were for real. They said we'd better not meet Bill and Jude here. The neighbors don't appreciate loose behavior, hippies or Negroes. They said they can't guarantee our safety."

After that, cars drove by at all hours, the occupants yelling insults from their open windows. The real estate agent who'd rented us the apartment came to meet with us and Dad.

"Are you blockbusters?" he asked.

After the agent left, I had to ask my father what the man meant. Dad explained that blockbusters go into White neighborhoods and tell the homeowners that one of their neighbors is ready to sell to a Black family. The blockbuster offers to buy their property at a significant loss, then resells it to a Black family at an inflated price.

The agent gave us a clear message: Move or get kicked out. This time we had to find a place on our own, but it wasn't hard. We found one in Uptown, another all-White neighborhood. The only really integrated neighborhood, Hyde Park, near the University of Chicago, was too far from the hospital. We paid by the week for a first-floor apartment that had its front windows nailed shut. On the second floor was a group of Chinese students. The landlord, Mr. Feeney, probably thought he was renting to three of them. The rest of the dozen or so occupants came and went by the fire escape, terrifying us the first couple of times we heard them rattling up and down the stairs. On the third floor lived two young men with elaborately styled hair who always came and went together. Lynn and I dubbed them interchangeably "Prince Valiant" after a comic book character with a similar hair style. Mr. Feeney's hearing was bad, and he didn't pay close attention to comings and goings so long as we paid the rent on time, in cash.

Lynn and I were more careful in the new apartment. Jude and Bill visited rarely—after dark... wearing hats. One Friday Bill and I went to a movie downtown. I unwisely put my small handbag on the seat next to me, and when the movie was over, it was gone. It had only a few dollars—no wallet or ID—and my keys.

"That guy must be really pissed that he chose you to steal from," Bill said. "You're sure there was nothing with your address?"

"Nothing."

I tried to phone Lynn, but she was out too. I kept calling her until midnight and then we gave up and went to a motel. Spoiled suburban brat that I was, I didn't consider that this extravagance might seriously stretch Bill's budget. I didn't feel pressured because of the circumstances—I felt I could have said no if I wanted to. He was a careful, gentle lover, even though there was no passion between us. I'd call it consolation sex.

Bill brought me a fake ID, and we went to bars and blues clubs in Old Town most weekends. One Sunday we went to brunch with another couple. I realized within a few minutes that the three of them had been smoking pot before they picked me up. I didn't care, and Bill knew I didn't smoke, but all they did was laugh, and they couldn't stop eating once the munchies kicked in. They put away an incredible amount of food that day. Not for the first time, I realized how boring it was for a sober person to hang out with people who were high.

* * *

Toward the end of the internship, my high school friend Norman came for a visit, and we went to see *The Pawnbroke*r in Old

Town. Norm went to Tulane in New Orleans, so I didn't see him often. I told him about Jackson, the breakup, and Bill.

"This doesn't sound good, Galinda," he said, using my old high school nickname.

"It's just... for now," I said.

"You can't do anything in a vacuum," he said. "Everything matters. I can tell you still love Jackson. You need to go back to him."

"Really?"

"I'm very sure."

Norm could tell I missed Jackson. Bill and I had fun, but that was all. From the beginning I knew the affair would end when I left Chicago, and I realized I wouldn't miss Bill at all when I left. A few weeks later, I went to Kalamazoo for a weekend to see Jackson. We really had missed each other, and the reason for our separation now seemed trivial. Somewhat warily, we agreed to start over when I came back after Spring Break in June. I saw the coming summer as a test. We had to decide whether to continue our relationship long distance or not.

That Monday when I walked into the workshop, Jane took me aside in the office.

"I want to tell you something before you see the daily report."

My stomach clenched.

"It's Eric. He killed himself."

Eric! My favorite patient, the former music professor, traumatized by shock treatments.

"But he's been here for years!"

Jane shook her head. "He saved up his medications and overdosed. Probably put them under his tongue and stashed them."

"How could the ward let this happen? Isn't that their job?"

Jane sighed. "Let's face it—he was smarter than they were. And it's very hard to keep a determined patient from committing suicide."

I felt tears coming on. In my head I ran through my conversations with Eric, looking for a clue. Had there been anything different about him lately? Was he able to talk to me because he hadn't been taking his meds? Was there something I should have noticed? Did I somehow cause it?

"I know what you're thinking," Jane said. "There was nothing you could have done. Sooner or later, everyone who works here goes through this."

The workshop wasn't the same without Eric. I kept going over our conversations in my mind. I didn't realize until then what a hard job Jane and the others had. It wasn't like working in a lab or an office. No matter how well they did their jobs, there would be heartache. I felt only admiration for people who could do this type of work without breaking down themselves.

Before I left Chicago, one of the aides threw a party at a fancy apartment looking out on Lake Michigan. The week before the party, I told Bill I was going back to Jackson, and he didn't seem surprised or disappointed. He came to the party with Shelley. They were smoking pot and laughing wildly. The two of them ignored me and everyone else, lost in their own little weed world. I could have been happy for him, except that I was sure Shelley would use him and dump him again.

Chapter 5

The Last Summer

Some people called it the Summer of Love, when the hippie era reached its heights. For others, it was the Long Hot Summer, when race riots shook American cities after years of civil rights struggles. For me the summer of 1967 was the Last Summer: the last summer I spent in Kalamazoo, my last summer with Jackson before he went back to Congo, possibly the last summer we would be together. Did it have to be? I began to wonder. *What if...*, I thought, and changed my Foreign Study location from Spain to Kenya. Mom and Dad didn't react to the change. I suppose one foreign country was the same as another, in their view. They knew Jackson was going back to Congo, and I'm sure they hoped the upcoming separation would pull me away from him for good.

As White resistance stalled progress toward desegregation, Africa started to look like a place where I could contribute more than I could in the US. Between Martin Luther King's failing Chicago Campaign and the devastating riots in Detroit, I did not have much hope that racial and political conflict in the US would end. The civil rights organizations like the Student Nonviolent

Coordinating Committee (SNCC) that fought for change didn't welcome Whites, and I didn't know of any integrated or White organization that was doing significant work to improve the situation. I didn't believe strongly enough in the American political process to work within it. I understood the need for armed revolt in South Africa, and after looking carefully at the situation, I could not believe that acts of violence would advance the civil rights cause in the US. Even though non-violent protests and marches brought only minimal and achingly slow progress, I couldn't see how violence could be any better.

I had come to Kalamazoo thinking I would train to be a translator. I had abandoned that idea in the space of three months, disillusioned with the Spanish department, and switched to Sociology, with the vague idea of becoming a social worker. When Jackson entered the picture, slowly everything changed. In a way, Jackson seemed like a safe choice. He would go back to Congo, and I would go on with a life as yet unplanned, in the US or elsewhere. I underestimated the power of love and overestimated my capacity to resist its capacity to change my mind. Now I couldn't imagine my life without him.

"I want to marry you," Jackson said. "Could you live in Africa?"

"I don't know," I said. "I have to finish my degree first."

"We could get married after your Foreign Study. I want to get my PhD here, so we could come back next year," he said. "I've been here for seven years without seeing my family or my country. I need to go back."

Jackson and me, 1967, at Kalamazoo College.

In 1967, there was hope for Africa. Educated Africans like Jackson were returning in increasing numbers from study and exile to build their countries. Optimism and hope increased, even for Congo, as one African colony after another became independent. Was I cowardly, running away from a problem I should help to solve, or was I running toward a place where I could help develop a country, leaving behind a lost cause?

"So you think you can save the world?" my more cynical friends asked me.

"I have to do what I can."

Jackson explained it better, in mixed metaphors. "What we can do is only a drop in the ocean. But we can't just sit on our hands."

I didn't have to marry him to carry out that idea, of course. My idealistic friends had the same goals. But turning away from the US meant that I could live in a country where I could do more… with Jackson. For my Foreign Study, I chose Nairobi, Kenya, instead of Freetown in Sierra Leone where K College had a more established program, because there were very few flights between Freetown and Kinshasa. I still wasn't sure I would marry Jackson. I planned to go to Congo for Christmas and then decide. I couldn't consult anyone at the college because they would veto the idea and, of course, I didn't discuss it with my parents. Once I made those decisions, I tried not to think about the future and just enjoy the summer. Jackson and I spent most of our time together, more in love than ever, while Detroit rioted and racial tensions in Kalamazoo reached a peak. The ridiculous police surveillance of Jackson's apartment continued.

I took Swahili lessons from a Tanzanian student and otherwise studied very little—my courses seemed so far from the real world. I earned the only D of my college career, in Statistics. That came back to bite me later. I studied the history of Kenya, planned a compact wardrobe, filled out reams of paperwork, and negotiated an allowance with my parents. Of course I said nothing to them about visiting Congo or getting married. They would never have let me board the plane. Three other students were going to Kenya—an engaged couple and another student named Steven. None of them shared my political views, so after some initial conversations, I kept my opinions to myself. According to K College rules, we had to travel together. The couple and I agreed to spend two days in Rome and two in Athens. Steven received permission to visit family in London and joined us in Athens.

On our last night in Athens, we went to the Acropolis, open to the public during the full moon. It was utterly magical, and I wished Jackson could be there with me. We could see people dancing at rooftop cafes all around the Acropolis. Afterward, we went to a late dinner at a small family restaurant in the neighborhood—my idea, and not the best choice, as it turned out. Food poisoning had us throwing up most of the night on the plane. Unable to sleep, I watched the lights of Europe below us fade into the distance as we flew south. Soon only a few lights twinkled along the main roads and in the centers of the larger cities. Early the next morning, we landed in Nairobi.

* * *

Jackson and I exchanged letters as often as the erratic postal services between African countries permitted, writing on semi-transparent blue aerogrammes. He taught at a mission school far from any town in Congo, near the border of Congo-Brazzaville, the smaller country to the north. A messenger employed by the mission walked twenty-five miles every week to the nearest town on the other side of the border to get the mail and twenty-five miles back.

I wanted to decide if I would marry Jackson after visiting Congo at Christmas. He wrote that he wanted to get married in March and go back to the States together in the fall. I did not agree with that idea. I wanted to finish out the summer term at Kalamazoo and wait for him in Chicago. No doubt we would have had a serious argument if we had lived in the same place, or could even talk on the phone. Carrying on an argument through letters forced us into a more thoughtful exchange. Jackson backed off. Married or not, I was going back to Kalamazoo in March. I needed permission from my parents for the trip to Congo on Christmas break, and then from the Foreign Study Program because I would be traveling alone, normally not permitted. The whole exchange took place on flimsy aerogrammes.

"If I don't get permission, I'll get kicked out of the program," I wrote to my parents. "Then I'll have to decide whether to come home or stay in Congo."

It was close to blackmail, but I felt justified. My parents invaded my privacy by reading my diary and had used their financial support as a weapon to impose their beliefs on me when they found out about my affair with Jackson. Since they believed sex should only happen in marriage, how could they logically object to a marriage now?

Meanwhile, I made friends in Nairobi, even then a cosmopolitan city of many ethnicities and nationalities: English, Tanzanian, Ugandan, South African, Rhodesian, Canadian, American. I met several members of the African National Congress, exiles from South Africa. I knew they went to training camps in Tanzania and sometimes disappeared for weeks at a time on mysterious missions that they refused to discuss. I once asked them if I could enlist in the struggle. They smiled politely and shook their heads. No foreigners allowed.

Several months before I arrived, Kenya had announced that British passports were no longer valid for permanent residence. Whites and Asians had to obtain Kenyan citizenship or leave. If they left, they could exchange only a minimal amount of Kenyan shillings into foreign currency. During colonialism, the

British brought thousands of Indians and Pakistanis to build the railroads and other infrastructure. Now many of their frightened descendants took what they could and left. I saw them at the exchange counter at the bank, withdrawing their meager funds. Most White Kenyans and wealthy Asians gave up their British passports, unwilling to abandon their farms and businesses to start over in a country where they'd never lived. They knew they had higher living standards in Kenya than they would in England. An Asian population of 180,000 when Kenya became independent in 1963 shrank by half during the late 1960s, and to fewer than 80,000 by the mid-1970s. The exodus had just begun when I arrived. The Asian students like my Ismaili roommate came mostly from wealthy families, descendants of immigrants from many areas of India, Pakistan and Goa and from different religious traditions. The three main communities—White, African and Asian—lived in separate enclaves, and though I was determined to get to know students from all three groups, they would not socialize with one another. Juggling my inclusive social life proved even more difficult than it had been at Kalamazoo. Reading about Kenya's history had not prepared me for the racial situation there, even at the University. As interesting as my classes were, the experience of living in Nairobi and getting to know the other students proved far more valuable. I met several American students, including Tricia, an African American from Antioch College who also stayed in the dorm. We didn't spend much time together because we both wanted to get to know people of other nationalities.

Kampala, Uganda's capital, was the departure point for all flights to Kinshasa. It was also the site of the nearest Congolese Consulate. In 1967, the Entebbe airport on the shore of Lake Victoria looked like a makeshift shack. I basked in the warm, humid atmosphere on the hour-long bus ride into Kampala. We drove through lush tropical vegetation with the unmistakable scent of tropical plants, fresh and slightly decaying. Bananas and plantains grew everywhere. In Nairobi's dry climate, only thorn trees and grasses grew without irrigation. None of my Ugandan friends lived in the city, so they advised me to stay at a mission hostel. A bus dropped me near the Namirembe Mission, and from there I made the daily trek to the Consulate until the Consul finally issued my visa for Congo.

Friends of all nationalities, including some who knew Jackson, thought a week in Congo—not to mention my encounter with the Consulate in Uganda—would make me change my mind about marrying him. Congo had a scary reputation, even in Africa. I convinced myself that the country wasn't as bad as they thought. I'd made up my mind to follow my plan, no matter how dangerous, illogical and ill-advised it looked to anyone else. I loved Jackson, but even then, I did not believe the popular romantic notion that love conquers all. It was his dedication to improving life in Congo that clinched it for me.

I'm sure my friends' doubts had a lot to do with the fact that I hadn't exactly been pining away in my dorm room since I landed in Nairobi. Everyone wanted to go out with the new American girl, and I was eager for new experiences. With the best of intentions, my friends presented attractive opportunities, and I seized as many of them as I could. Anyone who knew me in Kenya must have known that I wasn't ready for marriage. They certainly weren't considering it for themselves. My American friend Tricia had no intention of marrying the American diplomat she spent most of her time with. Tricia had an Ismaili roommate who actively avoided the arranged marriage her family planned. She couldn't fathom why I was in such a hurry.

She hoped for a scholarship to attend grad school in England. Ismaili men value modesty, so on the blind dates arranged by her family, she would flip up her skirt to show some leg, and if that didn't put them off, she'd light up a cigarette. That worked every time. I told myself her situation was different. I had no interest in graduate school. I had found my calling: working to improve life in Africa, with Jackson. I couldn't imagine anything that would convince me to abandon that plan now.

I made good use of my last few months of freedom. One weekend a White Kenyan student invited me to the Nakuru motorcycle races with her brother, his friend Ian, and a transplanted South African coffee plantation manager. I was mightily hung over from a night of drinking and dancing the night before, and during the ride they alternately teased and indulged me. Ian trained animals for films (could it get more glamorous?) and that day was nursing a cut on his handsome face that had required several stitches. At the races, he sat with me, away from the others. I had no interest in motorcycles, but seeing a race in person was exciting, and the unfamiliar setting offered opportunities to observe White Kenyan culture. During the races, the engine noise made it impossible to talk. During the breaks between races, one beautiful woman after another came over to flirt with Ian; he responded in monosyllables and barely made eye contact with any of them. Their contemptuous eyes swept over me; they must have been thinking, *What does he see in this pale, bedraggled American?* I wondered the same thing. When they finally drifted away, Ian and I joked around as we had in the car. On the way back to Nairobi, we stopped for tea at a former estate, where we looked seriously out of place in our disheveled traveling clothes. It was a taste of old colonial Kenya, and that day I welcomed it.

When we dropped Ian off, he invited me to come to see his animals.

"Well, you've made a hit," said the plantation manager. "He doesn't invite just anybody."

I didn't follow up. A week or so later I ran into Ian on the street, and he repeated the invitation, but still I didn't go. It wasn't just a fear that I might be swept away—there was that—but I never really liked animals, except in the abstract. Could I have learned? I'm sure I could have. But I didn't want to be tempted.

A month or so later, a fellow student invited me to participate in a Kenyan radio show and introduced me to his friend Elliot, who drove a Jaguar with all the extras. The friend told me that Elliot's father was a high-ranking government official. Elliot, who was gorgeous, easygoing and soft-spoken, had just finished a BA in the States and was going back in a few months for graduate study. I went to parties with him, and sometimes to visit his friends and relatives. He knew about my engagement and gently tried to talk me out of it. I wavered for a while, but in the end, I didn't change my mind.

My Ismaili roommate encouraged me to join a trip that the Geology Club was planning, an overnight on the floor of the Rift Valley. Any student could sign up, so I joined about thirty other students, mostly Ismailis and Sikhs, to ride a rickety bus into Masai country, a near-desert from which they planned a hike the next day to a series of caves farther inland, reachable only on foot. Few tourists ever saw the Rift Valley from this vantage point. When we arrived at our campsite in the late afternoon, I saw giraffes running through the landscape in the distance, as well as the occasional elephant lumbering past. From a nearby village, Masai men and women in full ceremonial dress came to our camp to pose for photos in exchange for money. Paying people so I could take their pictures felt wrong to me, so I refused.

A few people slept in tents, but most of us spent the night in the open, under a sky so full of stars they didn't seem real. Away from the city, or any other light, they sparkled as I'd never seen anywhere else. No insects disturbed us, either, in this patch of desert. With a Sikh friend from one of my classes, I moved my sleeping bag away from the chattering crowd, leading the others to assume, mistakenly, that we had plans other than stargazing. The friend came in for more criticism than I did—he was a good Sikh boy, and I was just a crazy foreigner leading him astray. He did want to share my sleeping bag, but when I said no he didn't push it. We just watched the fabulous sky until we fell asleep.

The next morning, the gung-ho spelunkers, all men, set off early. I've been claustrophobic since childhood, so nothing would have convinced me to go into a cave, but I wanted to hike there with the main group. A few students with disabilities and a couple of organizers stayed in camp. As advised by my roommate, I wore slacks, a long-sleeved white shirt, and a hat—the sun was especially strong and there would be no shade. We took water with us. About two hours later we reached a rocky area below a small mountain where the others had gathered. The cave entrance lay at the bottom of the rocky ravine, essentially a hole in the ground that appeared to lead straight down. Several students had already gone in. The rest of us settled on nearby rocks with sack lunches brought by the organizers. After a while, some students started to worry about the spelunkers and went in after them. An hour later, they all emerged together.

"The passage was so narrow, I had to turn sideways to get through," said one thin student.

“I’m too big. I couldn’t get through,” said his heftier friend.

“I saw that tunnel and just couldn’t do it,” said another.

“Maybe that passage comes out somewhere interesting, but I was getting scared,” said the chief spelunker. “It was hard scooting backward and uphill. In the end they had to pull me out like a cork from a bottle.” I imagined myself in that cave and shuddered. I wished my spirit of adventure extended to spelunking, but I could not bear the idea of being trapped. I was never physically adventurous. I had no desire to hang-glide, bungee-jump or parachute out of an airplane. Once the spelunkers all returned, the organizers rounded us up and hurried us back to camp. They had a deadline to get the rented bus back to the depot. By the time we boarded the bus we’d exhausted our water supply, so it was a very thirsty ride back to Nairobi. I had protected everything but my hands, which glowed red with sunburn for three days.

Over a long weekend, Annette, a newly arrived Canadian student, proposed a trip to Mombasa in her car. We had only just met her, and we hesitated, but eventually four of us agreed to sign on: Tricia from Antioch, a Mennonite from Iowa, Steven from my group, and me. Annette rented a cottage at an oceanside resort called the Twiga Lodge. The cottages there were far apart—we could barely see the next one over. Ours had a simple living room and several bedrooms, all fully supplied with sheets and blankets—an amenity we hadn’t yet experienced in Kenya. Annette pulled out a bottle of Drambuie, her drink of choice, and we all drank a little before walking along the beach to the restaurant. Up a couple of flights of stairs from the beach, the bungalow-style restaurant had a steeply pitched thatched roof and brick half-walls, the rest open to the ocean breeze and the sound of the waves below. We splurged on a wonderful seafood dinner. It was the most romantic place I'd ever seen, and I wished Jackson were there.

On the way back, Annette proposed a skinny dip. My sense of adventure didn't extend to group nudity, and I declined. So did Steven. There were a few jokes about us staying behind together, but it didn't bother us. We'd become friends over the months we'd been in Nairobi, but there was no romance, and no tension. It didn't occur to me then that he was gay—he was way back in the closet until much later. I was just grateful to have a platonic male friend and didn't think more about it. The next day we lounged in the ocean, wonderfully warm and shallow, and then set off to explore Mombasa. We wandered a bit through the streets of the old city—there were hardly any tourists then—and to Fort Jesus, a 16th-century Portuguese fort. Technically, it was a museum, but it appeared untouched since its early functional days. Back at the lodge, we spent the rest of the weekend lolling in the surf. Farther out there was a coral reef, and the better swimmers (not I) went to look at it. I paddled around in the shallow water until time for our uneventful ride back to Nairobi.

All that time between December and March, a voice in my head kept saying, "See all the great adventures out there? Marry Jackson and you'll miss them." But another voice said, "Miss this chance to marry Jackson, and you'll miss the greatest adventure of all." I didn't doubt that I loved him, but should I marry my first love and preclude any others? Certainly I could have explored other options, and I met attractive men almost daily, but I still didn't change my mind. The potential dangers of living in Congo seemed preferable to living in the US with its seemingly immutable racism and the turmoil of the Vietnam War. The civil rights marches had been thus far ineffective. The Tet Offensive and the battle of Khe Sanh dominated the news.

Disturbances continued on college campuses. All of that only fed my determination to marry Jackson, despite everyone's advice against it. I knew I was too young, and even in my determination I knew I was taking a big risk. Beginning with my high school trip to Mexico, I had launched myself into adventures partly to overcome my childhood fears and anxieties. My parents, my teachers, my church warned me of dangers, but they did not equip me with the confidence and skills to face them. To most adults, I was only a pale and fragile girl in need of protection. As a result, I had not learned to distinguish a calculated risk from a downright crazy one. My affair with Jackson was my first serious relationship, and I still knew little about living in Congo. I did my best to suppress my internal conflicts and uncertainties.

In January, I wrote to my parents and told them I planned to marry Jackson in March, then go back to Kalamazoo to finish my junior year. I expected a strong reaction, and possibly a threat not to pay for that last quarter. They surprised me with a carefully worded aerogram voicing their disapproval but acknowledging that I would be twenty-one and could make my own decisions. I would turn twenty-one two days before my flight to Kinshasa. I expected only to have a civil ceremony with a couple of witnesses, so I did not ask them to attend the wedding, and they didn't ask to come.

Chapter 6
Omens

At the end of Kalamazoo's winter term in March, I flew from Nairobi to Kampala. An African friend from Uganda suggested that I stay at the Kampala YWCA. Full of young women like me, it was much more fun than the Namirembe Mission, and this time I didn't have to spend every day at the Congolese Consulate, since I already had a multiple-entry visa. Unlike the Namirimbe Mission, the YWCA cafeteria served Ugandan food. I loved *matoke*, the Ugandan national dish of mashed plantain. At the Y, I met Bridget, a seventeen-year-old Californian traveling solo around the world, in a 1960s version of the gap year, with her parents' blessing. She'd only been in Kampala a couple of weeks, and she already knew her way around in ways I couldn't imagine.

"I have to go to the bank to change some money," I said one day.

"It's a bank holiday today, remember? Never mind. I know a guy who'll give you a much better rate."

"I don't think it's a good idea to—"

"Oh, come on. Everybody does it. Here's a taxi."

The taxi dropped us at a gas station where Bridget asked for someone by name—the owner, it turned out. She introduced us, we went to his office, I wrote a check, and he gave me East African shillings. Five minutes.

"See?" she said. "Easy."

Next we went to the Air Congo office downtown.

"We have no flights until next week," the young Ugandan clerk said apologetically.

"But I need to get to Kinshasa before that," I said. "Are you sure there's nothing available?"

"Wait here." He went into a back room and returned with a ticket form.

"In two days, there's a cargo flight that will take passengers," he said.

"I'll take it," I said. I paid in cash for the ticket that he wrote out by hand.

"I'd better take you to the airport, just to be sure you get on," he said.

"Really? Would you do that for me?"

"I have to go anyway," he said. "It's not a regular flight, so there won't be any announcements or anything."

"That was pretty weird," said Bridget after we were on the sidewalk.

"Very weird. A lot of things about Congo are weird."

"Do you think he'll show up?"

I shrugged. "Who knows? If he doesn't, I'll run to the hotel down the street and get a taxi."

"Well, what should we do now?" Bridget asked.

"It's my birthday," I said. "The big two-one."

"Come on, then. I'm taking you to lunch. I know a good place close by."

We walked half a mile down the main road, where Bridget led me down a flight of stairs beside an ordinary office building. On the ground floor in the back, a large open-air restaurant overlooked a wild, hilly garden. The trees appeared to be laden with a type of large fruit I didn't recognize.

"Let's have a beer," Bridget said. We took our time with my birthday lunch and had another beer. Suddenly I heard a muffled whooshing sound and looked up. The large fruit on the trees had suddenly taken flight. What I had thought was fruit turned out to be a colony of very large bats. Bridget laughed at my astonishment.

"That's the first time you've ever seen fruit bats?"

"Yes! They're huge! And gross!"

"Hey, they eat the mosquitoes."

After flapping around the tree for a while, the bats settled back onto its branches. I wondered what had disturbed them. Half an hour later, Bridget and I made our way lazily to the street to walk back to the Y. At the top of the stairs in front of the building, we both gasped.

There was no sign of the usual noisy traffic, and no one else was on the street. Two charred, smoking cars lay on their sides, their lights and windows smashed. Glass from shop windows, windshields and first-floor offices sparkled on the sidewalk.

"Maybe we should go back to the restaurant," I said.

"We have to get back to the Y eventually. Let's walk a little further."

Thirty yards down the street, we saw an Asian man in an office pecking at a typewriter behind what had been a large plate glass window. Its glass lay shattered on the sidewalk.

"Hello, excuse me… what happened here?" Bridget asked.

The man looked up, startled, and glanced around nervously.

"A riot. Didn't you hear it? It started as a protest against President Obote." He looked up and down the street. "You really shouldn't be here. You need to get off this street. Take a side street."

Infected by his anxiety, we took a parallel street back to the Y. The next day shops and offices opened as if nothing had happened. The Ugandan news reported on the riot, though not in great detail. I already knew that East Africa's press enjoyed more freedom than Congo's. I could imagine a similar riot in Kinshasa. From discussions with my Ugandan friends, I knew that President Obote's popularity had waned. But unpopular leaders lasted a long time in Africa; riots and protests didn't always lead to change, any more than they did in the US. Still, when Idi Amin deposed Obote three years later, the only surprise was that it took so long.

Two days after the riot, I said goodbye to Bridget and my friends at the Y. My flight was leaving early in the morning, so I hoped the Air Congo agent would show up. I didn't want to rush around looking for a taxi. It didn't occur to me to call Mom and Dad before I left. They hadn't asked me to either. The Air Congo agent arrived on time, in his Volkswagen Beetle. He stationed me in the airport cafe while he bustled off, returning fifteen minutes later with a boarding pass.

"All set," he said with a broad smile. He seemed so relieved that I realized he hadn't been absolutely sure he could get me on this cargo flight. Alone on the tarmac, I walked up the portable staircase into the first-class section of the plane, where the crew and an Indian family waited. I glanced into the coach section—it was full, top to bottom, with cargo. What could Uganda possibly be exporting to Congo? After the plane made a brief stop in Bujumbura, the crew served a meal, the same as on a regular flight. Just as I had at Christmas, on landing I whizzed through the airport and found Jackson waiting outside.

"They told me your flight was canceled," he said as we stood surrounded by taxi drivers. "I almost left, but I thought you might be on this flight." He chose a taximan from the ten or so clamoring for his attention. "We're staying with Mary Bobb and her family, at Isaac Kalonji's house."

Isaac Kalonji was then president of the senate, and a famous figure in the struggle for independence in Congo. The taximan let us off in front of a large duplex in the Quartier des Ambassadeurs.

"Nobody's home," Jackson said as we climbed the stairs to the front door. "They'll be back for lunch—the kids are in school, and Mary is at the church office. Senator Kalonji is traveling, so we'll stay in his apartment, in back. After the wedding, I mean."

An old cook in a white apron nodded to us as we passed the kitchen. Jackson led the way down the hall and through a small office to a bedroom.

"Here's where we'll stay." Finally alone, we held each other in a long embrace.

"Can't we...?"

"No, they'll be back any minute."

Soon footsteps and slamming doors mixed with children's voices. Jackson introduced me to Mary and her four children, the youngest an adopted Congolese boy of about nine. Mary, sleek and stylish, was unlike any missionary I'd ever met. Missionaries had different roles—teachers, doctors, pastors—but I never figured out exactly what Mary's job was. She acted more like a diplomat, and in fact socialized mostly with the Embassy staff. In any case, the family would be going back to the States permanently in a few months. Mary's husband had already left for the US to look for a house, and Senator Kalonji had graciously offered his house to the family in the meantime.

"Wonderful news! You can have the wedding reception here," Mary said.

"We can just have a civil ceremony at the Zone office, can't we?" I said, somewhat alarmed. I did not plan on anything more.

"Well, you have to do that," Mary said. "This is separate. We're Protestants, so you need the church wedding, but you can only get a marriage certificate from the civil authority. And if you were African, there would be a traditional wedding too! With a band of old women checking to make sure you're a virgin!"

I must have looked shocked. Mary laughed.

"We will have the religious service at my uncle's church in Bandal," Jackson said. "I already spoke to him about it."

"Then we can have the reception here."

"A church wedding? Really?" I hadn't planned on all this. "I don't have a dress."

"Hmm. There's not really time to order one either," Mary said.

"I can make one, if there's a sewing machine."

"There is!" Mary said, delighted. "Tomorrow I'll take you to get the fabric and the pattern. We need to go to the Embassy and find out how to get the Consul to certify the marriage."

"We do?"

"Yes, we do. Jackson will need a marriage certificate later when he asks for a visa, won't he? And you will need one, too, when you come back here."

Mary Bobb knew everybody who mattered in Kinshasa, and she moved twice as fast as anyone else. At our first stop, she and I bought the makings of a white lace dress. When we stopped to fill up the car, the attendant called, "*Oui, chérie, j'arrive!* (Yes, sweetheart, I'm coming!)."

"*D'accord,*" Mary called. "And I'm not your *chérie*," she muttered.

We breezed into the Vice Consul's office with no appointment, and he agreed to attend the civil ceremony the next day. In a place where nothing moves fast, Mary Bobb and Jackson arranged everything in two days, while I whipped up a simple cotton shift and a white lace tent dress to wear over it. Jackson took me to a Senegalese goldsmith near the main market to get a gold filigree ring, made on the spot. Mary organized the reception around the pool in Kalonji's front yard, and Jackson sent word to his Kinshasa relatives.

Civil marriage ceremony at the Zone of Ngaliema. Left to right, top row: US Vice-Consul, Pastor Biandudi, Mary Bobb. Bottom row: me, Jackson.

Everything happened on schedule. I would have gladly skipped the church wedding, but Jackson insisted on it. I did not realize until then how important church weddings were to Congolese Protestants. I learned to appreciate traditional rituals much later, but then, at twenty-one, I had no use for them.

"You will be sorry later if you don't do it. What pictures will you show your children?"

The service lasted nearly an hour, and Pastor Biandudi ignored the carefully worded vows I had written, reverting to the traditional "love, honor and obey." I tried not to wince. The excellent men's choir sang spirituals in English.

"Nice choir, although 'Swing Low, Sweet Chariot' isn't the best choice for a wedding," Mary said afterward. "They probably don't realize it's a funeral song. I suppose they have a limited repertoire of songs in English."

Jackson went to sort out transportation for the family, so I went back to the house with Mary. "I'm glad you don't mind coming back without your husband," Mary said. "A lot of women would be upset at that."

Since I had no expectations of the church ceremony, I was free from disappointment. I saw it as just another ritual that social norms demanded. That night, after the guests left and we thanked Mary and the children, we went back to Senator Kalonji's apartment where Jackson and I argued as we never had before, about who would sleep closest to the door. Of course, we were really fighting about something else—control. I knew it wouldn't be the last time, but like so many newly married women, I convinced myself that we would argue less once we were living together.

On the plane the next day, I chatted with my seatmate, a middle-aged British woman.

"You married an African? Beautiful ring. These mixed marriages almost never work out, you know," she said.

I closed my eyes and pretended to sleep.

When we stopped in Monrovia, the plane stayed at the end of the runway instead of moving to a gate. The crew stood near the open door by the cockpit. Two workers were rolling a mobile staircase toward the plane.

"Why aren't we going to the gate?" I asked a flight attendant who was smoking a cigarette in the doorway, gazing at the far-off terminal.

"Didn't get permission in time," she said. "WAWA."

"WAWA?"

"West Africa Wins Again."

It matched the French equivalent I frequently heard from Belgians in Congo, spoken almost as one word, "*Que voulez-vous dans ce pays*?" (What can you expect in this country?). As if Belgium didn't have its own problems, not to mention what its colonial policies did to Congo.

Jackson planned to come to the States in August. He'd arranged a scholarship for graduate school through the Embassy, and I had every confidence in that plan. That would be Lesson Number One in how wrong things could go in Congo.

Chapter 7
No One to Watch Over Me

Eighteen days after my wedding, Martin Luther King was murdered in Memphis, and riots shook a dozen American cities. Two months later an assassin killed Robert Kennedy. In August, the entire nation watched as police beat up protesters (my friends among them) outside the Democratic National Convention in Chicago. I had no hope for the country after that. The only reason to stay in the US was to finish my BA and Jackson's PhD.

By the end of the summer, Jackson still had no scholarship and no ticket, despite earlier promises from the US Embassy. The marriage certificate, as Mary Bobb predicted, allowed him to get a visa, and instead of waiting for a Washington bureaucrat to issue a ticket, he traded his precious stereo system to the local Congolese program representative for a ticket to Chicago. During the year and a half he spent in Congo, Jackson had learned to work the system. The Congolese said there was an unwritten fifteenth article in their fourteen-article national constitution. Article 15 is *Débrouillez-vous*, meaning "Figure it out" or "Get by somehow." There was even a noun for it: *Débrouillardise*. That idea dominated our lives from then on.

My parents, to my surprise, agreed to house us temporarily while Jackson applied to graduate schools. Focused on starting our new life, Jackson and I had no more arguments like the one we had the night of our wedding. My youngest sister Jo was still in high school; Beth was a sophomore at Valparaiso. Jo told me later that Dad convinced Mom to make this partial reconciliation. I could hardly be surprised that Mom barely tolerated me. I should have known from the way she talked about her father throughout my childhood that she could carry a grudge for a long time. I half-expected my parents to disown me, but they clearly accepted my marriage as a *fait accompli* and had no intention of cutting off contact.

Jackson and I both took jobs at the department store where I had worked the summer after my freshman year at Kalamazoo. I went back to selling children's shoes, and Jackson worked in the furniture department. He showed almost exaggerated respect for Mom and Dad, since respect for your parents-in-law is an absolute obligation in Kongo culture. Their attitude toward him evolved from tolerance to wary appreciation. They silently applauded his willingness to work at a menial job. Mom believed in humility.

"Everyone should work at a menial job so that they appreciate what it's like," she repeated to me and my sisters. She thought of humility as an essential Christian quality, but I thought it stemmed from the constant self-effacement I observed in Norwegian–American culture.

Jackson wanted to study African History at Temple University, but admissions had closed for the winter semester, and Temple did not give financial aid to PhD students in the middle of the year. Instead, he used his Baptist connections to get accepted into a master's degree program in Comparative Religions at the Eastern Baptist Seminary on the western edge of Philadelphia. In January, Jackson and I moved into a large studio apartment in a building owned and subsidized by the seminary. I took a clerical job and looked for evening classes to finish my degree. Jackson finagled a small stipend from the State Department, a fraction of what they had promised. Together we had just enough money to live on, $750 a month.

The only time I'd ever had my own apartment was during the three months of my internship in Chicago. In my ignorance of what it takes to maintain a household, I agreed to do all the housework and cooking, a concession (as I saw it then) to African gender roles. I had no idea what that commitment meant. I couldn't even make spaghetti sauce. The recipe I followed when I made it for the first time called for a clove of garlic. I didn't know what a clove was, so I put in the whole garlic head, rendering the sauce inedible. The first time I did laundry, Jackson watched me folding his T-shirts and asked, "Aren't you going to iron them?"

I laughed. "I'll try to iron dress shirts, but if you want undershirts ironed, you'll have to do them yourself."

It took me half an hour to iron a dress shirt, and I made such a mess of it that he did it over himself. I proved incapable of learning to iron shirts to boarding-school standards, so that became Jackson's share of the housework. Later he also started doing the laundry, because thieves regularly broke into the coin-operated machines in the basement, and he worried about my safety.

Jackson worked hard at the seminary, but he still aimed for a doctorate in African History. Through his Kalamazoo professors and local African friends, he lobbied all the professors of African History in Pennsylvania—the American version of

Article 15. He and I quickly fell into the routine of married graduate students. We made friends with the other families in the building. I took the bus to work and applied to the only college close to us that catered to evening students, St. Joseph's. My D in statistics from the Summer of Love did not transfer, of course, and I lost other credits switching systems, so it would take me two semesters and a summer to finish. Mom and Dad paid my tuition, and when I held that first $700 check, I felt it represented a new level of reconciliation. I don't know what motivated them. They probably couldn't bear the thought of having a daughter who didn't finish college.

Despite our poverty, Jackson and I were happy. We finally felt we were on the path to the life we wanted. Then, just as we were getting accustomed to our new life, news reports came out about strokes in healthy young women caused by birth control pills, and Jackson wanted me to stop taking them. The reports were scary, even though I'd taken the pills for three years without problems, so I looked for another means of birth control. My doctor advised against an IUD, still experimental in 1969. He thought my risk of getting pregnant was low because of a "tipped uterus," believed at the time to be a cause of infertility. So I stopped taking the Pill and went back to older, less reliable methods. The doctor was wrong. In August, after weeks of nausea and abdominal pain, I consulted an internist, who prudently did a pregnancy test before ordering an X-ray. It came back positive, and he referred me to an OB/GYN.

"Congratulations," said the gynecologist's nurse. I was three months pregnant. I burst into tears. The gynecologist never sent me a bill. I had nausea every night until well into my fourth month. The nausea should have tipped me off much earlier—I was clearly in denial—but I had a history of stomach problems and convinced myself I couldn't be pregnant. Jackson seemed pleased about the pregnancy, although most of the time he seemed distant and troubled. I had absolutely no desire to have a child while I was still trying to finish my degree. I wanted an abortion, but Jackson wouldn't consider it. Legal abortions were not yet available, and, having delayed too long, I didn't have enough time to figure out how to get an illegal one. I had unwisely opted out of the pregnancy coverage offered by my health insurance, so the gynecologist referred me to a low-income clinic at a nearby hospital where I could get prenatal care and delivery for $300—a real bargain, even in 1969. I was grateful to him—and miserable.

* * *

Although we had many friends, Black and White, Jackson and I faced hostility whenever we went out together, especially in our mostly White City Line Avenue neighborhood. Philadelphia had high crime rates and serious racial tensions. In many areas, including the downtown area around city hall, I didn't feel safe alone even during the day. Civil rights advocates won a court case in 1968 that desegregated an all-White college located in the largest Black neighborhood in the city. The White majority in Philadelphia reacted violently to this important legal victory, propelling the rise of racist police commissioner Frank Rizzo, who later became mayor, with disastrous results. Jackson often talked about his resentment of the discrimination he faced. One night he said, "I've joined a new Black Power organization. You know I have been looking for a group of people to work with."

"How did you know about them?"

"They contacted me," he said. "This group follows some ideas of the Nation of Islam, but they are not religious. They talk self-defense instead of non-violence like the old-style groups."

"How big is the group?"

"At the meeting I went to, about ten people, all men. They don't like the fact that I'm married to a White woman."

"Well, what did you expect?"

"Maybe getting married to you was a mistake," he said. "Maybe they're right, and I have betrayed the cause by marrying you."

For the first time since we were married, I thought about everything I had given up for Jackson and felt a ball of rage grow in my chest.

"Nobody wanted me to marry you," I said. "And I ignored them."

"It's not the same thing," he said.

"You made a promise to me," I said. "Are you going to listen to people who don't even know either of us?"

He didn't answer and offered no reassurance. Whenever I cried, almost every night over the next few weeks, Jackson left the room. I wondered how he could even talk about his doubts when he knew how the pregnancy had already upset me. He didn't want me to get an abortion, but he didn't want to be a father to his child. How could he do this? He could only hurt me so deliberately if he no longer loved me, I reasoned. Why was he so eager to get married if he had ideas like this barely a year later? I certainly had my doubts about the marriage, but I never imagined he could be ready to break a whole series of promises so lightly.

One night, about two months after we found out about the pregnancy, we were taking a walk in the neighborhood when he suddenly said, "I want a divorce."

I couldn't speak for several minutes. Then I took a deep breath. No tears, I told myself. By that time anger had replaced my initial sorrow at his betrayal.

"You're the one who wanted me to stop taking birth control pills. This pregnancy is your fault. The least you can do is stay until this baby is born."

He said nothing. He didn't mention divorce again, but I felt the word floating between us like a cloud of acrid smoke. It never left my mind, and I went through the motions of everyday life in a kind of trance. I couldn't really think, couldn't plan, and couldn't talk about it to anyone. In my head, I could hear my mother saying, "I was right. You should have listened to me."

Within a month, Temple University accepted Jackson in the African History PhD program, with a scholarship and a stipend. It meant little to me, since I believed that he would leave me in a few months. I would be raising our child alone and prepared myself emotionally for that future. I would not go back to my parents. I located an agency that offered counseling to low-income women and began seeing a social worker who happened to be a young Black woman. Her insights into racial attitudes helped me understand what could be going on with Jackson. Before I talked to her, it never occurred to me that the racial situation in the US could affect his mental health. Toward the end of my pregnancy, she asked to meet with Jackson, and, to my surprise, he agreed. I don't know what she said to him—he wouldn't talk about it—but after he met with her, his mood lifted, and he left the self-defense group. His admission to the PhD program could have been a deciding factor, but I never asked. By that time I had entered the strange, floating serenity of late pregnancy and couldn't focus on anything but the upcoming birth.

The baby came a week early, after barely four hours of labor. We named him Kiame, which means "mine" in Kikongo. Jackson explained that since the Kongo traced their lineage through the mother, and as a non-Kongo I did not have a clan, Kiame would belong to Jackson's clan. When he was a month old, I asked Jackson, "So when are you leaving?"

"What do you mean?"

"You said you wanted a divorce."

He looked embarrassed that I had brought it up, and said, "Oh. Don't worry about that."

Relief surged through me. From then on, our lives revolved around our difficult, delightful baby. Jackson never mentioned divorce again. I pushed the memory of those anguished months to the back of my mind, wishing I could forget them, but I couldn't. He had put a space between us, an area of doubt that I couldn't breach. I knew I could never completely trust Jackson again. At what stage of life can you believe nothing will ever shake your trust in someone? Maybe only when you're young and in love for the first time, and even then, not for long. At twenty-three I realized—far later than I should have—that I had to look out for myself. Nobody was going to watch over me—certainly not Jackson. And now I had to protect someone else—baby Kiame. And he wasn't an easy baby. I had to feed him every three hours for months, and he never slept more than eight hours a night. He took only short naps during the day. Always ambitious, Kiame became frustrated when he didn't succeed on his first try at anything. He became furious when he couldn't roll over. When we started to give him baby food, he immediately grabbed the spoon, so the food ended up mostly in his hair or on the floor. He never cried when anyone else held him. He just gazed at the person with obvious curiosity, his eyes wide and bright. He talked early and embarrassed us by reaching out to any Black man nearby, yelling, “Daddy!” and to any blonde woman, calling, “Mommy!”

With four younger siblings, Jackson knew far more than I did about childcare. He gave Kiame his baths, fed him, rocked him and took him along whenever he went out, even to his classes. When Kiame was a little older, Jackson would throw a coat over his head and pretend to be a monster, walking toward Kiame like Frankenstein. Kiame loved it. Visitors, especially the Congolese, would hold out their arms and ask Kiame, “Want to come with me?” Usually, babies shrink back in their parents’ arms at that prospect. Not Kiame. He would lean toward the surprised visitor and hold out his arms too.

It’s hard for a mother to tear herself away from a new baby, but I needed to finish my BA. It was time for me to embrace Article 15. I would get by any way I could. I needed four more courses to finish, and I squeezed them all into a marathon summer session, while Jackson took care of Kiame. For three months, I barely saw either of them. For my Shakespeare course alone, I had to read all the plays. As soon as the last class ended, I started looking for a job. Jackson encouraged me to go to grad school instead.

“What am I going to do with a master’s degree in Congo?”

“You’d be surprised. You can never have too much education.”

I should have listened to him, but I didn’t have the foresight to imagine a future other than what we were planning—to develop Congo. I never for a moment thought about what I would do if my marriage broke up, or if we ended up living somewhere other than Congo. So I worked at temporary jobs for a few months and then took a bilingual secretarial job with a drug company. If there were better jobs available, I didn't find them. Without a nursing degree or a teaching certificate, I could find only secretarial jobs. Then I had to find a babysitter. Daycare barely existed in 1971. Fortunately, a young woman in our building who had a baby the same age as Kiame agreed to take care of him when Jackson couldn't. When she went away for a week and Jackson had classes, I had to put him in a home daycare forty minutes away, where they put him in a highchair in front of the television.

* * *

In October of 1971, President Mobutu announced his "Authenticity Campaign" and changed the name of the country from Congo to Zaire. He also replaced each old Belgian place name with an African name in one of the country's four official African languages: Kikongo, Chiluba, Kiswahili and Lingala. Stanleyville became Kisangani, Thysville became Mbanza-Ngungu, Elizabethville became Lubumbashi. While people were still adjusting to that change, he announced that everyone in the country had to abandon their European first name and choose an African one instead. That brought him into conflict with the Catholic Church, which up to that time baptized its members only with European saint names. He replaced his own name "Joseph" with a string of African names. He also banned religious youth organizations, radio broadcasts and publications, and forbade religious instruction in schools. He later banned short skirts and pants for women and banned the European suit and tie for men. After a protest by Catholic bishops, Mobutu increased restrictions and threatened to close any church that did not obey. Then he canceled Christmas and Easter, forbidding their celebration. The Protestants quietly obeyed and did not join the Catholic protest. Jackson initially approved of some of these changes, although he thought some regulations against the Church went too far. Kiame already had a Kikongo first name. For himself, Jackson chose the name "Kimpianga," after his grandfather.

Jackson finished his master's degree in African History and the course work for his doctorate a few months after Kiame's second birthday. Now he needed to conduct research in Zaire for his dissertation, which he planned to do part time while holding a teaching job. His advisors wanted him to finish his research in the US, but he refused. It was time to leave. Jackson didn't expect to have trouble finding a job in Zaire. By all reports the country was desperate for university graduates. While the local universities had expanded since Independence in 1960, when the country notoriously had only twenty-five college graduates, secondary schools also expanded, creating an enormous need for new teachers. Jackson wrote to an American missionary who had written an article in a church publication, complaining that he couldn't get teachers to come to his secondary school near Kimpese, because Zairian graduates didn't want to work outside the city. The man wrote back that there were no jobs open at his school.

"How is that possible?" I asked.

"Everyone wants to keep his job," Jackson said. "Even missionaries."

He wrote to another American missionary school director and received the same shocking response. Eventually an offer came from the Sundi Lutete secondary school where he taught in 1967, while I was in Kenya, but as director rather than teacher. In that role he would have less time to work on his thesis, so he would have preferred a teaching job closer to Kinshasa, but clearly there were not as many job opportunities as we expected. He decided to take the job, and I would teach English at the same school. I knew the history of missionaries in Zaire, and that they ran nearly all the schools, but until Jackson's job search, I didn't think much about how they might influence our life. The Protestant Church sponsored Jackson's education, and in his first years in the US he lived with families who worked in the church. He remained grateful to those who had helped him, but he believed it was time for Africans to replace missionaries, especially in the schools. When he taught at Sundi in 1967 and 1968, he clashed frequently with the missionaries. Everyone in Sundi would remember that, and I did not expect a warm welcome from the Swedes. The job was open because José Dianzungu, who taught at Sundi with Jackson and became director the year after he left, was moving to a bigger mission school in Kimpese.

Evangelization began in the 16th century with missionaries from Portugal. Conversion continued with Italian missions in the 17th and 18th centuries and intensified in the 19th century with Catholic missionaries from Belgium and Italy, and Protestant missionaries from Britain, Sweden, Canada and the US. Even though the Belgian colonial government favored Catholic missionaries, the Catholic Church couldn't evangelize the whole country. Colonial authorities tolerated Protestants because they built schools and hospitals and had a pacifying and Westernizing effect on the people in the areas where they worked. Mission churches, both Catholic and Protestant, still had immense power in the late 1960s. All missionaries targeted African traditional religion, which they regarded as "superstition" and "idolatry." Before the missionaries, Kongo religion centered on a spiritual relationship with Nature and communication with deceased family members. The Kongo did not believe in a pantheon of gods. Instead, they performed rituals to invoke the intervention of ancestral spirits and of spirits in Nature, especially water spirits, believed to be the souls of long-dead ancestors who had passed through a complex series of afterlives. Other rituals centered on more recently deceased family members, seeking their intervention through libations and prayers.

Missionaries worked to replace these beliefs with Christianity, of course, but they also took aim at traditional healers and diviners. I've seen old Swedish missionary photographs of smiling Africans beside burning piles of carved wooden statues that would command thousands of dollars in today's art markets. The missionaries considered these "idols," even though in no way did the Kongo worship these statues, which were used as magical or symbolic objects in healing rituals, sometimes combined with herbal treatments. Belgium feared the power of healers and diviners because they were closely connected to traditional political and social leadership. Both missionaries and colonial authorities believed their own medical system to be "scientific" and superior to African ways of healing. They also misunderstood the Kongo concepts of witchcraft and sorcery and the practices used to control them. At the insistence of missionaries, Belgium outlawed the divinations and ceremonies the Kongo used to expose sorcerers. Africans felt threatened and exposed to evil, deprived of the protection that traditional religion and healing provided.

The Belgian colonial state knew that Protestant and Catholic missionaries facilitated colonial domination and encouraged obedience to colonial authorities. An important exception, William Henry Shepherd, an African-American missionary, militated against the atrocities committed by King Leopold and his surrogates in the Congo Free State, the name of the territory when King Leopold held it as his personal fiefdom. Shepherd's reports and lobbying created international pressure to remove the country from Leopold's direct control. As a result, it became a Belgian colony in 1908. Shepherd, though, stood almost alone. In the 20th century, those who disagreed with the colonial government either left on their own or were expelled. In 1972, Zaire was nominally independent, politically. In many other ways, independence remained a long way off.

Chapter 8
Land of the Kongo

I took Kiame for one last visit to my parents before leaving for Africa. I left him with Mom and Dad for a weekend to visit my sister in Milwaukee and confessed to Mom that my active and talkative two-and-a-half-year-old would not use the toilet. She took that information in without comment. When I came back on Sunday night, I was talking to Mom when Kiame came up and pulled on her skirt.

"Oh, you want to use the toilet?" she asked.

He nodded and gave me a look with a clear message: "Don't you dare say a word." I don't know how she did it.

Instead of flying directly to Zaire, we stopped in France to visit a family Jackson had stayed with in his first years in the US. Reverend Tuller was now pastor of the Protestant Church in Paris, on the Quai d'Orsay overlooking the River Seine. I marveled at its immense Gothic furniture and the 19th century tapestries that covered entire walls of the apartment that served as a parsonage. I took Kiame, now an active toddler, to the Luxembourg Gardens and to as many art museums as he (and the museum guards) would tolerate. From Paris we went to the Netherlands to visit the Dutch couple I'd met in Kinshasa. We also met with a Belgian who had worked at Sundi shortly after Independence. From the way the Belgian looked at me, I knew he didn't think I could adapt to Sundi Lutete. Nonetheless, I soaked up valuable ideas on how to adjust to mission life. The Dutch couple gave me a list of items they found useful, and I bought as many of them as I could. We bought a VW Beetle in France and had it shipped to Zaire. That was cheaper than shipping a car from the US. Buying a car in Zaire would have been even more expensive.

We had at least fifteen pounds of excess baggage, but the Air Zaire agent barely glanced at the scale. I felt relieved until it occurred to me that if she did that for everyone, the plane could be seriously overloaded. In fact, the 747 wasn't even half full. When Kiame and another child raced Matchbox cars in the aisle, the flight attendants just smiled and stepped over them.

I emerged from the Air Zaire plane into blinding sun and hot, humid air. At the bottom of the portable stairway, two soldiers confronted a passenger, a Zairian wearing an *abacost*—the Zairian version of the Mao suit. The soldiers looked ready to arrest him.

"Don't look. Don't stop," Jackson murmured behind me, as he carried Kiame down the rattling stairway. The man was still arguing with the soldiers as we passed.

The airport hadn't changed in four years: aircraft and equipment scattered across the tarmac, no signs or directions to Immigration and Customs. We followed more experienced passengers to Arrivals, as I had the last time, dodging vehicles on the way. Once through passport control and Customs, we took a taxi to the mission hostel, where José would meet us. There we found a message that he would come the next day because his wife

Suzanne had just delivered their fourth child. José drove us to Kimpese two days later, along a paved, two-lane road bordered by makeshift market stalls in front of one-story shops. Once out of the city, we passed through Kasangulu, a sprawling suburb, and into the hills of Mbanza-Ngungu, site of a big army base. Roadside vendors hawked small baskets of strawberries.

"They only grow here in the hills," José explained. "It's too hot everywhere else."

Soldiers manned roadblocks at every bridge, as if they expected convoys of rebels to rumble across any minute, even though the rebellion was fifteen hundred miles away. The only purpose of the many roadblocks seemed to be to intimidate the population and allow the soldiers a chance to make extra money by stopping cars and demanding bribes in exchange for permission to pass. José made this four-hour trip so often that they knew him and exchanged a salute as they let him through.

"The mission plane will take you to Sundi tomorrow," José said. "There's no time to arrange other transportation. They need you there."

"There's a plane?" Jackson asked.

"Yes, the Missionary Aviation Fellowship. They have hangars in Kinshasa and Kimpese, and two planes with American pilots. You're lucky they're available tomorrow. Otherwise," he said, turning to me, "you'd have to drive two hours to the river, then wait for a ferry to get to Luozi. From there it's another six hours by road."

"At least," Jackson said.

I didn't appreciate the plan to fly to Sundi Lutete as much as I should have. I hated small planes and did not yet realize how difficult the road trip could be. José arranged for some of our baggage to go by road, and we showed up the next morning at the MAF hangar. Two American pilots in white jumpsuits bustled around, checklists in hand. They greeted us and went on with their work. One named Scotty brought out a bathroom scale and weighed us and our baggage. At Scotty's invitation, we boarded the six-passenger Aztec, José in front, Jackson and I in the second row, Kiame on my lap. The plane taxied out of the hangar and onto the rough dirt runway. Kiame fell asleep before the plane lifted off.

Ahead of us lay the Bangu, a tall butte that marked the route toward Sundi, and we flew directly over it. Scotty and José chatted amiably, but I couldn't hear them over the noise of the plane. Jackson, who hated planes even more than I did, clutched my hand and closed his eyes tightly. Fifteen minutes later, we crossed the Zaire River against a strong headwind and followed the River along the North Bank.

"Look at the river, Jackson," I shouted.

"I can't."

The plane had no radar. At a landmark that I could not distinguish, Scotty turned the plane north along one of the many tributaries flowing into the immense Zaire River. The terrain below rose swiftly from a narrow riverine plain to a plateau. Beyond, hills and gullies alternated as far as I could see. Scotty veered sharply east, and I could see the runway below us, a wide cleared space on top of a large hill with a miniature Land Rover at one end. Tiny figures ran back and forth across the runway as Scotty buzzed the site and circled over it. He brought the plane just below the level of the runway. We flew straight toward the wall of vegetation on the side of the hill, and my heart thumped until Scotty lifted the plane at the last moment. The plane's wheels touched down and rumbled along the dirt runway.

A welcoming party surrounded the plane, headed by the pastor of the church, as I handed the sleeping Kiame to Jackson and climbed out.

"Tell them they have to keep those kids off the runway or one day they'll be hamburger," Scotty said to José, who nodded and translated.

After handshakes all around, we got into one of the Land Rovers, and a taciturn driver in a tropical print shirt drove down a hill so steep that we had to brace ourselves against the front seat to keep from falling forward. At the bottom, where a shallow stream crossed the dirt track, the driver splashed across without slowing down. He shifted to four-wheel drive to get up the bank on the other side. We drove through the hospital complex first. A group of women waved to the driver to stop. Hands came through the window to greet us; a woman began talking to Jackson in Kikongo.

"My cousin," he said, when we started up again. "She works at the hospital."

Down another hill and around a few corners, we stopped in front of a red brick house. The driver put our suitcases inside the front door. We followed the pastor into a living room with European-style windows at both ends. At the near end, by the front window, stood a large dining table and chairs. At the far end by the back window, several Swedish-modern chairs clustered around a coffee table. I wondered why there was a fireplace against one wall. As we approached the kitchen, I understood. A Husqvarna woodburning stove occupied an entire wall. Outside the window, three fifty-five-gallon barrels stood on bricks, fed by a gutter that channeled rainwater into them during the rainy season. The group continued its tour, back across the living room to the bedrooms.

I decided to get a change of clothes out of my suitcase, and as I flopped it onto the floor, a huge spider ran out from under it. I screamed, and everyone ran back into the living room. Without interrupting his conversation, the pastor stomped on it and kicked the corpse into a corner.

"There are two bedrooms," he continued, "one in the front of the house, the other in the back. In here... "

I'm not usually bothered by bugs, but that spider was a good eight inches across.

"When people haven't lived in a house for a few weeks, the bugs start to multiply," Jackson said. "Remember that spiders eat mosquitoes."

I was still shaking and tried to pull myself together. After the others left, I went to look at the bedrooms and bathroom. I knew there was no running water, so I was surprised to see a toilet. I looked at Jackson with raised eyebrows.

"There's a cistern up there," he said, pointing to the outside wall.

"Ingenious," I said. "What happens in the dry season?"

"Buckets," Jackson said. "Someone brings water up from the spring."

Although the house had basic furniture and linens, it had no cooking equipment or dishes, and the nearby shops didn't carry them. According to mission custom, we would take all our meals with the Swedish missionaries and teachers until we could get our own equipment.

When Jackson first came to teach at Sundi Lutete in 1967, only Europeans lived in this section of the mission. Zairians lived in smaller, unfurnished houses on the other side of the mission. The Swedish director of the school allowed Jackson to have a room on the Swedish side only when he threatened to leave. After that breakthrough, all college-educated teachers lived on the missionary side.

Two missionary families lived at Sundi, plus four Swedish volunteer teachers. Two Zairian university-trained teachers were due to arrive, one of them married. Jackson and I occupied the house where the Dianzungus had lived before moving to Kimpese. Though simple, it was bigger and furnished better than I expected. There was even a large wardrobe with shelves and space to hang clothes. A hallway off the living room opened onto a large pantry, with the kitchen on the left and an office to the right. It felt downright luxurious compared to our two-room apartment in Philadelphia.

The next day we took a walk around the mission, ending our tour at the dispensary. Jackson stopped and greeted two old women sitting on a bench. I followed suit, shaking hands with them. Their skin was callused and hard as wood.

"This is my paternal aunt, Mama Eliza," Jackson said. "She lives near Luozi, so I'm surprised to see her here. She came with her friend here."

They spoke in Kikongo for a few minutes, and we walked on.

"Her friend is here for treatment of bad dreams," he said. "The hospital in Luozi couldn't help her. Her husband died a few years ago, and she says he comes back at night, wanting to have sex."

We laughed. I wondered what the dispensary could do for that.

We had our first dinner with Swedish volunteer teachers, Sara and Elias, their young son, and two other Swedish teachers. Everyone knew Jackson's history, and anti-American feeling ran high among the Swedes because of the Vietnam War. We were not desirable guests, and I felt the tension. Kiame got off to an unpromising start by biting the Swedish child's face.

"He's never like this," I lied. "It's so unlike him. I'm so sorry."

Jackson gave Kiame a look that would have reduced any other child to a puddle of tears. I knew it was normal for children to regress in stressful situations, but I had no experience with a violent child. I didn't know how to get him to stop his anti-social behavior. Kiame scowled and crossed his chubby arms. We didn't stay for coffee.

The next day the Swedish volunteers talked about the latest developments in the war in Vietnam.

"I wonder what the latest withdrawal of American troops means," said Olav.

"South Vietnam can never win the war without them," said Elias.

I took a deep breath.

"Nixon has to get out of Vietnam if he wants to be reelected," I said. "He won the election on that promise. Whatever you hear in the press, the majority of Americans want out. I'm surprised it hasn't happened already."

"Did you protest against the war?" Elias asked.

"Of course," I said. "Nearly all the students at my college did."

The Swedes relaxed a little.

Over dessert, Sara said, "Did you hear bandits attacked a truck near the border of Zaire and Congo-Brazzaville?"

"Was anyone hurt?" asked Jackson.

"No, they just took whatever they could carry. The bandits didn't even have a vehicle, it seems."

"It's that failed coup in Brazzaville spilling over the border," said Olav. "It's Diawara's gang. The soldiers from Congo-Brazzaville are afraid to cross into Zaire to pursue them."

"What about the Zairian soldiers?" Jackson asked.

"There are only a few of them right at the border on the main road," said Elias. "They're not going to go chasing a bunch of guerillas in the bush. They don't have a vehicle either."

On the way home, I asked Jackson, "What's this about a failed coup?"

"A couple of ministers and a few army officers decided the president wasn't far enough to the left, and they staged a coup that failed," he said.

"You knew about it and didn't tell me?"

"I didn't want you to worry. And I didn't know they were anywhere near here. Diawara comes from an area further east. That's where he took his men after the coup failed."

"So how many of them are there?"

"Nobody knows, but there can't be very many. Diawara expected the workers and the students to rise up and follow him, but they didn't. He thought he had the unions in his back pocket. Hah!" Jackson said. "Ideology makes some people blind. Diawara didn't have the army or the population behind him. What kind of coup is that?"

I was concerned. I already had enough to deal with without worrying about a band of guerillas.

"What's to stop them from coming here?" I asked. "Clearly they are looking for food and money. There's more to steal here than out in the bush."

Jackson sighed and gave me a look of exaggerated patience. "The border is thirty kilometers away. I know that doesn't sound far to you, but here, without a vehicle, that's far. And lots of traffic crosses the border."

"What traffic?" I asked.

"I mean *traffique*—smuggling. Merchants take flour, salt cod and sugar across the border and sell it for twice what they can get here. And what do you think that laundryman does when he's not washing clothes? He distills alcohol and sells it across the border." A week passed, and I heard no more about the guerillas.

After days of Swedish oatmeal for breakfast, rice and Swedish stew for lunch, and bread and cheese for supper, Jackson had had enough.

"I can't take any more of this white food. We need to go to Luozi—I left all my things at my parents' house there when I went to America. We can at least get some pots and pans that we can't get here. And I need to see my parents, anyway. It's been four years."

I was eager to make the trip. Keeping Kiame in check took all the energy I could muster, and I was curious to meet Jackson's family. We wouldn't have another chance until Christmas break. Jackson grew up in Luozi, the regional capital of the Luozi Territory, called "Manianga" by its inhabitants. The town of about ten thousand sprawled along the North Bank above the Zaire River. Manianga and the neighboring area of Mayombe to the west are the only areas of the country that lie north of the Zaire River.

Friday, the day we left for Luozi, I found Jackson in the kitchen packing snacks and bottles of water.

"Why all the food and water? It's only seventy miles, right?" I asked. "We should be there in a couple of hours."

"Hunh," Jackson snorted. "You'll see why. It will take six hours if we're lucky."

Jackson paced the living room, waiting for the Land Rover that he had rented from the mission. François, the driver, pulled up an hour late. He ignored Jackson's scolding and loaded our luggage without comment. I was surprised to see Mama Eliza in the back seat.

"I forgot to tell you," Jackson said. "My aunt is coming with us."

Between Sundi Lutete and Luozi, the altitude dropped fifteen hundred feet, so we drove mostly downhill on a dirt road that frequently degenerated into a track with grass growing in the middle, clay soil at first, sand and rock closer to Luozi. We crossed bridges made of logs laid lengthwise from bank to bank, with wood planks nailed crossways over them. In the heat and humidity, wood deteriorated fast, and often the planks barely covered half the bridge. Before every dubious bridge, we all got out and walked across, because we could be injured or killed if the Land Rover suddenly tipped with us inside. One bridge across a nearly dry stream was simply a pile of earth between the two banks, in such bad condition that we had to hire villagers to shore it up. They conveniently showed up with shovels, eager for work, at the sound of our approaching vehicle.

Three hours into a bone-shaking ride over deeply rutted roads, François pulled over beside a small settlement called Sundi-Mamba, really only a row of small shops near a Catholic mission. François started collecting money from some people waiting for a ride by the side of the road, all surrounded by bundles and boxes.

"He can't take paying passengers," Jackson grumbled. "We've already paid for his time." He followed François and told him to stop. The would-be passengers joined the discussion, all pleading an urgent need to get to Luozi. Finally, Jackson chose three that he allowed to board. He plucked the money out of François' hand, leaving two lonely bills, and returned the rest of the money to the startled travelers. The lucky three passengers climbed into the back, after Jackson vetoed most of their bundles.

Half an hour later, François stopped the Land Rover in the middle of the road, opened the door without a word, and walked into the vegetation on the side of the road.

"Bathroom break," Jackson announced. "You go to that side of the road."

I'd learned how to pee in the woods during years of camping with my parents. I hiked far enough into the bush not to be seen from the road. Unfortunately, I hadn't looked toward the other side. I turned when I heard voices and saw that people on a footpath below had a clear view of me. I moved further into a clump of bushes until I found a small clearing. Just as I finished peeing, I noticed some large ants crawling up my shoe. I tried to brush them away, but one clung stubbornly to my index finger with pincers like a big staple. I rearranged my clothes with the other hand and crashed through the vegetation to the road.

"Jackson!" I called. "Help!"

Through an opening in the bushes, he stepped onto the road, Kiame in tow.

"What is it?" he said, looking worried.

"This! Get it off me!"

His face relaxed. "I thought you got bit by a snake. This is just a soldier ant. Where did you go?"

Jackson picked up a short stick and prodded the ant. It let go of my finger and latched onto the stick, which Jackson threw into the bush.

"I found a little clearing where there wasn't too much undergrowth," I said.

Jackson laughed. “That was an ant hill. Couldn’t you tell?”

“How would I know what an African ant hill looks like?”

“Mommy peed on an anthill!” said Kiame, laughing.

Jackson turned to Mama Eliza and said something in Kikongo. She grabbed the edge of her cotton shawl and covered her mouth to hide her laughter.

“Jackson, I don’t think this is funny.”

“Soldier ants guard the army ant column,” he said. “Their jaws are incredibly strong. You can’t pull them off—you have to trick them into biting something else. At one time they used to use them in traditional medicine, like stitches, to close cuts. If you pull off the body, the head and pincers stay locked in place.”

Down the road, we picked up two road workers. They proved useful farther on when they were able to guide François around a pond that covered a hundred feet of road. All of us clambered out, and François drove through uncleared vegetation at the side of the road, crushing small bushes along the way. When we came to another pond, the road workers walked ahead, using long sticks to test its depth. We drove through that one. I noticed how François navigated big puddles. The trick was to drive slowly and not stop until reaching dry land. If he stopped, the backwash would kill the engine.

Toward dusk, François stopped on a ridge. Below us, the Zaire River and the town of Luozi glinted in the dust-laden sunset.

“This last part of the road we call ‘Chicken Guts,’” François said. He threw the transmission into four-wheel drive and began to inch down the slope. The town seemed so close, and yet we drove another hour, crawling down the steep hill, dodging rocks and boulders. As it grew darker, a few pale lights—kerosene lamps—-appeared in the town. Pools of light appeared in the distance—generators, used only at the missions and a few bars. Altogether it took seven hours to drive less than seventy-five miles, and that was a routine trip.

Just outside the town, Jackson told François to stop in front of a large house set back from the road. A young girl stood on its veranda, pounding something in a large mortar with a six-foot pestle. She looked up but didn't wave. Mama Eliza pulled her cloth bundle from the back of the Land Rover and walked away without a word.

"She could have said 'Thank you,'" Jackson muttered. "She's put out because I didn't want her to come with us to my father's house."

Near the center of town, we stopped in front of the large house Jackson's father had built when he was a prosperous merchant in the 1960s. He was sitting in a deck chair on the wide veranda when we drove up, digging out coconut from its shell and feeding it to a cluster of small children. I knew immediately who he was. He picked Kiame up and gestured to his face. We all laughed at the resemblance.

"You call your parents-in-law *nzitu*," Jackson said.

"*Nzitu*," I repeated.

"Other in-laws are *nkwezi*. You can call everyone *nkwezi*. Nobody uses names."

I repeated the words to myself as a crowd of family members and curious neighbors gathered. A smiling teenager came up to shake my hand.

"My brother, Ronsard," Jackson said.

I heard a woman shouting on the road outside. The buzz of conversation in the room ceased.

"What is she saying?" I asked Jackson.

"She says to stay away from the river," he said.

"The Zaire River?"

"No, the Luozi River, a smaller one. With no running water, people have to go to the river to bathe," he said. "A crocodile attacked a woman just now at the bathing place. It happens often here."

Someone called him, and he drifted off. Ronsard appeared and handed me a Fanta.

"Three men are in jail now because of the crocodile attacks," he said.

"I don't understand."

"There are men who train wild animals to do their bidding," he said. "There are also sorcerers who can change their form and become crocodiles."

At first I thought he was joking, trying to shock me. I almost laughed, but Ronsard's face showed only concern.

"How is that possible?" I asked.

"A sorcerer gains an animal's trust, little by little, by feeding him," he said. "Then he uses magic to change himself into a crocodile, so that he can kill his enemies and escape punishment. The men arrested today live in a village famous for it."

I wondered how people could really believe such nonsense, but I said nothing. I wanted to ask Jackson about it later. Eventually the visitors left, and Tata Mahaniah called us to dinner. Now I could see who actually lived with Jackson's parents: Ronsard, their youngest child; their oldest grandson and five of their granddaughters. We had chicken and cassava greens for dinner, all of it so heavily laced with red pepper that I could barely eat it, even though I was used to spicy food. The cuisine of Luozi, it turned out, had a reputation for its liberal use of *pili-pili,* red pepper.

"Rice will help," said Ronsard. He was right. Kiame ate only rice and some of the sweetest pineapple I'd ever eaten.

***Chikwanga*, or *kwanga*, cut in pieces. The major staple food in the Kongo Central region, made from cassava (manioc) root that is peeled, fermented in water, pounded into a paste, formed into batons, wrapped in maranta (prayer plant) leaves, and boiled.**

***Nsombe*, a delicacy in Western Congo, are the larvae of the palm tree beetle. They are sautéed or braised in a sauce and taste like shrimp. The adult beetles are harmful to the tree, so their consumption also serves as pest control.**

As we were finishing dinner, the girls in the living room fell silent. Everyone turned to see Mama Eliza at the door, dressed in black. Nobody said a word. She shook hands all around, an odd smirk on her face. She greeted Jackson's father with respect so exaggerated it bordered on mockery. He pulled up a chair for her and she sat down, then made sure all eyes were on her before she spoke. Everyone except Jackson and his father looked at the table. She finished talking and sat with her hands folded. A few moments passed before Jackson spoke a few gruff sentences in reply. Ronsard frowned. Mama Eliza stood up and walked out, trailed by muffled giggles from the girls in the living room.

"She wants me to give her some sugar and salt, and a few other things for her grandchildren," Jackson said.

"And she couldn't have told you that during the seven-hour drive?"

"Not with François and the passengers there," he said. "She's not asking for much."

"Maybe not, but she came to show your family that she has a claim on you," I said. "No wonder they can't stand her."

"Look. She and her children belong to my father's clan and have nowhere else to turn. I will support them because my father asked me to, and I already get enough flak from my clan. I don't need it from you too."

No one else understood English, but they picked up on the tone. Everyone looked from me to Jackson and back, trying to decode the conversation.

"I'm just making an observation," I said. "I don't care who gets sugar and salt—I don't know any of these people." But Jackson turned his back to me and started talking to his father. It was easier than I had imagined to get embroiled in a family squabble.

One by one, the other people drifted out of the room. When Jackson's father stood up, Ronsard showed us to a room that opened off the veranda. A bed with a large, grass-filled mattress occupied all but a sliver of the space. No doubt we displaced someone, although I couldn't tell how many rooms the house contained.

Kiame fell asleep as soon as his head hit the pillow.

"Jackson, what's this about men being arrested for changing themselves into crocodiles?"

"Oh, the Crocodile Men," he said, and chuckled.

"You don't really believe that," I whispered.

"No. I believe that men can train wild animals to attack people though," he said, and described how people in Luozi believed it was done.

"What will happen to the men they arrested?" I swatted at a mosquito buzzing over my head despite the closed shutters. The windows had no glass or screens, and we had no mosquito net.

"The soldiers will keep them for a few days and then quietly let them go," he said. "They arrested them to keep other people from beating them up."

"So it's more like protective custody?"

"You could call it that."

Luozi was even stranger than the Sundi Lutete mission. The way people lived, the family dynamics, what they believed—it was all so alien. I wondered how I would ever get used to it.

An army of mosquitoes dive-bombed us all night. If sorcery was so powerful, why didn't they use it to kill mosquitoes? When I woke up, Kiame and Jackson were gone. The nylon bodysuit I pulled out of my travel bag had a huge hole in the middle. Bugs had eaten through it. I took everything out of the bag and shook it upside down, but the bugs had finished their meal and moved on. Cockroaches love nylon, I learned. I had to wear a top that didn't match my skirt—it was the only other one I'd brought.

On the veranda, I saw half a dozen conical baskets resting against the wall. In the living room, a corresponding number of women sat on the floor, legs stretched out straight in front of them, while Ronsard set the table and made breakfast. Saturday was market day, so the rest of the household had already gone to the market.

Fishing basket, used by men to carry tackle and small fish.

I learned that these women walked fifteen miles with baskets on their backs, held in place by a woven grass band around their foreheads. A standard load was ten to fifteen kilos—twenty-two to thirty-three pounds. They carried these baskets so often that some women had the weave pattern of the band pressed into their foreheads. Men carried loads on their heads, as both men and women did in Sundi. Custom even dictated the way women sat on the floor—legs together, straight in front of them, never crossed or spread out. Jackson told me to walk around them, because stepping over the women's outstretched legs brought bad luck. I shook hands with each of them, as they continued their loud discussion.

"This is my sister, these are my cousins, this is my aunt," Jackson recited. "They're on their way to the market."

"What are they arguing about?" I asked.

He laughed. "They aren't arguing," he said. "That's just the way they talk."

By the time we finished breakfast, they were gone.

"You need to go to the Zone to get your residence permit," Jackson said. "First we'll get pictures taken for our driver's licenses."

After the pictures, Jackson went off on another errand, and Ronsard walked with Kiame and me to the Zone office, something like a county office in the US. Ronsard gave the clerk the information, and we walked outside.

"Shouldn't we wait in the office?" I asked.

"It's going to take a while," he said.

"Why? There's nobody else here. All he has to do is write two lines in a ledger and two more on a card."

Ronsard shrugged. "That's just how it is."

While we waited, Ronsard told me some family history.

"My aunt, the one who came last night? She's my father's only sister," he began. "In our culture, a mother's brother is the head of the clan, and responsible for his sisters and their children. Our father tried to find a good husband for her, but she married a man against our father's wishes. His work often took him away from the village, and he died young, so my aunt's children came to live with us. They were always telling us they would inherit my father's wealth when he died. It was like they were wishing for his death, and we hated them. Our father sent them all to school, but they were like their father and didn't do well, except for one son who joined the army and one daughter who married someone in the city."

"If your uncle is responsible for you, why haven't I heard anything about him?" I asked.

"Ah," Ronsard said. "My father is modern. He wanted to take care of his own children. He himself was orphaned very young and took care of himself. Anyway, our *ngu'a'nkazi*, maternal uncle, is a villager who never went to school. He didn't have the money to take care of us. He hardly ever comes to Luozi. You will meet him if you go to the village."

"What happened to your father's business?"

"When my brother went to America, my cousin Louis went to work for my father," Ronsard said. "One day when the truck was loaded with merchandise, he stole it and ran away to another region. My aunt—the one you met—knew where he went, but she wouldn't tell my father."

He picked up a stone and threw it against a wall. Kiame started doing the same.

"He came back a year later, after he lost everything. He sold the merchandise, spent the money, then sold the truck, and spent that money too." He dusted off his hands.

"Didn't your father have him arrested?" I asked.

Ronsard shook his head. "He couldn't have his own nephew arrested. My father could have gone to get his truck back, at least, if he'd known where to find it. That's how he lost all his money. Now he still sells a few things at the market. It doesn't bring in much income."

"So where is Louis now?" I asked.

"In the village. He came back asking forgiveness when the truck and all the money were gone," Ronsard said. "Those people—we don't owe them anything. My father wants us to take care of his nephews and nieces, but I say no."

"And your brother Jackson?"

"He will do whatever my father wants," Ronsard said. "My mother and the rest of us don't want him to do anything for them. They had their chance, and they betrayed our father. Anyway, they will always be poor. They don't know how to do business, and since they never finished school, they can't get jobs."

He looked up at the sun. "That paper ought to be ready by now," he said, and led the way back to the Zone office. What should have taken half an hour took all morning. I would have to cultivate patience to deal with the Zairian bureaucracy. Life in Manianga involved a lot of waiting around.

After lunch (with more hot pepper) Jackson took me around town to meet his childhood friends and people at the church compound. That evening we had dinner with a family Jackson knew from childhood. Instead of African food, they had prepared what they thought was a European meal, based on the few imported foods available: canned corned beef, bread, canned Danish cheese, sardines and rice. I was touched by the effort and appreciated the lack of red pepper, even though I preferred African food to corned beef and sardines.

Back at the house, a family conference awaited us. Around the table sat Jackson's father, mother and brother. His father spoke first. Ronsard frowned, fidgeting. His face grew angrier as the monologue continued. Then Jackson spoke, addressing Ronsard. After a short, sharp exchange, Ronsard pushed back his chair and left the room. Jackson's mother made a *What can you do?* gesture and folded her hands.

"I want my brother to come to Sundi," Jackson translated. "They don't have enough teachers here, and my mother spoils him. He just hangs out with his friends and does what he wants. I need to make sure he gets an education."

"And he doesn't want to go," I said.

"He'll go," Jackson said. "We have a saying in Kikongo. 'No matter how big the ear, it's never bigger than the head.' I am his older brother, and he has to obey."

I found the image of the proverb a little grotesque. It turned out to be one of the proverbs I heard most often. Kongo culture had firm conventions about authority.

* * *

Miraculously, François drove up on time for the trip back to Sundi Lutete. This time Jackson was late, still out picking up our driver's licenses from the local official he had paid to produce them on a weekend. By the time Jackson tracked down the appropriate official—not easy on a Sunday—it was nearly noon. François paced, looking up every few minutes at the sun rising higher in the sky. I found it odd that François, so unpunctual up to then, was suddenly worried about the time. In a few hours, we would find out why.

After five hours, and still three hours from Sundi Lutete, we reached the place where we had picked up passengers three days before. Less than an hour later, night descended suddenly, as it always does in the tropics. François waited for total darkness to turn on the headlights; they barely cast a glow. Whenever we went around a bend, I felt a cool breeze rise from the gulley that I couldn't see below the edge of the road. Jackson and François began to argue in Kikongo. François drove more slowly. The moon rose, providing a bit of light, but not enough, even for a driver who knew the road well. Then clouds slid over the moon, and it began to drizzle. The headlights gave only feeble light, and after a few minutes, went out. François didn't stop.

"What's the matter with the lights?" I asked.

"I don't know, and I don't think he does either," Jackson said.

I understood from a sprinkling of French words that Jackson wanted to stop at a nearby Catholic mission to recharge the battery, at a minimum, and stay the night if we couldn't get the lights working. François wanted to drive on. It wasn't completely dark yet, but I couldn't see more than thirty feet ahead of us, and I could see almost nothing when I looked out the side window. The narrow roads had no railings or fences, and only a few feet separated the Land Rover from a sheer drop. Jackson stabbed the air to the left, and François reluctantly turned onto a side road that led to the Catholic mission of Bienga, two hours from Sundi.

After some discussion, a mechanic helped François hook the battery to a charger. A priest greeted us and led us into a large brick building, leaving François to deal with the Land Rover. Jackson explained the problem, and the priest invited us to supper in the refectory, where he asked the nuns to set three more places. François would apparently eat elsewhere with the mechanic. The nuns and priests were accommodating, though not friendly. Catholics and Protestants had been rivals in the region for fifty years, and they cooperated only minimally. As in many isolated regions of the world, though, travelers who worked in the missions of either faith always received help if they needed it.

"We'll let the battery charge for another hour before going on," Jackson said.

Meanwhile, we had supper with the nuns and priests, a silent meal except for Kiame's constant questions. As in Sundi, the buildings were made of local red brick, but these structures were far grander, some multi-storied. The organization of the place impressed me. The Catholics had a purpose and a schedule and made sure they had the material and human resources to implement their plans. After supper, I chased Kiame around the refectory for an hour before we left.

The newly charged battery gave out after less than an hour. From then on, we could have walked faster than François could drive. Whenever we came to a bridge, we got out, watched the Land Rover slip and slither across, and followed on foot. At last we descended a steep hill to the last bridge. It was raining harder, and this time we didn't get out of the vehicle, because the bridge was only a couple of feet above a patch of mud. I guessed that a torrent would flow here in the rainy season. I could see broken planks ahead and I held my breath. François stopped, changed gears and drove cautiously onto the bridge. Halfway across, the Land Rover skidded, and I screamed as I felt the right rear tire drop. François twisted the steering wheel and gunned the accelerator. The Land Rover skidded over the bridge and up the steep bank on the other side as I started to breathe again.

If you've never lived in Africa, you imagine danger from wild animals, flooding rivers, and rampaging rebels. Where we were, danger came mostly from ordinary life: tending the wood-burning stove, driving over poorly maintained roads and bridges, sitting outside at night and getting too many mosquito bites, drinking unboiled water. That trip to Luozi showed me that daily life here was tougher than I expected. I'd been in Sundi Lutete for two weeks.

Chapter 9
The Sealed Fortress

A language which we do not know
is a fortress sealed.

—Marcel Proust

Months before we left Philadelphia, I wanted to learn Kikongo, the language I would encounter most in Zaire, and found an old Kikongo grammar book, written in French. I already spoke Spanish, some French, and a little Swahili. How hard could it be?

"It's not the right dialect," Jackson said after glancing at it. "You should just wait until we get there."

"The vocabulary may be different, but the grammar rules will be the same."

Languages were not Jackson's strongest suit, so I didn't fully trust his opinion. I assumed he spoke French well, since most of his high school education was in French. In English, his third language, he had a heavy accent, and made quite a few mistakes in grammar, especially with articles and verb usage. I edited the papers he wrote for grad school, and often I had to ask him, "What are you trying to say here?" A closer look at my new textbook, though, showed Kikongo to be more daunting. The language had ten classes of nouns, and every adjective and verb had to agree with the noun. Instead of using a different suffix for a plural as in English, Kikongo used a prefix. That required a lot of quick thinking. The variety of verb tenses was equally daunting—several present tenses and even more past tenses. I read through the grammar to get the general idea and then put it aside, my head spinning. Now, after feeling deaf and dumb for three days in Luozi, I renewed my determination to learn this mysterious and difficult language. First I recruited one of the primary school teachers, but Jackson vetoed him.

"Not a man," he said. "It would not look right. Find a woman."

"Oh, for God's sake," I responded in irritation. "He's old enough to be my father."

Jackson remained adamant. "That doesn't matter. People will get the wrong impression." Was it "people" or just Jackson himself?

The adult women I approached for help claimed to be too busy or didn't consider themselves qualified. Later, I realized that they didn't feel comfortable accepting payment from me but couldn't afford to use up so much time without compensation. The best I could do was a high school senior, Henriette, who knew nothing about teaching a language. I really taught myself, with Henriette as my walking grammar book and dictionary.

I started by learning simple everyday phrases, repeating them until I could pronounce them to Henriette's satisfaction. I wrote them in a notebook. Once I had those down, I moved on to verbs in the present tense, basic nouns, adjectives and adverbs. Although there were indeed ten classes of nouns, most commonly used words fell into one of only two or three classes. That made it a lot easier. Pronouncing Kikongo words started easily enough. It was much like Spanish, except that there was no "r" sound, a potential pitfall in both Spanish and French. Pronunciation presented only two challenges. The first was that Kikongo combined consonants at the beginnings of words. Try saying *nzonzi* (mediator), or *mbwaki* (red). Second, and trickier, Kikongo is a tonal language. Hold onto a vowel too long, and you may say "excrement" instead of "no." I found that out the hard way. My teenage teacher didn't tell me about the tones—I learned that on my own. She knew when I mispronounced words, of course, but she couldn't always explain how or why.

I practiced with anyone who would talk to me. In the late afternoons, I joined my neighbor Josette on a mat in front of her house, shelling peanuts and practicing Kikongo. Other women would stop by to chat, and I practiced on them too. They laughed at me, but anyone learning a language can't let that stop them. I practiced on the cook and babysitter, but they were too deferential to correct me. Jackson could have been my best resource, but he would not speak Kikongo with me. He refused to explain why. Later I thought perhaps he didn't have confidence in his ability to explain Kikongo grammar and syntax. Most people learn their native language by example, and unless they also learn it in school, they often can't explain the "why" of verb tenses or rules of grammar. Kiame spoke more Kikongo than I did, within the limits of a three-year-old's vocabulary and grammar. When the babysitter tried to haul him into the shower, he shouted, "*Ngo ngwandi!*" (He doesn't want to!) because that's what he heard the babysitter say to the cook. Kiame also hadn't yet absorbed a sense of propriety in his new culture. One day he ran into the house, trailed by a friend who called, "*Kiame, kwe wele?*" (Where are you going?). Kiame shouted, "*Ngiele nena!*" (I'm going to poop!). The boy looked at me in shock and ran out of the house.

In learning a language, you learn a culture, if you're open to it. Early on, I learned that time, as Westerners understand it, has no meaning in Kikongo. There is no way to translate "on time." The closest Henriette could come was "*ntangu ifueni*" (the time is full). That doesn't mean that the hands on a clock have moved to a certain spot. It means that all the conditions are present for an event to proceed—the food or supplies are ready, and everybody important has arrived. In Kikongo, you cannot spend time, save time, lose time, or make time. You can't have a good time, bide your time, or have time on your hands. None of those expressions make any sense in the Kongo world. When people really want something to start at a particular hour, they say "Four o'clock. European time!"—an admonition routinely ignored.

English has a very large vocabulary relative to other languages, yet Kikongo has many more words in at least two categories: the natural world, and family relationships. My instructor knew a Kikongo word for even the tiniest, rarest insect or plant, and for every degree of family relationship. Kongo culture has rigid gender roles, so I found it surprising that everyday speech in Kikongo is largely gender neutral. I heard the word *muntu* (person) far more often than "man" or "woman," just as *mwana* (child) is most often used without specifying gender. To complicate matters, the word for "girl" (*ndumba)* became a synonym for "prostitute" sometime during the previous fifty years, so nobody used it anymore. The words for "man" (*bakala*) and "woman" (*nkento*) are the same as the words for husband and wife, but also designate directions, right and left, because, in the Kongo religion, the Creator of the world, Mahungu, turned three times to the right to create man and three times to the left to create woman.

Even more surprising, I found that there is no word for "to have." The work-around is a possessive pronoun. To say "I have a house" you must say "The house is mine," (*Nzo yena yame*). The absence of a word for ownership directly reflects the Kongo disdain for personal property and suspicion of accumulated wealth. Kongo culture did not encourage amassing material goods, and by tradition, almost any of a person's possessions is considered his clan's property, and clan members have a right to take it if they need it. Before colonialism, a person who accumulated too much wealth, even a chief, could be accused of selfishness—a grave defect—or even of being a *ndoki* (sorcerer). In the same vein, there are no words for "more" or "less," "better" or "worse," "higher" or "lower." Kikongo provides no structure for comparison. Although the word for "too small" is *ukeke,* for example, it has no link to the word for "small"—*fioti*. When Henriette told me this, I didn't believe her, so I asked Josette.

"Henriette's right," she said. "It's bad manners to compare. It causes jealousy, and that is the source of *kindoki.*"

Many of these language quirks relate to *kindoki*, for which no other language has an adequate translation. Missionaries translated it as "witchcraft," a drastic over-simplification. *Kindoki* means mysterious knowledge of any kind, good or bad. To the women around me, my contact lenses were *kindoki.* But most of the time, *kindoki* refers to a malevolent force used by a person with evil intentions, known as a *ndoki*. A person can be a *ndoki* without knowing it, but that was considered unusual. People believe *kindoki* to be the source of almost all chronic illnesses or conditions and any sudden, severe illness, death or other misfortune. People often attribute infertility, chronic unemployment and mental illness to *kindoki*. The Kongo acknowledge that minor illnesses can be cured by simple remedies, and I met several local herbalists, but Kongo people spend inordinate amounts of time, effort and money attempting to protect themselves from *kindoki*. Despite nearly universal Christianity, the concept of *kindoki* permeates the culture, even today, at every social, economic and educational level. Belief in the Christian God carries some degree of protection in most people's minds, but people employ traditional means as well. These include an unlit match lodged in a baby's hair, magical statues placed beneath a mattress, jewelry with magical properties, potions and powders to rub on the body or sprinkle around a room, and a variety of ceremonies and rituals in which an entire clan must participate.

The Catholic Church and all mainline Protestant denominations deny that *kindoki* exists, but I have not met any Kongo person who did not believe in its power to some degree. Partly because of the Christian taboo, and partly because it is seen as such a dangerous force, people hesitate to name it directly and employ euphemisms instead. *Mayela* means wisdom or knowledge, and *mayela ma mpimpa* (knowledge or wisdom of the night) is one most frequently used. Others include *kimpala mpasi* (extreme jealousy) and *ntima ya mbi* (bad heart).

"Do you believe in *kindoki*?" I asked Jackson.

"My God protects me," he said, "but yes, I believe there is something to it."

I concluded that evil intentions have greater power than most Western cultures acknowledge. Haven't most of us suffered from the toxic effects of a hostile supervisor? Or a determined rival for someone's affections? And over the years I, too, saw instances of that power. In Philadelphia, I knew a Kongo woman who couldn't get pregnant until her husband made a series of gifts to her disgruntled uncle who believed he didn't get the share of her dowry that he deserved. In Sundi and later in Kinshasa I saw ceremonies of reconciliation when family conflict had affected a person's health. I also knew people nearly paralyzed with fear, some of them Europeans and Americans, unable to lead normal lives because they were so obsessed by the conviction that someone wished them harm. In nearly every interaction, I had to keep these beliefs in mind, to be careful of the words I used. And although the Kongo would make fun of almost anything, they never joked about *kindoki*.

Learning the language gave me more confidence when I interacted with both the mission residents and the villagers. I no longer felt as though I had cotton stuffed in my ears. I could bargain with the women who came to sell fruits and vegetables. I understood Kiame's conversations with his friends and the whispered exchanges of my students. Most foreigners never learned Kikongo or Lingala, even when they had lived in the country for years. They didn't realize how much they were missing.

Chapter 10
Honeymoon

Culture shock is often split into four stages:
honeymoon, uncertainty & doubt, adaptation,
and acceptance.

—internations.org

After we returned from Luozi, we had a week to set up the household before school started.

"First we have to hire workers," Jackson said.

"I really don't want servants," I said.

"Don't be ridiculous. Everyone has help. How will you teach classes, shop for vegetables, and cook a meal on the wood-burning stove? We'll need a wood and water carrier, cook, babysitter, and laundryman."

"Do we need that many?"

Jackson gave me an exasperated look. He slipped back into mission culture without missing a beat. I had to adjust to the idea that I would depend on strangers for most of my basic needs. It made me feel helpless. Only after several months did I realize how much everyone at the mission depended on other people. In the villages around us, men and women worked in the fields all day, cultivating only with a short hoe, and left grandparents and older children to cook and take care of small children. Supporting teachers who neither farmed nor hunted required a great deal more of other people's labor.

Since I didn't speak Kikongo yet, and knew nothing about hiring servants, Jackson had to recruit people. The wood and water carrier and part-time laundryman were the easiest. They both lived in the neighboring village and had worked for missionaries before. They did all their work outdoors, so we had minimal contact with them. Only men did these jobs. Hiring a cook, though, became problematic because Jackson insisted on hiring a woman. The missionaries all had male cooks.

"Why do you want to hire a woman?" I asked.

"The missionaries didn't hire women, even though, traditionally, cooking is women's work, except for grilling meat," Jackson said. "I don't want to ask a man to do it."

Men in the neighboring village would have loved to have the job—and asked for it. They took his decision as an insult. The Belgians never hired women for any paid work, even though women played a prominent economic role in traditional culture. That changed very slowly, and even in 1972, the local schools had only a few women teachers. Most nurses, too, were men. When I learned more about Kongo culture, I realized that Jackson would have felt uncomfortable giving orders to a male cook, especially one older than he was. He heard about a woman who worked for a Swedish missionary nurse and sent for her, despite the nurse's warning that she had caught the woman stealing. Jackson's cousin, who worked at the dispensary, had a teenaged daughter, so he hired her as a babysitter.

My new neighbor Josette, wife of the art teacher, showed me how the wood-burning stove worked, even though I could only boil water. I didn't know how to cook Zairian food, and Western food wasn't available. I went to the so-called Centre Commercial about a mile away and took the babysitter with me. The merchants there sold staples and a few processed foods: corned beef, sardines, pilchards, tomato paste, flour, salt, rice, sugar, coffee, tea, canned margarine, oatmeal and powdered milk. They also sold ten-kilo boxes of salt cod, the main protein source throughout the region. At the biggest shop, villagers gathered around me to see what I would buy, whispering comments to each other. The clerk did not know how to add more than two numbers at a time, so his calculations took a while. Finally, I offered to add up the column of figures, and he accepted gratefully. As we were wrapping up, the owner, Melia, appeared and introduced himself. He was Protestant, and his children attended the mission schools, so the missionaries trusted him, and he did many favors for them, and for us.

Most of our food came from vendors who came to the door and from two local markets: a daily one near the mission for fresh vegetables, and a weekly market at Mangembo, the Catholic mission a couple of miles away. At that market I could get pork, chicken, produce and imported necessities. I could get beef only at the monthly market near the Centre Commercial, in a good month. In most of Zaire, the main protein was fresh fish, but because it was so far up in the hills, Sundi Lutete had only a few small streams that didn't produce fish large enough to eat. Almost every household kept a few chickens, but nobody raised them commercially because it was difficult in a tropical climate without access to processed chicken feed and veterinary medicine. Village chickens foraged for their food, so of course they picked up all kinds of diseases. Villagers could afford to lose one or two chickens now and then, but not thirty of them all at once. They didn't have the resources to invest in larger operations, or to absorb the losses if they failed, and chickens were delicate.

"You're a chicken here, you lead a tough life," said one of our Peace Corps teachers.

For the monthly market, a merchant brought a cow or a bull from the neighboring region of Mayombe on foot—a three- or four-day trip—and slaughtered it on the spot, early in the morning. The missionaries always received the best cuts because they bought the biggest quantity. We usually bought eight or ten pounds of fresh, tough beef. After experimenting, I discovered that I could age it myself by leaving it in the kerosene-fueled refrigerator for a week before cooking or freezing it.

Soapstone carving by our neighbor Bakala Kalundi Daniel.

In between domestic tasks, I met our neighbors and colleagues. Josette lived with her husband Bakala and two children, in one of the oldest mission houses, built on stilts half a story high. Under the passageway between the kitchen and the living space, Bakala set up his studio—a table and a set of chisels—where he carved thick hardwood planks into bas-relief plaques. Later, as hardwood became more difficult to find, he switched to soft stone.

Across the road on the other side lived a Swedish missionary, Jan Nilsson, and his wife Emma. Nilsson considered evangelization his real function, although before we arrived, he taught Religion classes at the high school. The previous year, he argued with the students, and he dropped the class. He was not an ordained minister, and the students probably knew the Bible and theology better than he did. Emma taught Geography, but also dropped her class, in solidarity with her husband. Jackson eventually coaxed her back. In the meantime, she held popular weekly knitting classes for village woman. Once I learned a few words of Kikongo, I realized that the women believed that the infant caps and sweaters they knitted carried the protective power of the Christian God, because the wool and instructions came from a missionary. No wonder her classes were so popular. I wondered if she realized it, but I never got to know her well enough to ask. The Nilssons' son attended the Swedish boarding school in Pointe Noire, in neighboring Congo-Brazzaville, so we saw him only during vacations. Their daughter Tina, a year older than Kiame, belonged to his preschool gang. Nilsson had a Land Rover with the slogan "*Leka minu mu Yesu Klisto*" (Put Your Trust in Jesus Christ) emblazoned on the sides. The local population found this amusing, and behind his back, called Nilsson himself *Leka Minu* (Put Your Trust). The Kongo love sarcastic nicknames. I often wondered if they had one for me, but I never found out.

Three new university-trained Zairian teachers arrived that year, recruited the year before by the tireless José. They taught pedagogy, math and history. That first year, we acquired one Peace Corps volunteer who arrived unexpectedly, wearing a denim jacket with a marijuana leaf embroidered on the back. He ended up in Sundi by accident when something went wrong at his original posting. Jackson disapproved of the attire, but the volunteer turned out to be an excellent biology teacher. High school graduates with teaching certificates filled in the gaps and performed all the administrative duties, running the office and supervising the students and the dormitories. The one I saw most often was the good-looking *prefet de discipline*, Jean Balekita, who was also the soccer coach. He came to report infractions a couple of times a week. Always cheerful, he obviously loved his job. I had a bit of a crush on him.

"I confiscated a note," he told Jackson. "Let me read it to you. 'I am happy every day in class to see your fat thighs.'" Then he would double over with laughter, oblivious of—or perhaps enjoying—Jackson's discomfort. I became friends with Balekita's wife, Christine, who taught primary school and supervised the high school girls' dormitories. Along with their two small boys, they stood out as the perfect family.

Ernest Badia ran the office, and I have never seen a more loyal and able administrator. The school had a very tight budget, and Badia kept such a firm grip on its resources that some of the teachers resented his control. Who was this *secretary* to tell *them*, university-trained teachers, what to do? Jackson trusted Badia completely and always defended him.

In addition to the Swedish volunteers Sara and Elias, who fed us for two weeks after we arrived, there were two other Swedish volunteers, Hannah and Olav, and another missionary family whose function I never quite understood. A middle-aged Swedish nurse ran the dispensary, and a Swedish midwife led mobile clinics in the surrounding villages.

The cistern on the side of the house had run dry weeks before we arrived, and rain would not fall for at least another month. We had electricity only three hours a night, if the diesel generator was working and fuel was available. Most cooking took place on the large wood-burning stove. We asked Melia to buy us a kerosene-powered refrigerator on his next trip to Kinshasa. The mission supplied a small gas stove, fueled by a cylinder, like the ones people use in the US for gas grills. Exchanging empty cylinders for full ones was one of the favors Melia did for the missionaries, and for us. Availability of all supplies depended on the state of the roads, the condition of Melia's trucks and the reliability of his drivers.

Any device powered by kerosene required constant surveillance and maintenance. Reservoirs had to be filled and wicks adjusted. A little too high and the device would produce choking smoke; too low, and the flame would go out. The gas cylinder and its tubes and connections had to be checked constantly, because gas cylinders occasionally blew up. In the US, whoever sells a gas cylinder must ensure its safety; in Zaire, consumers were on their own. The tropical climate accelerated decay of components such as rubber and soft plastic, so I had to do a safety check every time I used the gas stove, which I found unnerving. For the wood stove, we needed a reliable supply of dry wood, and the ashes had to be scraped out and emptied daily, a hot and messy job. When the generator wasn't working, we used hurricane lamps, familiar to most Americans, and the more complicated Aladdin lamps with tall chimneys that provided whiter light and smelled less but required constant attention. The wick in the open chimney of the Aladdin flared up at the slightest breeze and set fire to anything nearby. Curtains were a frequent casualty. The local shops carried only selected parts for the Aladdin, but Olav advised us to buy whatever parts were available and complete the set over time. Over several months we had bought enough parts for two lamps.

I felt as though I had dropped onto another planet with unfamiliar surroundings and a way of life I had never experienced, not even on my earlier visits to Zaire. Even the sky and the ground looked different. At the same time, the need to adapt as quickly as I could insulated me from any homesickness that might have surfaced. I felt more excited than fearful.

Classes started at seven thirty, and I was often late because the babysitter, Marie, rarely arrived on time. We came home for breakfast at eight thirty because it took an hour for the cook to get the wood-burning stove hot enough to boil water. We usually ate Swedish-style oatmeal, sweet and milky; bread baked by the cook; instant coffee or tea; eggs if we had any; and whatever fruit was in season. We had bananas all year round. In the rainy season, we had a fruit paradise: mango, pineapple, avocado, papaya, and local fruits and berries that have no English translation. *Nsafu,* harvested during a short season in February, became my new favorite: dark blue, the size of a large egg and boiled or roasted until the blue skin burst to reveal the green flesh. It tasted a little like an olive. In the dry season, from May to October, we had oranges and sometimes grapefruit.

Classes resumed at nine thirty and continued until twelve thirty, when everyone went home for the main meal of the day and the *sieste* until two o'clock. For lunch the cook usually prepared a green leafy vegetable (the market offered many types) cooked with palm oil, peanut butter, or both, mixed with either canned pilchards or salt cod, and rice. Twice a week we had chicken, or beef if we were lucky. One afternoon a week, I taught eighth grade English from two to three o'clock. Students who didn't have an afternoon class reported for two hours of manual labor beginning at two o'clock Monday through Thursday, supervised by teachers and administrators, including me. The mission needed that student labor. Schools' fees would have been unaffordable if the mission had hired workers to pick fruit, cut the grass, and do everything else the students did. Students' work varied according to the season and the shifting needs of the school. Women students cleaned the classrooms and offices. In the upper grades, girls comprised about 20 percent of the classes; in the lower grades, half the students were girls. Education for girls became more popular once parents realized their daughters could help support them just as their sons did. Sometimes girls dropped out to get married at fifteen or sixteen, but child marriage had declined, partly because of pressure from the government and partly because of better opportunities for girls.

On Friday afternoons, students cleaned their dormitories. At four thirty teachers and administrators inspected the dormitories and checked for contraband. Christine, Balekita's wife, invited me to join her to inspect the dormitories. The first time I went with her, Christine began sniffing the air as soon as we walked in.

"I smell *chikwangue.* Who's hiding *chikwangue*?" she called and followed her nose. To make *chikwangue*, a local staple, women fermented manioc (also called cassava), by soaking it for several days, then pounding it into a paste, shaping it into a short baton, wrapping it in a particular kind of leaf, and boiling the resulting packets. A pungent *chiwangue,* also called *kwanga,* is about the size of a small baguette. *Chikwangue* is dense and filling, easy to store and transport, although unfortunately it has little nutritional value. It has a shelf life of about a week, becoming increasingly smelly, like stinky cheese. We never had it in the house because Jackson hated the smell.

"Aha!" Christine cried, pulling a small bundle from a coat pocket. "Whose coat is this?"

A timid hand went up.

"Lisette, you know you are not allowed to have food in the dormitory. It attracts vermin," Christine said, shaking the half-consumed *chikwangue.* "Get rid of it—now!"

In another dormitory, she chided the girls for traces of colored chalk on the windowsill.

"They use it for makeup," she said with a sigh. I nodded but silently sympathized with the girls. They were teenagers, after all, and real makeup could only be bought at great expense in Kinshasa, where few of these girls ever traveled. In the markets, I saw only skin-lightening cream, much of it banned in the US because it contained toxic levels of mercury.

In the evening, we ate bread, eggs, or leftovers warmed up on the gas stove. Rarely, if I had nothing else, I opened a can of corned beef or sardines, but I didn't like either, so they were really a last resort. After I learned to use the wood stove, I made cakes and cookies once in a while. After supper, I prepared lessons and Jackson worked on his PhD research until nine, when the lights went out. If the generator wasn't working, we lit the Aladdin lamps. On Saturdays, we had classes in the morning and often went visiting in the afternoons. Until our car arrived, we walked around the mission, stopping to talk with anyone we ran into, or walked to Tadi, the village that bordered the mission. On the first few Sundays, I went to church, but I didn't often go after that because the service was two or three hours long—too much for me and definitely too much for the hyperactive Kiame. The workers ("servants" sounds too grand) had Sundays off. After our car arrived in November, I usually drove to the weekly market at the Catholic mission.

Kiame had an enviable daily schedule: play, eat, sleep, play, eat, sleep. Marie didn't follow him around or play with him. She just turned him loose, and he roamed the mission with his friends until he was hungry, or night fell. The kids spent hours taking imaginary trips in an old Land Rover chassis near the missionary garage, worn smooth by time and weather. The pastor kept a herd of pigs in a pen, and Kiame's preschool gang often went to watch them, learning the facts of life the old-fashioned way. Then they would stop at the carpentry shop, where the workers gave them cast-off pieces of wood the size of children's blocks. They took them home and played with them in the dirt path. When they lost the blocks they'd go back and get new ones. If Kiame didn't show up for lunch, Marie would go and look for him. One day she couldn't find him.

"What do you mean, you can't find him?"

"They all went together, him and his gang. We can't find any of them," she said.

"Don't worry," Jackson said. "Nothing can happen here."

I could think of all too many things that could happen. Finally, at two o'clock, Kiame walked through the door, sweaty and smelling of dirt.

"Where were you?"

"Dadi took us to Luozi," was all he could tell me. I couldn't expect him, at two and a half, to know that they couldn't have walked to Luozi, seventy-two kilometers away. Josette's son Dadi was a year or two older and a bit wild.

"They probably went to the stream," Jackson said. "Don't go there again, Kiame. It's dangerous and you can't swim. And Marie, you have to watch him more closely."

For a few days, all the babysitters kept closer track of their charges. Inevitably, their supervision reverted to benign neglect. Fortunately, the children never disappeared all at once again. Kiame usually played hard enough that he'd fall asleep during the *sieste* but if he didn't, I allowed him to play quietly in the house until two o'clock. Then he was back outside, roaming free until dark. What child wouldn't love a life like that? For a hyperactive boy who didn't know how to lower his voice, Sundi Lutete was paradise.

Sundi-Lutete preschool crew, 1973. Left to right: Dadi, son of Bakala Kalundi and wife Eugénie (Josette); missionary child, name unknown; Masika, daughter of Bakala Kalundi; Esaïe, son of local evangelist; Kiame; Nzuzi, adopted daughter of Swedish midwife Barbrö; missionary child, name unknown.

Kiame with Masika in Kimpese, forty-nine years later.

I'd never lived in a more beautiful place. The houses all faced the large grassy quadrangle, crisscrossed with paths, along which missionaries had planted flowering shrubs, local and imported. There were three large rosebushes and, nearby, a gardenia bush five feet tall and four feet across. I never knew gardenias could grow so big. Alongside one house, a row of poinsettias grew six feet tall. In the backyard of Nilsson's house grew a large tree with flowers like small pink orchids. I never found out its name, and I never saw another one like it. The courtyard of the school had a row of flame trees, with wide canopies of bright red flowers. Frangipani and other flowering trees dotted the quadrangle.

I was impatient to begin the work that we had planned for so long. Maybe as a result of all those years of religious indoctrination, I believed that everyone should have a higher purpose, that we should all find a way to contribute to a more just and peaceful world. I didn't believe in working just to amass a fortune and buy more possessions, or in fame and recognition as goals in themselves. I knew we would make sacrifices. I accepted the living conditions I knew I would find in Sundi. In the beginning, it was all a great adventure. I had not yet thought about sacrifices I might not choose to make that would be forced upon me.

Chapter 11

How Not to Teach English

The audio-lingual method of language learning made its debut in the 1960s, and through it I learned Spanish and French. The best way to learn a language, so the theory went, was to speak it from the beginning, the way I was learning Kikongo. In Zairian schools, though, the old-fashioned emphasis on reading and grammar exercises prevailed. Written exams mattered most, and daily work—actually speaking the language—counted for less than a third of a student's grade. Even worse, at the end of their high school studies, students had to pass a written State exam to get a diploma. Students didn't need to speak a word of the language for the exam. Any student who failed had to repeat the year and take the exam again. No exceptions.

Nearly everyone wanted their sons and daughters in school, although boys took precedence if the family could not afford school fees for all their children. Most boys and girls had at least four or five years of primary school. Fewer than 20 percent of primary school graduates went on to secondary school. There were simply not enough places for them.

Overall, education expanded after Independence, but the fledgling State had bigger worries than overhauling the colonial educational system. Naturally, teachers tailored their lessons to the type of questions students would find on the State exam, a practice characterized critically in the US as "teaching to the exam." In the US, opponents of Statewide and national exams deride this practice, for good reason. Students quickly forget material simply memorized for an exam rather than learned by using a language. The English exam included only standard reading comprehension, a short text followed by questions. It included no measure of the student's ability to understand spoken English-—exactly the opposite of my own language training.

The Government did make one change. It did away with the old textbooks glorifying Belgium and colonialism. In the new textbook, that apparently borrowed heavily from an earlier Nigerian series, each lesson began with a dialogue or story, followed by an explanation of grammar points, a vocabulary list, and questions about the text. One story began, "We are all familiar with the petrol pumps at the filling station in our neighborhood." Only one of my freshman students had ever seen a gas pump. In Sundi and Luozi, workers siphoned fuel out of a metal barrel with a garden hose. The other stories were equally inappropriate for students in the African bush. One recounted the life of Marie Curie. My students needed a lot of imagination to relate to these texts.

Mom and Dad must have appreciated the irony that I had refused a teaching career, and now gladly threw myself into teaching English. But I still didn't see it as a career. I didn't know what I would do in Zaire once Jackson had his PhD. I didn't think about it—I had more immediate decisions to make. I had two weeks before my classes started, so Jackson encouraged me to get advice from Hanna, the Swedish volunteer who had taught most of the English classes before I showed up. Now Hanna would be teaching math instead, and English only to final-year students.

"The students find English so difficult," Hannah said every time I talked to her. "They need translation to understand. We did a lot of exercises, but they still found it *so difficult*."

Hanna painstakingly translated all the texts in the book into French. I didn't know enough French to translate anything more complex than "hello," but I did not see translation as a valuable learning tool, anyway. English was a third language for most of these students and a fourth for some, after Kikongo, French and Lingala, the lingua franca of the cities, the army and popular music. People who already speak more than one language usually find it easier to learn another, and I could not believe that English would be *so difficult* for these students. I wondered with some anxiety what I was in for, so I walked into my first class—sophomores—with my nerves on edge. The students jumped to their feet like soldiers and chanted, "Goo mow-ning, Cheecha." Taken aback, I barely managed to say, "Good morning, class. Please sit down." Like a deflating balloon, the entire class sank onto their chairs. Thirty students crammed themselves into the room, the desks so close together nobody could move between them.

The school administrator insisted that I take roll the first day, since he was never sure who would be back from the long vacation. Students and their families couldn't always find the money, so the administrator had anxious parents at his door every day, begging for any open spot. Unfortunately for me, this was the first year that students had to use African first names instead of European names, part of President Mobutu's Authenticity Campaign to replace Belgian cultural elements with African ones. When a student didn't recognize his new *nom authentique,* or pretended not to, the others called out his nickname. With each new name provoking more hilarity, taking roll took me twenty minutes. These students had lived together for at least three years. Some had been together since grade school, and I didn't stand a chance against their collective telepathy. And they weren't kids. Some of them were close to my age, having started school when they were ten. Others lost years of schooling to illness, lack of money, or failed exams. One student was over forty, a teacher back in class for additional qualifications. He abstained from the hijinks but didn't try to stop them. The few girls stayed aloof too—one junior, two sophomores and three freshmen.

With roll call mercifully over, I asked the students to take turns reading the first text in the book, each student reading a sentence. The room suddenly hushed. No one volunteered, so I called on a boy in the front row. He stumbled through the sentence. Had they never done this before? I prayed the next student would read better, but he was worse. Had this class really studied a whole year of English?

"Did your class finish the first book in this series last year?" I asked.

They shifted in the chairs. I asked an older boy directly.

"We still had five chapters left," he replied, looking at the floor.

I knew we couldn't go back and catch up, because last year's book was in the hands of the incoming freshmen. I didn't know what to do, so I told them to write the answers to the questions at the end of the lesson for the next class.

The juniors read just as badly, although they didn't act out. In fact, they barely spoke at all. The freshman class went better. Since they had only an hour a week of English the previous year, they didn't worry about my expectations. At lunch, I told Jackson about my classes. He shrugged.

"Nearly all Hanna's students passed the State exam," he said. "Her methods can't be so terrible."

The next day, again getting no volunteers, I chose students to write their responses to the questions on the blackboard. I could not explain why "They did quickly their homework" was incorrect. Embarrassed that I did not know the grammar rules of my own language, I spent that afternoon poring over old English textbooks in an airless shed behind the school office. Some of the old colonial books, despite their outdated stories and colonial point of view, provided better grammar explanations than the current book. How, I wondered, could I use them? I wandered into the next room and found the answer—an old-fashioned mimeograph machine.

"Do you have stencils for that mimeo machine?" I asked Ernest Badia, the administrator.

"Yes," he said, reaching for a shelf behind him. "Don't use too many, though. We have a budget."

Gratefully, I accepted two. I knew I had no natural gift for teaching and had never taken an education course, yet here I was, teaching English six days a week to three levels of high school students, and one hour a week to eighth graders, with no one to replace me if I quit. I would do the best I could. Thank God Hannah taught the seniors. At least I wouldn't be responsible if any of them failed that all-important State exam.

Most of my students came from villages within a twenty-mile radius of the school, although a few came from farther away. Teachers like Jean and Christine brought their younger siblings from their village. Church employees in Luozi sent another half dozen. All the students had one thing in common:

their firm sense of identity. They were proud of their Kongo heritage, and every student knew his place in his clan, his future responsibilities, and his family's expectations. Nothing in Kongo culture is more important than the welfare of the clan, a principle drummed into them from babyhood. When they finished high school, they knew they would be part of an elite. They had anxieties about their appearance and their academic abilities, like young Americans did, but there the similarities ended. None had ever driven a car, and most probably never would. They rarely argued or fought and cooperated more than they competed. I don't recall ever seeing students shout at each other.

Their material life at Sundi had few advantages over life in the village. They lived in old one- or two-room dormitories, each with eight to ten students and the outhouses a hundred feet away. At dawn, students bathed in a stream half a mile away. From a spot further upstream, they filled plastic jerry-cans with drinking water. Mornings and evenings, the sound of students drumming on their jerry-cans resounded along their path like a percussion band. They washed their clothes downstream from the bathing place whenever they could find the time.

The government did not require children to attend primary school, but nearly everyone in Manianga did. Since Independence in 1960, many more secondary schools sprang up, but the number still didn't meet the need. The missionaries used to limit classes to twenty or twenty-five students. When José took over at Sundi, he admitted thirty in the upper classes and even forty in the middle school classes. School fees paid by the families had to cover books, office supplies, school maintenance and medical care at the dispensary, since the central government only paid staff salaries. The school fees represented a large chunk of a family's income. A few villagers called on wealthier relatives in Kinshasa for help with those fees. When a student failed to pay, he was sent home until he could come up with the payment. Those whose families were too poor simply didn't return.

Students had to cook for themselves, or buy prepared food in the market, unless they lived with relatives near the mission. The wife of my forty-year-old sophomore had a thriving business selling beans in tomato sauce, cassava greens, and rice to students in the late afternoon, charging four cents for a large ladleful. My neighbor Josette sold Swedish-style knotted rolls made with palm oil instead of butter for ten cents. When they could afford it, students ate these with their morning tea, which they prepared themselves, using generous amounts of powdered milk and locally processed sugar.

From all the walking they did, and carrying loads on their heads, both boys and girls had beautiful posture and muscular bodies. None were overweight. During the years they were born, between 1952 and 1960, nearly 25 percent of children died before their fifth birthday. These were lucky survivors, and they knew it. The girls steered clear of the boys, who often teased them to get their attention. Jackson punished the boys when he caught them harassing the girls. In one of my freshman classes, a girl once lost her temper and started whacking the offending boy on the head with a book, to his great amusement. According to the rules, I should have sent her to the *prefet de discipline*, but I thought her life was hard enough already. Some of the older girls were already engaged to be married, and the boys avoided them. One already had a child, cared for by her family in a nearby village. She would marry the father when she graduated.

One day, the Peace Corps biology teacher and I were supervising a group of students who were cutting the grass on the mission quadrangle.

"Can you see yourself in the States supervising twenty teenagers with machetes?" he asked. "And these kids are strong. Last week I was teaching them about blood circulation, and I showed them how to take a pulse. The first kid had a heart rate of fifty-two. I thought he was an exception, so I took another kid's pulse. Same thing. That's the heart rate of an athlete! So I had one of them run around the school for ten minutes and took his pulse again. Still under sixty. They're in fantastic shape."

Extreme formality dominated relationships between teachers and students. Kongo culture demanded that children show respect for adults and those in authority such as chiefs, pastors and teachers. The other women teachers and I were always "Madame," Jackson was "Citoyen Directeur" and the Zairian male teachers "Citoyen Professeur." Mobutu's Authenticity Campaign had replaced the French "monsieur" with "citoyen"—a form of address borrowed, oddly, from the early days of the French Revolution. When I entered a classroom, the students stood up until I told them to sit. On the rare occasions when Jackson walked in, they stood at attention and stayed there until he left. Outside of class, the girls dropped a little of the formality, but the boys, never.

These social norms flowed naturally from Kongo culture, and the students showed no resentment. The entire mission had a sense of shared vision and purpose in which everyone had an important role. Disagreements occurred—especially in faculty meetings—but a path to resolution could always be found in a culture built on cooperation and consensus. I sometimes wondered if the same spirit would prevail if the region became more prosperous. Despite our efforts, that was unlikely to happen any time soon.

Chapter 12
Kinshasa by Road

Our car arrived in November, and Jackson spent a week in Matadi getting it out of Customs, using every political connection he could find. With a car, we could drive to André Fukiau's independent school at Kumba a few miles away on weekends. He had written a book describing the Kongo world view, much beloved by the educated Kongo, and his school attempted to teach Kongo history and culture in addition to the subjects taught at schools like Sundi. Visting him and his family provided a welcome break from the insulated mission station. The car also enabled me to drive to the Mangembo market on Sundays and to the Commercial Center. More importantly, we could now drive to Luozi and on to Kimpese during Christmas vacation. For me that meant crossing the river on the ferry for the first time.

The large flat platform, just big enough for two trucks and a small car, rested on three pontoons that looked like giant canoes. After the workers tied up the ferry, they threw down a few long planks between the deck and the riverbank. The fast current made a floating dock impossible, and the level of the river varied widely between the dry season and the rainy season, so a fixed dock wouldn't work either. Drivers crept slowly up the rickety planks, guided by a ferry worker. Once the crew secured the vehicles, pedestrians clambered on, some on deck, most in the pontoons below. The crew guided the ferry slightly upstream to avoid a sandbar in the middle of the river and to make it easier to tie up the ferry on the other side. It was easier to float downriver to the docking point than to reach it going upriver. Unloading and loading the ferry took about an hour if all went well; the crossing itself took fifteen minutes. Usually the ferry made four round-trip crossings a day, starting at dawn and stopping at dusk. Passengers in the pontoons scanned the water, shouting out if they saw a water snake or a crocodile, which happened often. Fisherman plied the backwater close to shore in their small dugout canoes. Pictures from the 19th century show huge pirogues made of giant trees, with twenty or more rowers. Those trees disappeared decades ago, and today's canoes are not much bigger than kayaks.

From the south bank, we drove an hour and a half over a well-maintained dirt road in a nearly empty landscape to Kimpese. Few people settled in the area because there was little fresh water. After an overnight with the Dianzungus in Kimpese, we drove to Kinshasa—altogether twelve hours of travel over two days. Kiame, normally hyperactive, slept through every car ride, no matter how rough the road. Jackson shopped for schoolbooks, mimeograph stencils and other supplies at the Protestant book and stationery store near the hostel. We could buy these supplies only in Kinshasa. I shopped at a European-style grocery, careful to stay within my limited budget.

Pedestrians debarking on the south bank of the Congo River across from Luozi. In the dry season, the level of the river is too low for the ferry to reach the ramp, so pedestrians must wade through thirty feet of water to reach it.

Road between Luozi and Kimpese.

I could not resist a can of Danish bacon and a tiny canned ham, in addition to staples like baking powder. In between shopping trips, we visited family. Kiame always found other children to play with. Jackson interviewed informants for his research, including one unpleasant man who claimed to have helped organize the murder of Patrice Lumumba in 1961. We visited only one person more than once, a Ministry of Education official who lived in a modest neighborhood near the former "Green Space" that separated the European quarter from the African city before Independence. Tata Nsingani wanted help from Jackson and José to establish more schools in the Manianga region. Unlike younger Zairians (Jackson included) he never wore an *abacosts*, only polyester shirts and khakis. Despite his modest manner, Nsingani had considerable influence in the Ministry. Like many older Kongo, he survived in Mobutu's government by downplaying his importance.

"I'm just a simple functionary," he would say with a shrug, as he conducted diligent maneuvers behind the scenes. The national government, said Nsingani, wanted to open more schools across the country and would pay teachers to staff them if the villagers provided the buildings.

"You need to move fast," he said. "Not many people know about this yet, and we don't know when the Government will change its policy, so if we don't want other regions to get ahead of us, we need to open as many schools as possible."

He and Jackson had long discussions about strategies and priorities: which villages to target, which village notables to approach, what message would be most convincing. Nsingani had nothing to gain personally from this effort. He was a Kongo nationalist who simply wanted to ensure that the Kongo obtained as much of the nation's resources as they could. In fact, Kongo Central was one of the three regions that already had the most schools. Even before Independence, its proximity to the Atlantic Coast ensured a strong missionary presence, both Catholic and Protestant. The other two favored regions included Kasai, with its vast diamond mines, and Katanga, site of copper and cobalt mines. The comparatively neglected regions of Bandundu, Haut-Zaire, Equateur, and Kivu had greater need, but like the Belgians before him, the Mobutu regime had no political or economic interest in developing them. Equateur, Mobutu's home region, had the fewest hospitals and schools of all. Its population of isolated ethnic groups lived mainly in the forest, subsisting on hunting and fishing. The Kongo elite feared that Mobutu and his cronies would eventually direct resources to their own region, so they felt pressure to move quickly. Jackson had a new project.

* * *

Christmas in Zaire is a religious holiday, with none of the commercial glitz and gifting frenzy of American culture. Cyclists decorated their bicycle handlebars and sometimes their heads with bits of tinsel, and a few churches put out crèches. The main event in Protestant churches, though, was an all-night Christmas Eve service. The Catholics also had all-night services, but I don't know if they had the Nativity plays cherished by the Protestants. We went to a Christmas Eve pageant in Bandal, where a relative lived. The play unfolded in numerous scenes, interspersed with singing and Bible readings, and continued until dawn. The pageant participants made not-too-subtle historical comparisons. In one scene, Herod wore a leopard-skin toque like Mobutu's. The audience understood.

Ferry ramp on the south side of the Congo River, across from Luozi.

Car driving off the ferry onto the Luozi ramp.

We left Kinshasa in time to catch the ferry and get to the big New Year's celebration in Luozi. New Year's Day reigns as the country's most important national holiday. If they can afford it, families buy meat for the occasion, which most of them don't see the rest of the year. People party on New Year's Eve, and on New Year's Day they show off their new clothes, pitying those who can't afford to buy them. We stayed at the mission hostel instead of at the family house—not any more luxurious, but the rooms had screens on the windows. Showers and outhouses were a hundred feet away. Robert Diyabanza, who lived nearby, ran the Protestant Church garage, and his wife Ruth, a Swedish missionary, did liaison work with the Protestant Church Headquarters. They had a daughter Kiame's age, Hélène, who became his lifelong friend. To ensure that the town's poorest families could celebrate the holiday, Jackson, Robert and other friends pooled their money to buy a bull and drew up a list of recipients. Robert located an animal for sale, negotiated the price, arranged to haul the live animal from the farm to Luozi, and had it slaughtered. Robert and a few others distributed the meat early on New Year's Day.

At the Mahaniah family house, a hired cook roasted a goat on a spit in the backyard, and all the women were busy cooking. We passed houses where people danced to loud Zairian music. People must have stocked up on C batteries to power those boom boxes. Before Independence, Protestant churches didn't allow dancing. Jackson's friends joked about getting suspended from school if anyone caught them even nodding to the music in the village. That prohibition ended, but the habit remained. Hardly any Protestants older than twenty ever danced, and the Church still prohibited alcohol. The holiday meal started in mid-afternoon, with food distributed according to social hierarchy: oldest men first, then the younger professional men like Jackson, then the children. Women ate last, in the kitchen, except for me. As a special guest, I ate with the men, and so did Kiame.

"What about the women?" I asked Ronsard. "Will there be enough left for them?"

"They're in charge of the food. Don't worry—they keep enough back for themselves."

After the meal everyone sat around talking. Three months into learning Kikongo, I could catch a word here and there, enough to understand the subject of a conversation, but not enough to follow it. We stayed until dark when the mosquitoes started to buzz.

The next day after breakfast, Jackson's father called a family meeting about one of his grandchildren, the fourth daughter of Jackson's sister Malakidi, who lived in the village. Five of Malakidi's six daughters lived in Luozi with their grandparents. The two oldest did most of the family's cooking and housework, under their grandmother's direction.

Eight-year-old Julienne, Tata Mahaniah explained, needed medical care, and he thought she should go to a better school than the one in Luozi. He asked us to take her with us to Sundi. I was stunned. How could I take on a little girl I couldn't communicate with? But from a traditional Kongo perspective, Tata Mahaniah was making a reasonable request. All the teachers' families in Sundi had at least one young relative living with them. Now the whole family looked at me, gauging my reaction to this request. I didn't know what to say, but Jackson read my face.

"I don't like it either," Jackson said. "But how can we refuse?"

I glanced at Julienne, a thin little girl with a swollen belly, a sure sign of intestinal parasites. The girl looked miserable, whether from illness or fear, I couldn't tell. She gazed at her feet during the entire discussion.

"We have to take her," I conceded.

Jackson turned to Julienne. "Pack your things," he said. She slipped out of the room without a word, never meeting his eyes. Ten minutes later she returned with a bundle smaller than a child's backpack.

"That's all?" Jackson asked. She nodded. Her sisters tittered in the background, embarrassed for her. All the way back to Sundi, Kiame chattered at her in Kikongo, delighted to have company. Julienne didn't say a word.

Before the second semester started, I had to get Julienne settled. The first stop was the dispensary. Everyone called it a hospital, and while it had fifteen beds and an operating room, it had a doctor only one day a month, when a Dutch missionary doctor flew in for the day, mainly to perform hernia surgery, a consequence of carrying heavy loads. A middle-aged Swedish missionary nurse managed the hospital, and a young Swedish nurse-midwife led an outreach team in the surrounding villages, performing pre- and post-natal exams and well-child visits. The Zairian nurse practitioners, two women and a man trained at the nursing school in Kimpese, did most of the work, with the help of several aides. The Catholic hospital a few miles away had a doctor, but he was often away, and many Protestants didn't have confidence in the Catholic hospital. Both missions had only the most basic equipment and drugs. Religious rivalry gave this enclave two hospitals and two sets of schools, a rarity outside the major cities.

In the clinic, Julienne and I waited on a long wooden bench. Except for emergencies, nurses treated people in the order they arrived. Sometimes when the nurses saw me, they brought me to the front of the line, but I never asked for special treatment. I found it embarrassing, even though no one else objected. That day, though, they were busy with a bad malaria case. We waited half an hour before Angel, a nurse practitioner, called us in.

"Your husband's niece?" Angel said. "What's your name?"

"Julienne," she said, looking at her feet.

"Madame, I must use her *nom authentique*," Angel said, and asked the girl a question in Kikongo.

"Dilubenzi," the girl whispered. Angel wrote on a chart.

"She came from Luozi to stay with us, and she's really not feeling well," I said in French. Dilubenzi didn't understand what I said and looked slightly alarmed.

Angel examined her quickly and asked a few questions in Kikongo. She pulled out a lancet from a sterilizer, pricked Julienne's finger lightly, and smeared blood onto a slide.

"Most likely, she just has worms and malaria," Angel said. She reached into a cabinet behind her and pulled out two bottles. "Do you have aspirin and paracetamol?"

"Yes."

She nodded as she counted pills from two bottles and wrapped each set in a small cone of brown wrapping paper. "This one is Vermox. Most people give their children a cure every six months. It's probably time for Kiame to take some too. She will feel sick to her stomach, but she needs to finish the cure. This one is Nivaquine." After reciting the instructions to me in French, she turned to Julienne, aka Dilubenzi, and repeated them in Kikongo.

After lunch, we drove to the Centre Commercial. It just took twenty minutes to walk it, but I only walked when I had to. My neighbor Josette recommended a particular tailor, so we stopped in front of his shop. We needed two uniforms and three dresses, and Julienne gazed, eyes wide, at the bolts of fabric behind the counter. Luozi had bigger shops than this, but she had probably never entered them. No one had ever bought her a new dress. She wore only hand-me-downs from her three older sisters. The tailor pulled out four or five bolts he considered appropriate and laid them on a counter. She looked at me expectantly.

"No, you choose," I mimed. Kiame, our usual translator, had not come along. I approved her choices. The tailor took her measurements and promised a quick turnaround.

At another shop we bought flip-flops. Underwear would have to wait until the Sunday market. On the way back, we stopped at the mission carpentry shop. The head carpenter was a grizzled man in his fifties who called me *nkwezi* (sister-in-law) and brought me mushrooms from the woods.

"Can you recommend a carpenter who can make a bed for this girl?" I asked. He rubbed his chin.

"*Nanga*, (maybe)," he said. That was usually a polite version of "no," but this time I knew it was worker-speak for "The missionaries have an extra one. Let me work out how I can get my hands on it." By nightfall, he delivered it.

Julienne stayed in that bed for the rest of the week. I checked on her every couple of hours because she looked so miserable. She was taking toxic medications that make most people sick, and she wasn't yet accustomed to our diet. In our Sundi Lutete micro-region, people made their beans and greens a little differently than in Luozi, and we ate rice instead of *kwanga*. I had to make sure she ate and drank enough. During her treatment, she ate only bread, rice and bananas.

Jackson said a few words to her at lunch, and again at night when he came home, but that's all. He didn't joke or play with her the way he did with Kiame.

"Why don't you talk to her more?" I asked. "She's lonely."

"I am her *ngu'ankazi*, her maternal uncle, the head of her clan. She will never relax with me," Jackson said. "Or you either. I can't treat her the way I do Kiame. It would make her very uncomfortable"

It was true that she seemed more comfortable with the babysitter and the cook than she did with me, although she did play with Kiame when she felt well enough to sit up. After two weeks of treatment, Dilubenzi started to perk up. Jackson enrolled her in school. We picked up her clothes from the tailor, and I could tell she was pleased. She still didn't talk to us, but she played with Kiame in the evenings. Slowly, she made friends, and when I walked past the school at recess, I saw her jumping and clapping with the other girls.

Chapter 13
Fever

In this, O Nature, yield I pray to me.
I pace and pace, and think and think, and take
The fever'd hands, and note down all I see,
That some dim distant light may haply break.
The painful faces ask, can we not cure?
We answer, No, not yet; we seek the laws.
O God, reveal thro' all this thing obscure
The unseen, small, but million-murdering cause.

—Ronald Ross, 1897, winner of the Nobel Prize in 1902 for his research on malaria.

At the first faculty meeting in January, Jackson presented the plan to increase the number of schools in Manianga by convincing villagers to build them, as he had agreed with Nsingani. The four Swedish teachers objected, claiming there weren't enough qualified teachers to staff any new schools.

"The Government will staff them, but it wants us to build them first," Jackson said. He didn't disguise his impatience. In the discussion that followed, Jackson won over the Zairians but not the Swedes. Some Zairians volunteered to do the rounds of the villages with him.

"I can go to the villages too," I said.

Jackson shook his head. "It's the same problem as with my research. If you come along, it becomes a social visit instead of an official one."

"I'm a teacher, just like the others," I said. His argument didn't make sense to me. Was that the real reason, or did he just want to ensure that he was the center of attention on those trips? I fought harder over this than I did over the research, because I knew what would happen if I lost. He still refused. So for the rest of the school year, Jackson and his team of teachers traveled to the villages every weekend, and sometimes during the week. Now we rarely visited the independent school at Kumba, and I found myself alone even more than before. I visited Josette and Christine when I could, but women at Sundi had a lot of work, and the Swedes did not include me in their afternoon tea gatherings on their veranda. I would not have felt comfortable there anyway.

On top of that, we had intermittent news of attacks on commercial trucks by Diawara's band of guerilla fighters near the border. The Swedish nurse continued her outreach clinics in the villages, and she didn't see any sign of the guerillas. Then a missionary was shot in the leg near Mbanza–Ngungu, 100 kilometers from Sundi, near the Zaire-Congo-Brazzaville border further west. Around that time a Belgian couple were killed in their home in the same area. The Swedes didn't think the rebels killed the Belgian couple and suspected Angolan soldiers instead. For several years the poorly paid and undisciplined troops of one Angolan civil war faction occupied an army camp in the middle of Kinshasa. In Zaire's cities, Angolan soldiers frequently invaded homes and robbed residents. To ensure public safety, the Central Government stationed more Zairian soldiers on the border and near the larger Catholic missions and gave them AK47s and ammunition. The only person shot after that was a Zairian soldier who dropped his rifle and shot himself in the foot.

I spent more time with Christine and my neighbor Josette. Every day around four o'clock I joined Josette on a raffia mat between our two houses, shelling peanuts or gourd seeds, the children playing nearby, while Bakala carved sculptures in his makeshift studio in front of the house. Women stopped by to talk and correct my Kikongo, and men chatted with the artist as he worked.

Bakala could go to the bar at the Centre Commercial and drink beer with the teachers from the Catholic mission because he was a Catholic, the only Catholic teacher at Sundi. The Protestant Church forbade alcohol, so Protestant teachers couldn't go to the bar, although Melia, its owner, was a Protestant.

"Doesn't it bother you that you don't go with your husband to the bar?" I asked Josette.

She startled me by whooping with laughter and putting a hand on my arm. "*Nkwezi*, it would be so boring. Why would I want to sit around listening to all those men?"

"You could talk too," I said.

She shook her head and wiped her eyes. "I am not interested."

On weekends, I visited Christine, while her husband Balekita supervised soccer practice and matches. She took me to her garden and arranged for me to have a small plot of land next to hers. I brought my own flower and vegetable seeds and planted a few greens that Christine gave me. I enjoyed digging in the dirt, each of us in her own garden, yelling comments back and forth like the village women did. Women at Sundi didn't spend much time with their husbands during the day. As Josette's response showed, men and women lived essentially separate daily lives. My life began to resemble theirs, and it was not the life I had dreamed of. Still, I felt grateful for their company.

One day after lunch, Kiame and Dilubenzi were playing a game, sitting on the floor. Kiame looked flushed, and I put a hand to his forehead. It was burning hot. I ran to get a thermometer, but before I reached the bedroom, Dilubenzi called me back. Kiame had fallen to the floor, his back arched, arms and legs shaking. His teeth were clenched, his head turned to one side.

I scooped him up and ran outside, shouting, "Josette!" I didn't call "*Nkwezi*" because that could have meant almost anyone. She hurried down the steps from her kitchen.

"He's having a convulsion. Give him to me and get your car keys," she said.

By the time I got back, he was limp in her arms, and a trickle of blood dribbled from a corner of his mouth. I quickly felt his chest for a heartbeat.

"He's sleeping," Josette said. "Let's go."

At the dispensary, we jumped the line, and Angel did a quick physical exam. She pricked his finger and took the slide to the lab.

"Just in case, because I'm sure it's malaria. This is his first infection, isn't it?"

I nodded.

"Don't worry. He's breathing normally, and he's not dehydrated. He'll be all right. The convulsion has already brought his temperature down, and we'll make sure it doesn't go so high again."

Angel gave him an injection—probably an anti-malarial, but I didn't ask. She counted out some aspirin and Nivaquine and dropped them into a paper cone.

"Give him half an aspirin as soon as he wakes up, and give him one tablet of Nivaquine tonight," Angel said. "If his fever goes up, bathe him with lukewarm water. You can just use a towel. You don't have to get him into the shower. What are you using for malaria prevention?"

"Daraprim."

She shook her head. "The parasite has developed resistance to it. You can switch to Nivaquine, but that has its own risks. It would be better to let him develop his own immunity. Nivaquine taken over a long period of time is not a good idea. Is the Director traveling?"

"Yes. He's due back tomorrow."

She nodded, and looked at Josette, who nodded back. I followed Angel's instructions, and Kiame recovered within a week, although he lacked energy for another week after that. Josette stopped by several times over the next few days. When Jackson returned from his trip, I said, "This is what can happen when you're away."

"What could I have done? You have Angel and Josette," he said. "You don't need me."

"I do. I need you for moral support. And Kiame needs you," I said.

He launched into his usual lecture about the importance of the work he was doing, how urgent it was, and how the future of education in Manianga depended on him and his colleagues. But when he said "You don't need me" he didn't realize that he had planted a seed. It would slowly grow into something neither of us expected.

* * *

At the beginning of spring vacation, we dropped Dilubenzi off at the family house in Luozi and drove to Jackson's ancestral village, Kindezi, half an hour from Luozi. I was delighted to find the women making pottery, which they did only once a year, and I photographed the final stages of their work, which stretched over many weeks. That included a long walk to the source of the clay, gathering the plants they needed to prepare the dye, and forming the pots, using the coil method.

Kindezi, 1973. The potter has just finished spinning the pot in the dye solution heated in the wide, shallow pan in the background. She used the sticks to twirl the pot in the dye and then to remove the pot from the pan.

Kindezi, 1973. Finished pots drying. The dyeing process creates a unique pattern of irregular concentric circles. These pots were used mainly in the village, although a few were sold in the Luozi market.

We stayed overnight in the village and left the next day for Kimpese, where we visited José and Suzanne. A few days later, Kiame and I both came down with fevers.

"It's malaria," Suzanne said. "Come on, we're going to the clinic."

They put us in the small Guest House, where missionaries and other people of means stayed instead of the main hospital wards. Kiame and I both had high fevers.

"Mommy, make the spiders go away!" Kiame shouted as we sat in the emergency room. I was too dizzy to sit up. Jackson showed up an hour later; he and Suzanne conferred in the corner with Dorothy, the American missionary nurse.

"Sandie, I need to go to Kinshasa," Jackson said. "Suzanne and the nurse here will take care of you."

"No," I said. "You can't go. We're too sick. Stay with us."

"They will take good care of you here," he said. "I have to pick up documents for the school, for the State Exam, and supplies."

"Just wait... a day or two," I pleaded, weak from speaking just two sentences.

"I can't," he said. "I have to go."

I turned my face to the wall and cried until long after he left. I could not understand why he would still go to Kinshasa when we were both so sick. Was it perhaps normal for a Kongo man to do that? I was too sick to think clearly. That night Kiame's fever spiked. Dorothy put a cold cloth on his head and stood over his little body, praying.

If she's praying, he must be dying, I thought, in my malaria-addled mind. And I could do nothing for him. I cried until I fell into a feverish sleep. When I opened my eyes, I saw Kiame sitting propped up with a pillow, a big white napkin tucked under his chin, eating cereal. When I lurched to his bed to feel his forehead, he pulled away. The bed stretched into a trapezoid, and the bedclothes undulated like an ocean wave. Kiame's eyes didn't line up right, and the shape of his face kept changing.

"You go *you* bed," he ordered, his face solemn.

Dorothy came into the room and led me firmly back to my bed.

"His eyes..." I tried to say, but only garbled French came out.

"He's fine. It's the malaria distorting your vision. Now it's you we're worried about. You need a bath to bring your fever down."

"No. I'm too cold," I protested.

She called in another missionary to help her. I kept resisting, and they had to coax me into the water.

"Too. Cold," I said, my teeth chattering.

"Yes, it's the fever. This will help," Dorothy insisted.

They wrapped me, still shaking with malarial chills, in a towel. The bed, when I finally lay down, rocked uncontrollably. That night I slept very little. Dorothy made me take small sips of tea and Coke. I couldn't eat.

"Why is Kiame still sleeping? It's not like him," I said when the sun came up.

"He'll be fine," Dorothy said. "Let him sleep."

In the afternoon, Suzanne came to visit. I tried to talk to her, but I kept getting my languages mixed up. The light from the doorway hurt my eyes. I squinted, watching the lavender and pink stripes of Suzanne's dress undulate and shimmer. The motion nauseated me, and I shut my eyes. That night the bed rocked again, and the room spun around me. This time Dorothy came to pray over me. *Was I dying?* I wondered. I couldn't bear another day of chills, nausea and vertigo, and I thought, *Yes, just let me die. Not another day of this.*

When I woke up, the bed had stopped rocking, although I still felt too weak to sit up. Kiame sat propped up on pillows, playing with his hands. Dorothy came in with breakfast.

"Why is he...? What...?"

"Nothing's wrong," Dorothy said. "Children do that when they're sick."

One spoonful of Cheerios and I felt like I'd eaten the whole box. I sat up and looked around, seeing the room in its normal state for the first time in three days. I tried to read, but the words jumped around on the page. I thought about Jackson going to Kinshasa, and my anger and disappointment flared. How could he have left us?

Jackson came back on the fourth day, when Dorothy was giving Kiame a sponge bath. When we were alone, I said, "You shouldn't have left us. Kiame almost died, and I was too sick even to hold him."

"I didn't know it was that serious," he said.

"Suzanne and Dorothy told you. You didn't want to listen. And you left."

"Dorothy and Suzanne took better care of you than I could have," he argued.

Would this man never stop arguing? Did he ever express regret or remorse?

"That's not the point! You knew how sick we were, and you decided your school shopping was more important. We needed you here. Now I know I can't trust you."

He did not answer. When my temperature finally dropped to normal and I could walk a few steps, we drove back to Sundi, picking up Dilubenzi in Luozi. Kiame's usual energy returned in a week; it took me much longer. I couldn't stand for an hour of class, so I asked the carpentry shop to make a wooden stool for me. I still couldn't eat much, lost weight, and couldn't work up an interest in anything. Malaria can cause temporary neurological changes, but I believed my symptoms resulted mainly from my shock at Jackson's betrayal. For several weeks I could barely keep up with my classes. Josette told me to talk to Sara, one of the Swedish teachers, who had a bad malaria attack the year before.

Not expecting much, I went to see her and told her I was having trouble recovering and heard that she might be able to give me some advice. She looked off in the distance for a minute and then said, "It happened last year, on the day of the hospital picnic, when all the staff were having a party near the stream about ten miles from here. I had a fever in the morning, and by noon it shot up and I had the most tremendous headache. It was a Sunday, so nobody was around. The teachers all went to their villages, and the Nilssons were out evangelizing. Elias knew he had to get help, but we didn't have a car, and who would watch the baby? I took some malaria medicine but in the afternoon I started convulsing."

What must it be like to have a convulsion? I shuddered. "How awful."

Sara nodded. "By that time I was barely conscious. I have never felt so sick. Elias went for help and took the baby with him. He found a student to run to the picnic and get one of the nurses. It still took a couple of hours for a nurse to come." She sighed. "The treatment is awful, too, as you know. I was so weak. I talked to Elias about going back to Sweden. I was so afraid it would happen again, and I didn't think I could face it."

"I can certainly understand that."

"Then José Dianzungu came to see me. His family has been through a lot, you know. He talked about the school and how they needed me, how we all take risks working here, where there's no real hospital between here and Kimpese. Elias was very understanding, but he felt we had made a commitment, and he did not want to leave. After a while, I improved. I'm still afraid of malaria though."

"I'm so sorry this happened to you. Thank you for telling me about it," I said. "It makes me feel more hopeful, even if I don't feel very good right now. If I ever had convulsions I don't know if I would agree to stay."

She smiled. "I think you'll be OK."

I struggled to maintain my emotional equilibrium, with only my women friends to lean on. Jackson made no adjustments to his schedule, still touring the villages on weekends, lobbying village chiefs to build schools. He never apologized for abandoning us in Kimpese, and I never forgave him. I thought about Sara's story. She could have gone back to Sweden, either with Elias or alone. Not that it would have been easy. But Elias and José convinced her that their commitment was more important than a single bad experience. I had to convince myself of the same thing.

Now I was staying despite Jackson, not because of him. One night I dreamed that a bookcase fell on him and killed him, and in the dream, I felt the same indifference I saw him showing for me. I had never felt more alone.

Chapter 14

A Long Dry Season

In the last eight weeks of the school year, students crammed for their exams. Jackson opened classrooms in the evening to provide a quiet place for them to study. The other teachers and I organized review sessions, and all the students showed up, even the laziest who until then showed little concern. I had to write six exams, one for each of my classes. Exams for the two freshman and two sophomore sections were different, with an emphasis on business terms on the Commercial section exams that I would not include for the Pedagogy section.

The seniors took the State Exam at the beginning of June at Mangembo. All the teachers from Sundi, including me, had to serve as proctors, whether they taught seniors or not. A separate team of teachers from different schools graded the exams and submitted the results to the Department of Education, which would announce the results in August. The lower classes took their exams in mid- to late-June, and teachers had a week to submit grades. Students who failed an exam in any subject had to pass another in August to advance to the next grade. Any student who failed the make-up exam—even in only one subject—had to repeat the year.

I didn't expect many students to fail English. In the lower grades, a student who neglected homework but paid attention in class would probably still pass. English was a popular subject, because teenagers wanted to understand films and lyrics to American and British popular songs. After looking over the rules, I decided that no student should repeat a year just because he failed the make-up exam in English. The few who failed the first English exam generally failed other subjects too. Only two or three failed English alone. I was determined that they would pass the make-up exam.

After the students left for home, Jackson finished his government reports, and we prepared for a month of travel to Luozi, Kimpese and Matadi, planning to come back in August to administer make-up exams. The Zairian teachers went to visit their families in the surrounding villages or towns like Kimpese. Students walked to their villages, carrying their belongings on their heads, or if they were lucky, hitched rides on merchant trucks. We had very few students from Kinshasa, but those students had to find a spot on one of Melia's trucks.

In Luozi, we briefly attended a revival meeting. Many church members stayed in Luozi for nearly a week, spending all day singing, reading Bible verses, and listening to rousing sermons by pastors from around the region. The meeting took place outdoors on a hill, taking advantage of the dry season that lasted from June to late September. Cool breezes blew off the Zaire River, clouds covered the sun, and people found the seventy-degree weather chilly. Women wrapped thin cotton shawls around their shoulders. I opted for a cotton sweater at first, but the humidity made it uncomfortable, and I switched to a long-sleeved cotton shirt instead, the Western equivalent of a shawl. I found the revival meeting interesting for a few hours, but I would have had a hard time sitting through more than that. From Luozi, we drove to Kinshasa, with a stop in Kimpese. José greeted us with bad news.

"Jean Balekita had an accident, and he's in the hospital here. He was riding in the back of a truck, on top of the merchandise, and was knocked to the ground by the branch of a tree."

We visited the popular soccer coach the next day before we left for Matadi. He was in too much pain to sit up, although he had no broken bones. Christine prepared his food and cared for him, as family members must in a Zairian hospital.

"I hope he'll be all right," I said.

"IME is a good hospital," Jackson said. "He survived the fall, so I think he'll recover."

On an earlier visit, José had introduced me to a Peace Corps volunteer who taught English at the Kimpese school, so I went to see her. When I stepped onto the porch of her little house, she called from behind the screen door, "Don't come any closer. I have cholera."

"Cholera! And you're walking around?"

"I'm taking antibiotics and some other stuff. It's not really that bad, but I have to stay isolated."

"Where did you get it? Do you know?"

She shrugged. "No idea. There's an epidemic in Matadi, and IME has seen some cases come in from the village, but I'm the only case at the school."

"We're going to Matadi tomorrow. I suppose we'd better get vaccinated."

"Yeah, they have roadblocks up, and they check your vaccination card. If you haven't been vaccinated, they'll give you the shot right there at the roadblock, and who knows how clean those needles are. The vaccine isn't very effective, but it's better than nothing."

We got vaccinated, with Kiame kicking and screaming. While we were at the clinic, I asked the Canadian OBGYN to remove my IUD. Jackson and I had decided it was time for a second child. Despite my misgivings about Jackson and my marriage, I still believed in the mission to improve life in Manianga and had no intention of leaving Jackson. And I didn't want Kiame to be an only child. He was so wild and had so many close calls that I often wondered if he would live to adulthood. Sundi seemed like a supportive environment to wait out a pregnancy—plenty of time to rest, and no need to drive anywhere between January and June.

In Matadi, we stayed at the Swedish Mission's Guest House, a small, pleasant building at the top of a rocky hill. "Matadi" means "rocks" in Kikongo, and the town is built on them. It's a problem for sanitation and gardening because there is so little soil. Those who could afford it built terraces and trucked in dirt from outside the city. Boats cannot navigate upstream from Matadi because of a series of rapids that stretches from there to Kinshasa, with only small navigable sections between them, like the spot where we crossed to and from Luozi on the ferry. Nobody could dig a septic tank—all the household waste flowed into open sewers and down to the Zaire River, and from there into the Atlantic Ocean a hundred miles downstream. Matadi was Zaire's only port, which meant that the country's imports and exports were transported overland, either by road or by train. Minerals mined in the southeastern province of Shaba went overland to a port in Angola. Cargo flights came and went from Kinshasa and other large cities, but not Matadi. We visited the port, which Kiame enjoyed immensely, and even toured a large ship that had passenger quarters. Before air travel became common, most people traveled through Matadi to enter or leave the country.

I liked Matadi—its size, its sleepy provincial atmosphere, very different from Kinshasa's bluster and bustle and Kimpese's amorphous sprawl. The higher hills had a view of the Angolan border several kilometers away. The town had a small, charming market near the port, in a park built by the Belgians. The merchants there specialized in ebony, which grew nearby, and I bought a few items. Demand exceeded supply, though, and merchants learned how to use shoe polish to stain lesser woods to imitate it. Jackson showed me how to detect a fake by looking underneath a statue for evidence of a dye job.

On the way out of town, we had to show our vaccination cards at a roadblock. Then, halfway to Kimpese, a tire blew out. Jackson put on the spare, but fifty miles later we had another flat.

"You and Kiame could catch a taxi-bus to Kimpese and find somebody who can repair the tire," Jackson said.

"I don't know," I said. "I'd have to get José to help me. Wasn't he going to Kinshasa?"

Then a taxi bus pulled up. "Show me the problem," the driver said. He hopped out and examined the tire, apparently unconcerned about subjecting his dozen or so passengers to an unexpected delay.

"Do you have an extra inner tube?" he asked.

We produced one. On the damaged tire, he folded up the inner tube and wedged it between the tire and its inner tube with the hole, temporarily sealing the hole. He put the tire back on the car and returned to his patiently waiting passengers.

"Drive slowly. It won't last forever, but it will get you to Kimpese."

It worked. Sometimes Zairian adaptation to adversity was nothing short of brilliant.

* * *

Every morning at nine thirty, the Sundi mission participated in a short-wave radio call with all the Swedish missions in Zaire and neighboring Congo–Brazzaville. The radio call provided the only quick form of communication in a place without telephones or telegraphs. Mission business came first, then the personal messages. Most mornings, Jackson squeezed into Pastor Nsengi's office with everyone else waiting to send or receive a message. The Church could only use the frequency for an hour.

The day after our return from Matadi, Jackson came back from the radio call looking grim.

"What is it?" I asked.

He dropped into a chair. "Jean Balekita died yesterday in Kimpese."

"What... how...?" I spluttered. "They said minor injuries!"

"After we left, they found a perforated intestine," Jackson said. "They operated, but it was too late. He died of an infection."

Jean Balekita, the good-looking teacher and coach, gone before he turned thirty! He and Christine, an attractive couple, had two boys, a three-year-old and a baby. She was so young to become a widow.

"The funeral is today, in his village near Kingoyi," Jackson said. "I can't get there in time."

"How do you get there from here?"

"South to Bienga, then back north on a really bad road. The village is northwest of here."

We sat silent for a while. I suppressed tears with an effort.

"What can we do?" I asked.

"We'll make contributions to his clan, of course," Jackson said. "One from the school, one from us."

"What else?"

"I don't know yet," Jackson said.

For centuries, Kongo social and economic life has centered on funerals. Everyone contributed money, food or drink to defray the costs. At village funerals, people came from miles around and stayed for days. Each clan built the biggest memorial or tombstone they could afford. The head of the clan designated someone to handle the contributions and record them meticulously. Strict but unwritten rules dictated who must contribute to a funeral, and how much, based on the age of the deceased, a person's relationship to the family, the prominence of the deceased, and the wealth of the giver. A clan expected a higher contribution for an old person, especially if the person was well-known. They expected more generous contributions from the wealthy, which included Jackson and me. Any White person and any Zairian who owned a car was considered wealthy.

Contributions for funeral expenses, though, don't provide support for dependents left behind. Each person's clan takes responsibility for that. Traditionally, when a man died, his oldest brother would marry the widow. This custom, clearly intended to protect widows and children, remained current in 1973. But Balekita's brothers were all younger, and I knew Christine would have refused any such proposal. Because she was a teacher, she was better off than most widows. She would stay in the house the mission provided, and she had her teacher's salary. Still, everyone expected Christine, beautiful and still in her twenties, to remarry eventually.

Jackson sighed. "I need to find someone to do Balekita's work."

"His funeral isn't even over. Can't you wait a day?" I asked.

"I have a school to run, and I need to find someone to replace him until I can hire another teacher. It will take months." Jackson sat back. "And I need a soccer coach."

He started reviewing schedules to see which classes to switch around so that another teacher could take on the job. He chose our neighbor Bakala, the art teacher, as the new *prefet de discipline* and redistributed some of his classes. A younger teacher became the soccer coach. I would teach seventh and eighth grade art, each for an hour a week. Bakala handed me the curriculum.

"It's easy," he said. "It's just an introduction to art."

He was right, but it still meant two additional hours in the classroom every week, plus exams. I gave as little homework as I could justify in those classes.

As soon as Christine came back to Sundi, empty-eyed and subdued, I went to see her. She had shaved her head, a traditional sign of mourning for both men and women. Her older son, his head also shaved, looked tired and sad. Only the baby was too young to understand what had happened. I couldn't offer money—Christine would have refused it. Visits of this type, I knew, didn't require constant conversation. Women had no time to sit around and chat. Sometimes I helped Christine by shelling peanuts or helping with some other small task, or I went with her to work in the garden. Halfway through the school year, Christine's hair had grown out, and it didn't take long for a parade of suitors to start proposing marriage.

"*Nkwezi*, I am not ready to think about marrying again," she said. "These men act like they're doing me a favor. I don't need their favors."

So she shaved her head again for the rest of the school year whenever her hair grew out, a firm signal to her suitors that they were wasting their time. Christine never remarried.

Chapter 15
Buzzing the Bangu

Two more American Peace Corps teachers arrived for the new school year, both straight out of college, Jerri to teach English and Mike to teach math. The Peace Corps volunteers took over the house that a missionary had just left, giving the three of them their own kitchen. Most afternoons I played pinochle with them, when I wasn't working in my garden. My parents sent me seeds and gardening books, since I only wanted to grow vegetables I couldn't buy in the market: cucumbers, green beans, squash, lettuce. The new volunteers also brought seeds. At first, I wondered how they would adjust, but when Mike asked me if there was any rabbit to eat around Sundi, I knew he would fit right in.

The new arrivals had already lived through one adventure. They were among the 112 Peace Corps volunteers that Idi Amin detained in Uganda for two days, after their plane made an unexpected refueling stop. Amin suspected them of being spies or mercenaries and released them only after Mobutu assured him they were only teachers.

Jackson won the battle to get his younger brother enrolled at Sundi, and Ronsard entered the junior class. He stayed in the dormitory but became a frequent visitor. Kiame was thrilled, especially after Jackson increased his school-building trips to the villages.

"He's hardly ever here," I complained to Ronsard.

"What do you want?" he said. "Are you supposed to be together every day?"

"Yes, generally that's what people get married for, isn't it? I mean, otherwise, why get married?"

Ronsard laughed as if I'd said something hilarious.

"What's so funny? Why else do people get married?" I asked.

He shook his head.

"I don't need to be married for financial security—that would have been easier to find back home with somebody else. Even by myself."

Ronsard looked at me as if wondering why, in fact, we did get married.

When the nausea started in November, I groaned, even though the timing was good. I would have the baby in July. But I hadn't yet gained back all the weight I lost after my malaria attack. I wished I could just get sleepy like most other pregnant women, instead of throwing up all the time. Suddenly a whole list of foods went off-limits: coffee, anything made with palm oil, eggs, red pepper. And the local women, who had folk cures for almost any illness, had nothing for morning sickness.

"Tea. Drink tea," Josette said.

The Kongo don't talk openly about pregnancy, and they don't court bad luck by buying baby equipment before the child is born. Maternal and neonatal mortality rates were high, especially for women who lived far from medical care. Most village women traveled to the dispensary, or to the hospital at Mangembo, sometimes walking thirty or forty miles in order to give birth in a safe place. Of course, they didn't always make it in time, and Eva, the Swedish midwife, often went to pick up a woman who had given birth on the road.

Eva and the other nurses advised me to have my baby in Kimpese. I would need an injection of Rhogam, which prevents the formation of antibodies in women with Rh negative blood who are carrying Rh positive babies. In Zaire, very few people have Rh negative blood. so only the Swedish nurses knew about Rhogam. The medication needed refrigeration and had to be given within a few hours after delivery. All that meant I would be safer in Kimpese.

Staying at Sundi until my due date carried some risks. If an emergency arose requiring surgery before that, I could either go to the doctor at Mangembo, assuming he was there, or call the Missionary Aviation Fellowship plane to come and pick me up. Unfortunately, the small plane couldn't fly in bad weather and wasn't always available. During Christmas and spring vacations, I took the plane to Kimpese for prenatal checks with the Canadian obstetrician—a trip by road would have been too risky. By January the nausea had subsided, and I found teaching much easier the second year. My students were less exasperating than the year before, although sometimes they annoyed me. Sensitive to any weakness, they saw my pregnancy as an excuse to slack off whenever they thought I was tired or distracted. I used material from the first year for my English classes, and now I knew the students and the system. I still typed papers Jackson wrote for academic journals, but at least I didn't have his thesis to type anymore. Then a letter camc from Philadelphia. The PhD committee rejected the final version he sent them because it "needed more work," and they wanted him in Philadelphia for the revision, just as I had told Jackson they would. The committee included an initial critique asking for better documentation of sources, even if they were from oral tradition: a description of the interviewee, informant's age, village, etc. For the sources from the American Baptist Mission archives, the advisers wanted more details that he could get only from the archives. After a few days in a funk, Jackson began the revisions. Fortunately for me, the advisors insisted on a professional typing job done on an electric typewriter on a type of paper not available in Zaire. They would recommend a typist.

Jackson also had to look for the university teaching job that he wanted once he finished his PhD. That meant finding, reviving or creating a personal relationship with someone in authority. Even the most qualified candidate couldn't get a job in Zaire without a strong personal connection. After many letters and visits to Kinshasa, an old school friend hired Jackson as Professor of History at the Institut Pédagogique National (National Teaching Institute) in Kinshasa, beginning in October of 1974. We didn't know where we would get the money for the trip to Philadelphia until deliverance came from an unexpected source. The Leka Minu family went back to Sweden and another family arrived. They bought a Land Rover and had it shipped to Matadi but had not been able to get it out of Customs.

"I'm fed up. If you can get it out of Customs," the missionary told Jackson, "you can have it."

Jackson tapped into all his professional, family and social networks, and found a man from Manianga highly placed in the Customs Department. Through him, and some carefully considered gifts, Jackson succeeded in getting the vehicle. We would use it while we were at Sundi and sell it at the end of the year to pay for our trip.

In the last few months of the school year, Jackson started to lose weight. He decided he wasn't getting enough exercise and started jogging around the mission once a day. He quickly found himself out of breath.

"Something is wrong," he said, panting after a short run.

The nurse practitioner at the dispensary looked him over and found nothing. He went to the hospital in Kimpese where the radiologist found a shadow on his lungs but didn't know what it meant. He didn't have access to the tests needed to make a diagnosis. Jackson was vaccinated against TB, so that diagnosis was unlikely. While he struggled to find out what was wrong, we had to prepare for both the trip to Philadelphia and the birth of the baby. José Dianzungu borrowed a house for us on the hospital grounds from a missionary who would be away in July. I planned to leave for Kimpese the third week in June. Jackson would join us a few weeks later. We would store our things in Sundi. Everything was planned.

Two weeks before I expected to leave, Eva showed up at the door on her bicycle, out of breath.

"The plane is here, and it's going back to Kimpese this afternoon," she said. "You need to take it now, because it's going in for maintenance, and we don't know when it will come again."

I had three hours to pack everything I needed, find Kiame, and get the babysitter who would be coming with us to pack her things. The plane had a luggage compartment the size of a picnic basket, so I packed a suitcase for Jackson to bring later. Eva stopped by at lunchtime to tell me the plane would leave at two o'clock. The pilot always tried to leave by mid-afternoon, because a strong updraft from the Zaire River started around four o'clock every afternoon. I frantically packed, trying to keep

Kiame from wandering off. The babysitter returned, wide-eyed and clearly fearful, with her small fake-leather overnight bag, one handle missing. After quick goodbyes, we piled into the Land Rover.

At the airstrip, the pilot packed the luggage into the tiny compartment. I no longer have the picture someone took that day. I weighed 120 pounds and looked like a scarecrow with a basketball under my shirt. With Kiame, I'd weighed 160. We climbed in, the Dutch doctor next to the pilot, the babysitter and I in the second row with Kiame, and a pharmacist from Luozi, a big man, in the back seat. I knew we approached the maximum weight the pilot would allow, and I expected him to offload some of the luggage. But after his usual calculations, he pronounced us airworthy. The plane taxied along the bumpy ground to the end of the airstrip where the ground fell away to a gulley. As usual, Kiame fell asleep before take-off. The plane dipped slightly as it reached empty air. The pharmacist gasped and grabbed the back of my seat.

"Sorry, sorry," he said, forcing himself to sit back. "I am terrified."

Even on a relatively smooth flight, the small plane dipped every few minutes, and the pharmacist grabbed my seat with each dip, apologizing. Looking down always made me nauseous, but the doctor was pointing below us, so I flicked my eyes to the small window. We were crossing the Zaire River, buffeted by small gusts of wind that stopped when we reached the other side. Ahead of us lay the Bangu, a large butte that rose two hundred feet from the flat savannah floor. I couldn't hear the conversation between the pilot and the doctor. Then the pilot turned his head and shouted, "Hang on. We're going to buzz the Bangu."

The pilot accelerated as we approached a village on the top of the Bangu, and the plane dropped to just above the thatched roofs of the houses. I clearly saw a man standing between two rows of houses looking up at the plane, shading his eyes with his hand, a puzzled expression on his face. Then he smiled and waved as the plane passed over his head.

I imagined that I would come back to visit Sundi Lutete someday. Once we moved away, though, there were always more important trips to make. Most of the people we knew at Sundi went elsewhere. One teacher went back to his native Angola. Christine became the director of the primary school in a village near Luozi, where we saw her now and then. Other teachers moved to Kinshasa. After a while, I decided I wanted to remember Sundi Lutete the way it was when I left it. I never went back.

Chapter 16
Floating

I settled into the borrowed house for my unexpected vacation, enjoying the luxury of hot running water and twenty-four-hour electricity. Kiame instantly joined the local preschool gang, children of the hospital staff. On our first day, I found them snacking from a row of mulberry bushes in our new yard. The hospital had connections at the nearby German cement factory, which employed a butcher and a baker, so I could order meat and bread there. No more salt cod!

For the first time since my teenage years, I did nothing for two weeks. Jackson arrived from Sundi early in July, and his younger sister Céline came to stay when her high school term ended. The Canadian obstetrician (and father of one of Kiame's new friends) decided to induce labor on my due date, because it's better to get a baby with Rh problems treated as early as possible. After a minor procedure, I went home to wait. My back hurt all night, a sign of early labor, and in the morning I took a small bag to the private hospital where Kiame and I stayed when we had malaria. Nurse Dorothy proved as adept at OB nursing as she was with malaria patients. Mild contractions started, but I kept falling asleep and didn't time them properly. Dorothy took over the timing, and after a couple of hours, bundled me into her little Renault for the short drive to the hospital. An aide with a gurney met us outside the maternity ward, but as she pushed it toward the car, a wheel fell off, and she couldn't get it back on.

"We may as well walk in," Dorothy said, eyeing the aide struggling helplessly with the gurney. By then the contractions were a minute apart, and I winced as Dorothy guided me to the large delivery room, bare except for basic medical equipment. It felt odd to be climbing onto the operating table on my own. The obstetrician puttered at the instrument table with an assistant, but I didn't see an anesthetist. During Kiame's birth I appreciated the nitrous oxide I inhaled during the last few minutes of labor. Here, only complex cases merited that scarce resource. Then the compulsion to push took hold, chasing away all thought, and twenty minutes later, the baby's cries filled the room. We were back at the private hospital less than an hour after we left.

Jackson brought Kiame to the hospital that afternoon. He bounded in and immediately fixated on a Kleenex box decorated with prints of fanciful cars.

"Is there a toy in here?" he asked, shaking it.

"No, Kiame, only Kleenex."

"What's this?" he asked, attracted to the crank at the end of the bed.

"It makes different parts of the bed go up and down. OK, that's enough, Kiame. Come and see your new brother."

He glanced across the room. "I saw him. Does this other bed have a crank too? Why is there nobody in this other bed? Is there any candy here? Mommy, when are you coming home?"

Suddenly I felt very tired. "Jackson, I'm glad you brought him, but can you take him away now? And please think about a name."

We had hoped for a girl, but hadn't discussed names—something else the Kongo people don't do before a birth, partly because parents choose names based on events surrounding the birth. We had several students named *Biansatu* (Hungry Times) because they were born during a drought. I could have gone straight back to the house, but the baby developed jaundice, so the hospital brought in a homemade contraption with UV lights. The obstetrician was right to induce labor—the baby showed severe jaundice. We had to stay in the private hospital for another three days until his bilirubin levels improved.

The first morning back at the house, Kiame watched me change the baby's diaper.

"Why he don't say sum'sing?" he asked.

"He's too little to talk."

"He wants to walk. Put him down so he can walk."

I held the baby so that his toes touched the floor. "See? He's too little to walk too. Most babies walk when they're about a year old."

Kiame gazed at the baby for another minute, then shrugged and ran outside. After that he paid little attention to his brother until he started to crawl.

Céline became such good friends with Adolo, the babysitter, that the two of them got less work done than Adolo usually did alone, but with electricity we had much less work to do than we did in Sundi. The two girls prepared meals, did the housework, and rocked the baby when he cried. I had only to nurse him and wash out diapers by hand. Kimpese's amenities did not include a washing machine.

The hospital sent a messenger to get a name for the birth certificate.

“I want to call him Wakengo,” Jackson said. “It means ‘protected’ in Kikongo.” That sounded fine to me.

When Wakengo fussed in the late afternoon, Adolo and Céline put him in a portable crib beneath the tall trees by the house and sang as they accompanied themselves on maracas. The louder he cried, the louder they sang and the harder they shook the maracas. Apparently, Kongo lullabies were aimed at drowning out the noise rather than getting the baby to sleep. I learned a lot about childcare from these girls. They were only sixteen but had taken care of babies since they were six. I learned that the Kongo never allowed a baby to cry; someone always picked him up. Tradition required everyone in the household, including men and women of all ages, to take turns rocking, singing, cajoling and bouncing, so someone was always available to hold a baby. The unwritten protocol for dealing with a fussy baby starts with trying to feed him. If he won’t eat, burp him by laying him on your knees and patting his back. Still crying? Sing and rock him. If that fails, bathe him in cold water. Warm baths cause teeth to come in early, they believe, and when you’re breast-feeding, you don’t want to see teeth. If the bath doesn’t work, the protocol restarts. When one caregiver gets tired, she hands the baby to another. Eventually an infant will either eat or sleep, always in someone’s arms. When the baby is four months old, a woman can tie him on her back and bounce him there while she does other work. In the 1970s, American childcare experts were telling parents to lay babies to sleep on their stomachs to reduce the risk of crib death. I tried to get Adolo and Céline to do that, but they just smiled and went on laying Wakengo on his back. In 1992, the experts reversed themselves. The Kongo were right all along.

Mothers nursed their babies until they were pregnant again, or until the baby lost interest. Jackson claimed that his mother nursed his brother Benoit until he was nearly five, when other children (including Jackson) started to make fun of him. Once a child is walking and talking, at two and a half, the Kongo say "*Wabeki ngangu*"—he has developed reason. Only then do they expect a child to follow orders and understand reprimands. Until then, they simply remove a child from a situation or distract him. They don't bother with toilet training until the child shows an interest, usually around three. Latrines consist of long poles laid over a deep pit, difficult for smaller children to navigate. Children train themselves, motivated by the mockery of other children if they're too slow. No one punishes them for accidents.

Jackson went to Kinshasa to arrange our trip to the US and returned with tickets and a visa. Three weeks later, I took Wakengo's birth certificate to the American Embassy.

"You'll need a Certificate of Birth Abroad," the Vice Consul said. "This one doesn't meet American standards. But you don't need travel documents for a baby under six months. You can get a passport for him later in the US. I'll request the certificate. It won't be ready before you leave, but it will be on file when you request a passport."

After living in the bush for two years, I had forgotten about the pitfalls of international travel. Only rich people used credit cards in 1974, and we had only about thirty dollars in cash—Zairian currency did not trade on the international market, so we could not exchange zaires for dollars in a bank. Ignorant of Kinshasa's secrets, we didn't know about the informal currency market, illegal but tolerated, that operated openly two blocks from the Embassy. Anyway, I didn't think we would need foreign currency. We planned only to change planes in

Brussels. I had a bank account in the US that we could draw on once we got there.

The trouble started when we landed in Brussels. The plane landed so far from the terminal that we had to take a bus, carrying Wakengo and all his newborn paraphernalia. The transit bus had no seats, and no one offered to help us. The other passengers, mostly businessmen in suits, cast annoyed glances our way. In a thin cotton dress and flip-flops, I shivered in the cold air of early fall. I didn't even think to bring a sweater in my hand baggage.

At the check-in counter, I laid out the passports.

"You don't have a passport for the baby?"

"No. The Vice Consul in Kinshasa said we didn't need one."

The agent took the birth certificate, consulted with a colleague, and came back.

"We need something more official than this," she said. "It doesn't even have your full name on it. You'll have to go to the Embassy here and ask for an official document."

"But we don't have any money. How can I even get to the Embassy?"

"The airline has a driver who will go into Brussels in about an hour," she said. "Talk to that man over there."

I told Jackson the bad news and gave him half the twenty dollars I had. I hitched a ride with the airline van, and from the minute I left the airport I worried about how Jackson would fare with Kiame and the baby, stuck in the barren transit lounge, the only place to wait, because Jackson didn't have a visa for Belgium. He had plenty of formula for Wakengo, but only snacks for Kiame. The driver dropped me at the Embassy and promised to pick me up in two hours. We were lucky we arrived during the day. What would we have done if we'd arrived when the

Embassy was closed? I explained my problem to the receptionist and waited only a few minutes before she called me to the Vice Consul's office.

"Well, the Embassy in Kinshasa was right. Officially, you don't need a passport for the baby, but airlines get nervous because they pay return airfare when someone gets turned away at Immigration," said the Vice Consul, a woman with sculpted dark-blonde waves. She wore a tweed suit and heels, and I felt like a refugee in my flip-flops and flyaway hair. I'd worn the same clothes for twelve hours. "I'll write a letter to satisfy the airline. It will just take a minute."

Letter in hand, I waited nervously for the airline van. If it didn't come, what would I do? Hitchhike back to the airport? An hour later, it finally arrived. Back at the airport, I ran to the transit lounge where Jackson waited with the boys. Wakengo slept, and Kiame ran and jumped around the room in perpetual motion.

"Wakengo didn't cry much," Jackson said. "But it was hard to keep Kiame occupied."

"You look tired," I said.

He laughed. "So do you."

"We're a mess."

Somehow, the airline found three empty seats at the height of the tourist season. We had two hours to wait. I grabbed the boarding passes and headed for the transit lounge. We bought ice cream cones to celebrate. We didn't have enough money for a meal. We separated at the airport in New York, Jackson heading to Philadelphia and the boys and I flying to Chicago, where my parents picked us up. We went straight to bed in the middle of the day and slept until the next morning.

That afternoon I got a call—not from Jackson, but from one of his advisors.

"Jackson will call you later, but he wanted you to know what's going on," she said. "He's in the hospital. We took one look at him and sent him to a doctor, who then sent him for an X-ray. When the technician saw it, he took Jackson to a waiting room and called the doctor. He said he'd only seen X-rays like that in patients with advanced lung cancer, but if Jackson had that he wouldn't be walking around."

After more tests, the diagnosis arrived—sarcoidosis.

"We don't know yet what that means. He's still with the doctor," the advisor said. "They'll probably keep him overnight."

I sat on the floor of the hallway, under the wall-mounted phone where I'd spent hours as a teenager. I couldn't move; I felt numb, paralyzed. I had never heard of sarcoidosis. Like a sleepwalker, I went through the motions of nursing Wakengo and getting a snack for Kiame, unable to focus. Jackson called that night.

"I am taking medication."

"What kind?" I asked.

"I don't know. Red pills. I will be out tomorrow. The doctor said it is more common in the Southwest, this disease, especially where people breathe in dust. He thinks I may have picked it up from the archives when I was doing research. He has seen archeologists who have it."

"Do you feel any better?" I asked.

"I am relieved to know what disease I have."

"Should we come to Philadelphia?" I asked.

"Not yet. Let me talk to my advisors," he said. "I need to look for a place for us to stay."

"Will you…? Will it…?" I almost asked if he would recover before realizing I wasn't ready for the answer, so instead I asked, "How long will it take to cure the sarcoidosis?"

Silence.

"Jackson?"

"It will get better after some months."

"If the medication works."

"Maybe even without medication," he said.

"But they can't cure it," I said.

"I have faith. My God will protect me."

He said the same thing once when I asked him whether he believed in *kindoki.* Not that it didn't exist, or wasn't powerful, but that he had protection from it—not at all the same thing. I found a Merck Manual and looked up sarcoidosis. It is an inflammatory disease caused by an environmental antigen, treated with cortisone. Outcome—variable. Without treatment, often fatal. My brain refused to deal with the dangers ahead and went completely numb. I could only wait.

Mom and Dad loved playing with Kiame and Wakengo. Kiame was Mom's type of kid, athletic and willing to try anything. He loved riding Hot Wheels up and down the neighboring family's driveway with their son, a boy slightly older than Kiame. Mom and Dad both enjoyed Wakengo, an easy, affectionate baby. I told them about Jackson's illness, but we didn't talk about what the implications might be for the future.

In separate cities, Jackson and I watched the preparations for the Ali–Foreman fight in Kinshasa on TV, the famous "Rumble in the Jungle." There is no jungle in Kinshasa, only savannah, but that didn't have the same ring. Crowds followed Ali, chanting, "Ali, *boma ye*!" (Ali, kill him).

"The Boulevard du 30 Juin looks modern and beautiful. The city seems so green and lush on TV," I told Jackson on the phone.

"Because you can't smell it," he said, "or feel the heat and dust."

I saw more of the boxing spectacle on TV in Chicago than I would have in Kinshasa. When Ali won, Kinshasa exploded in celebration, despite a downpour that began just after referees stopped the fight. Men danced in the streets in the pouring rain.

* * *

Two months later, I flew to Philadelphia with Kiame and Wakengo. Jackson arranged a room for us in the married student apartments at Eastern Baptist Seminary, a block away from our old apartment. Kiame quickly made friends with children in the building, as he always did, and I signed him up for nursery school at a nearby church. Four-month-old Wakengo caught a cold that quickly worsened. The taxi I called broke down in the middle of a deluge on the way to the doctor. Apologizing, the driver called another cab for us. I held Wakengo under my rain jacket, running to the second cab, and remember thinking… *a husband with a potentially fatal disease, no money, no job, and a sick baby. Can it get any worse?*

It could.

"He has pneumonia," the doctor said. "If you had health insurance, I'd put him in the hospital. Just make sure you give him the antibiotic every four hours, even if you have to wake him up."

When I could find time in between childcare and cooking in the communal kitchen, I edited Jackson's thesis revisions and gave them to a typist. We'd been in the States for three months, longer than we planned, so Jackson had to negotiate with his new employer to hold his job—not easy with Zaire's erratic mail and phone service. Jackson and Wakengo slowly recovered. The committee finally accepted Jackson's thesis. So four months later than planned, we booked our tickets back to Kinshasa, Jackson's PhD at last in hand.

Chapter 17
Newcomers to the City

Back in Kinshasa, we sent word to the mechanic who was keeping our car, and he came to tell us he'd crashed it. He would repair it himself, but we didn't have a car for two weeks, a major handicap in a sprawling city of two million with poor public transportation. I couldn't hire a babysitter until we found a place to live, so I was stuck at the Mission Guest House with the boys.

Jackson started his job at the teachers' college, and when we had the car back, we moved to a house in Kintambo, a working-class neighborhood close to the city center. We soon discovered that the house did not have a modern electrical system, so we had to use a two-burner hotplate instead of a stove. That meant we could not install a hot water heater or an air conditioner, either. It was as if our house at the mission had been dropped into the middle of a city.

We enrolled Kiame in a kindergarten in Limete, a neighborhood on the other side of Kinshasa, so someone had to wait with him for the school bus in the morning, along with other parents, and wait again in the afternoon to walk him home. Jackson's brother Ronsard moved in with us, and that became his job. One day the children took the wrong bus by mistake. According to Kiame, the bus driver offered to take them where they needed to go but needed directions. Kiame, of course, directed the driver to the school.

"Some of the other kids were crying," he reported, clearly proud of himself. Kiame was learning Article 15—*Débrouillez-vous*—even though he was a *mapeka,* a newcomer to Kinshasa. People said it the same way Americans might call someone a hick or a hillbilly, gently mocking rather than malicious.

As soon as we found a babysitter, I looked for a job, and thought I found a good one as a receptionist with Morrison–Knudsen, an American engineering company that was building a high-speed power line between Matadi and the faraway mining province of Katanga. The manager who interviewed me told me I could get paid in foreign currency and could use the company's commissary, reserved normally for engineers hired in the US. This was a big perk because commissary prices for imported processed food were half of what the local shops charged. The job sounded great.

On my first day, the manager said, "I'm really sorry, but my boss says you can't use the commissary. Even though you're American, you're a 'local hire.' And that means you won't be paid in hard currency either." I nearly quit on the spot but decided to first see what the job was like. On my third day, while I was still in training on the switchboard, a couple of goons in black *abacosts* showed up, asking to see the director. They had little enameled pins of the Zairian flag on their collars, a signal that they were in Mobutu's political party. Like everyone else, I knew I had to be careful with people like that.

"We need to see the director," the lead goon said.

"Oui, patron," said the young man who was training me. He couldn't get the director on the phone, so he trotted off down the hall to fetch the highest-ranking manager he could find. One of the goons rattled on about the importance of his mission. I pretended to listen. Everyone in the lobby knew what these two were looking for—protection money. We were just dust on their path, but I found the encounter unsettling.

The receptionist returned with a middle-aged American in shirt sleeves. Nobody in that office wore a suit. I could tell that this man had experience with the goon squad. He welcomed them warmly, with no trace of anxiety, and led them down the hall to his office. More executives scurried down the hall. The flurry of activity lasted all morning, and a veil of tension fell over the building. Even though everyone knew what would happen, nobody wanted to be in the middle of it. Morrison-Knudsen had a direct short-wave radio connection to the Embassy. I knew this because on the day I came to ask for Wakengo's passport, I'd been in the Vice-Consul's office when they were finishing up their daily radio call.

I knew what would happen. The company Director would call the Embassy, and the Vice-Consul would call whichever Ministry handled the project and get the minister to call off the goons. Or, if they turned out to be from another Ministry, the Vice-Consul would put the director in contact with that minister. Only as a last resort would the company cough up the bribe the goons were looking for, and even then the company would bargain over the amount. When ministers received "commissions" themselves (which happened frequently) the arrangements took place at a much higher level, behind closed doors in the minister's office. I asked my trainer how often this kind of thing happened. He shrugged.

"A few times a year," he said.

If I kept this job, I would be fielding a visit from the Goon Squad every three or four months. And I would be paid in local currency. No perks. That wasn't enough to compensate for dealing with the goon squad.

"I'm sorry," I said to the young man. "I'm not staying in this job. This company already broke its promises to me, and this is too much."

"I don't blame you," he said. I marched into the manager's office and quit.

Someone told me that there was an opening at the Peace Corps office, strangely located near the Kinshasa Golf Club, next door to a formerly Europeans-only cemetery—segregation even after death. Zaire's colonial past jumped up and slapped me in the face everywhere in Kinshasa. Maybe the location dissuaded potential employees, or else bilingual staff was hard to find, because I was hired after a short interview with the director and another with a security officer from the Embassy for a security clearance. I filled out a long form with all the addresses I'd ever lived and everywhere I'd worked, plus personal references.

"They probably won't contact the references," he said with a shrug. "It's not like you're handling classified cables."

They did contact the references, I found out later. I worked with Maurice, the director's personal secretary, a West African in his late forties who typed like the wind and spoke perfect French and English. I wondered why on earth they needed me when they had superstar Maurice on the job. I would soon find out. On the Monday after our next payday, Maurice didn't show up, and nobody seemed surprised. Something was off, I thought. I scrambled to do his work and mine, including the daily short-wave radio call with the Regional Representatives, the only reliable way to communicate with volunteers. After three days, someone finally told me that Maurice, despite his talents, disappeared on week-long alcoholic binges every few months. During that particular bender, he called the director to get him out of a Brazzaville jail—which the director did, to my surprise. The following Monday, Maurice greeted me sheepishly from his desk, lowering his bloodshot eyes.

The central Peace Corps office in DC hired a coordinator for each type of volunteer, so we had three American officers, one each for Education, Health, and Rural Development. For every radio call and piece of mail, we created an "Action Form" and assigned it to an officer. The director had a copy and periodically demanded updates. Maurice and I both hated doing this, since the officers resented this micro-management, but I soon saw the reason for it. The education officer did about half the work he should have. Most mornings he showed up hours late, looking like he'd slept in his car, clothes rumpled and hair standing on end. No one knew where he was or what he was doing most of the time. That meant everyone else's workload increased, a source of tension among the staff consisting of several Zairians, a Belgian, and another American married to an Angolan. The director, a former military intelligence officer, had a low tolerance for poor performance, but since the mothership in DC did all the hiring and firing, he could do little more than complain and shout at the offender, which he did almost daily. The man's behavior reinforced the Zairian view of expatriates in Kinshasa. To the Zairians, expatriates were lucky slackers who did little to justify their outsized salaries and luxurious free housing. Years later, I saw the man's name listed as director of a well-known charitable organization. I'd never give money to that one! I've always been amazed at the way incompetent White men—and only White men—keep finding one good job after another, no matter how poorly they perform.

* * *

Jackson took a part-time job teaching History of Religions at the Protestant seminary, so we moved to a more comfortable house on the seminary campus. Unlike the house in Kintambo, our new house had no surrounding brick wall. A barbed-wire fence separated the campus from the military camp near the back of the house. A dirt road led from the front of the house to the entrance to the campus several hundred yards away, across from an open-air market. Kiame quickly made friends. Wakengo, now a toddler, trailed after him, calling "Ame, Ame." That summer, we began to look for a school for Kiame, unaware that parents in Kinshasa locked in their child's place in first grade a year ahead of time. I applied to the best private school in Kinshasa, run by the Belgian wife of a government minister, but it was too late and I had no political clout. Many highly placed government officials sent their children to that school, appropriately named *Les Loupiots*, the Little Wolves. I contacted the American School of Kinshasa, where American diplomats' and missionaries' children went. The American Baptist missionary who handled admissions told me that Kiame wasn't eligible because he had a Zairian father. In fact, children of other Zairians attended the school, then and later. Despite Jackson's good relations with the American Baptist headquarters, Jackson had never endeared himself to American missionaries because he challenged their assumptions and refused to kowtow to them. From then on, I vowed to stay away from American missionaries and their racism.

Through a friend, we found a new school for Zairian children started by a former Swiss missionary, Heidi Kabangu, also married to a Zairian. Immensely relieved, we enrolled Kiame, despite the long commute. He didn't adjust well to the discipline of a classroom. We were lucky that the first-grade class had only ten children. When I arrived early to pick him up one day, I heard the teacher say, "Now, class, we're going to read——Kiame, sit down. We're going to start with—Kiame, turn around and be quiet, please..." I cringed. What would we do if they kicked him out? I needn't have worried. Heidi knew how to control him, and he respected her.

While we were still frantically searching for a school, we started to hear rumors of a strange new disease identified in the Equateur region, near the town of Yambuku. Shortly thereafter, Kinshasa's elite hospital (formerly Whites-only—that colonial shadow again) admitted two Belgian nuns and a Belgian priest from Yambuku to a makeshift isolation ward, tended by one Zairian nurse. Within a week, all of them had died, including the nurse.

The Government blocked reports in the press about the new disease, called Ebola after a river area where it first appeared. We had only secondhand accounts and rumors via the *radio trottoir* (sidewalk radio). We found out about the nurse's death from a family who lived in her neighborhood. As always, we never knew how much of what we heard was true. This story that sounded like science fiction turned out to be spot on and soon appeared in the foreign press. Experts quickly realized Ebola was similar to the Marburg virus, known since 1967, when seven German scientists died after handling infected green monkeys from Uganda. Marburg transmission required direct contact with bodily fluids of an infected person or animal, so it was likely that Ebola transmission followed the same route. Oddly, I found this somewhat reassuring, since very few people in Kinshasa would have that kind of contact with an infected person or animal.

We had already lived through epidemics of cholera in Kimpese and Matadi, but cholera can be prevented by basic hygiene. The cholera vaccine wasn't very effective, but hardly anyone died of it, even in Zaire—rehydration and antibiotics treated it easily. We were all vaccinated against typhoid. From the available information, I still worried less about Ebola than I did about malaria. As news of Ebola circulated, though, people began to panic. A regularly scheduled boat towing a crowded barge from Equateur was not allowed to dock because soldiers guarding the dock heard rumors (soon debunked) that the disease could be transmitted by eating smoked fish from the region upriver where Ebola originated. Fearful of being kept on the boat, terrified passengers slipped off the barge, braved the dangerous current and swam through the crocodile- and snake-infested water to reach shore. We never found out how many didn't make it. The authorities finally allowed it to dock. Smoked fish sales plummeted until the rumor was declared unfounded a week later.

At the Peace Corps office, I found the Director on the radio early one morning with the regional representative in Equateur, ordering the evacuation of all the volunteers in that region and a neighboring one. The Zairian Government had already quarantined the area, but the next day, the Embassy quietly dispatched a small plane to fetch the volunteers from a remote airstrip, where the regional rep gathered them. Other foreign governments did the same. I was appalled. If anyone on board had been infected, everyone on the plane could have contracted Ebola. At the time, however, Ebola had not yet infected anyone beyond the Catholic mission and a group of isolated villages near the Sudanese border. None of those evacuated came down with Ebola. Years later, I learned that the evacuees were quarantined for two weeks in an Embassy house in Kinshasa. That must have been quite a party.

Soon after this evacuation, two young villagers evaded the quarantine and ended up in the isolation ward in Kinshasa. Fear rose again in the city. By this time, foreign experts began to arrive, and we heard that the mortality rate diminished by 50 percent with each person-to-person transmission. That would explain the lack of cases in Kinshasa, but the city remained on edge for weeks. Ebola had an 88 percent fatality rate; 318 people died in that first outbreak. Many outbreaks have occurred since, and the virus gradually became more transmissible, killing thousands in Sierra Leone and neighboring countries. Zaire already had enough endemic disease to deal with. Ebola was something altogether different. We had no idea then that AIDS was already spreading and would prove to be even worse.

After a year in the Peace Corps office, I became frustrated by the chaos of Maurice's binges and went to work as a bilingual executive secretary for INZAL, the Zairian affiliate of British Leyland. The company had a small office with European department heads, mostly British except for the administration, finance, and sales managers, who were Belgian. I worked for the director, although the headquarters in England made all the important decisions. The director just carried out their instructions—not that it was always easy. The office had puzzling dynamics. The Belgians didn't get along with each other, and the Brits didn't get along with the Belgians. The president of the company was a Zairian, a political appointee from Mobutu's region. He should have been called the government liaison since that was really his only responsibility. Europeans and Zairians all treated the president with wary respect. He returned the favor.

Among the expatriates, I was most friendly with two of the younger British staff: the assistant finance director and the assistant administration manager, the only expatriates with a sense of humor. I got along well with the Zairian staff, especially the women—there weren't many of us. Work relationships with the Zairian men always remained formal and scrupulously correct. I was always "Madame" to them, just as I had been for the students in Sundi.

INZAL ran a plant that assembled Land Rovers, a parts store, and a large garage that repaired Leyland vehicles. A Brit ran the garage, aided by an experienced Portuguese mechanic, and another Brit ran the parts operation, also assisted by a Portuguese mechanic. The pay was good, paid partly in foreign currency. I had a chance to buy a Morris Marina with a discount. I helped many friends and acquaintances get jobs at the company, an important social obligation in a city with a reported 75 percent unemployment rate.

Not long after I started working at INZAL, my babysitter arrived one day in a taxi with Kiame. He had a raging fever, and she didn't know what else to do. She had first gone to the Peace Corps office—she didn't realize that I had changed jobs. I dropped everything and drove him to the hospital. After a quick lab test, they began treating him for malaria. I discovered that even at Kinshasa's best hospital, a parent or other caretaker had to remain with a sick child during the entire hospital stay. I only saw a small section of the children's ward, and that was sobering enough. Kiame shared a room with a beautiful toddler who had also suffered from a high fever. Treatment at the hospital brought the fever down, but convulsions continued, and her condition didn't change during the time we were there. I thought she had brain damage and might not recover. Her distraught young parents took turns staying with her. Kiame's high fever persisted, and it was hard to get him to drink, but they didn't give him an IV.

Parents marooned with sick children acted like old friends by the second day, and they included me as one of them. Zairian culture runs on relationships, and you can never have too many. Where systems are weak or absent, relationships fill the gap. Kiame's two-patient room had a large window separating it from a room with ten or twelve cribs, all occupied by sick babies. On our third day there, a mother showed up in the big room with her face painted in red and white stripes and dots. She wore a traditional long, patterned skirt and a kind of sports bra decorated with magical symbols. She began to sing and dance around the room, in between the two rows of cribs, accompanying herself with maracas.

"Her twins are sick," a mother explained. "The healer told her she has to sing and dance so that they will recover."

Twins occupy a special place in most Zairian ethnic groups, including the Kongo, and the mother of twins has a special role. Twins themselves are believed to have supernatural connections, and once a woman has given birth to twins, she acquires a new name: *Mama a bansimba*, mother of twins. Even in the 1970s, a second-born twin rarely survived, because of poor obstetric and neonatal care, so this woman was particularly blessed. She sang in another language, not Kikongo, but clearly she occupied the same role in her culture as *Mama a bansimba* did for the Kongo. The other parents clapped and whooped, encouraging her. She moved into the hall and continued her ritual singing and dancing, with the hospital staff standing by, smiling. No one sought to stop her. They all knew the custom. The performance went on for more than an hour.

I recalled the "twin song" from Sundi, where the "twins' cult" remained particularly strong. Singers improvised verses, and everyone joined in the chorus:

Nsimba na nzuzi	First-born twin and second-born twin
Baana ba nlongo	Sacred children
Ey, eye	Oh, yes

The following afternoon, a high-pitched wail began in the hallway. A young woman, clothes awry, hair uncombed, walked down the hall shrieking and crying. The staff looked on with sympathy.

"Her child just died," another parent told me. Eventually, relatives surrounded her and led her away. I changed the compress on Kiame's forehead, willing him to recover. After five days, Kiame improved enough to go home, although he was still weak. The high fever left its mark though. He was six years old and still remembers very little of his life before that fever.

Chapter 18
Almost Dying

After two years in Kinshasa, Jackson and I at last had secure jobs, and his sarcoidosis did not recur. Life became easier. We had a comfortable house, surrounded by congenial neighbors, with plenty of space for the boys to play. It took me forty-five minutes in the morning to take Kiame to school and get to work, but that was a minor inconvenience, considering the location's other advantages. Though still subject to bouts of bronchitis, Wakengo fell sick less often, and at last began to talk, though in Lingala, not English. He still didn't say much, and his favorite word was "tala"—look. He spent a lot of time observing his world.

Ronsard stayed with us during school vacations, and Céline moved in when she graduated from junior college. Jackson treated her as if she were a wayward fifteen-year-old. He gave a hostile reception to any man who dared to visit her, and he refused to let her go out at night. He even reproached her for overly lengthy or excessively friendly conversations with our own visitors. Flirting didn't bother Jackson unless his sister was involved. I knew that a couple of Jackson's friends had mistresses. One of them once brought his young girlfriend with him when he came to visit. I told Jackson to make sure he didn't do it again. Another was a serial philanderer.

"This is a prison," Céline complained. I had to agree with her.

Then Jackson's brother Benoit finished his degree and came back to Kinshasa. His wife wanted to stay in the US to finish her accounting degree, so he came alone and—of course—stayed with us. After a few weeks, he found a room nearby, but he still came to us for his meals, and he had a huge appetite. With three extra adults in the house, our food bill skyrocketed. Jackson hoped that once Benoit found a job, he would take on some of the clan responsibilities and expenses. Benoit never stepped up. Instead, he seemed determined to extract as much from us as he possibly could. Soon Jackson started going out every night after supper, returning at ten or eleven, leaving me to deal with the boys alone.

"I'm alone every night with the kids," I told Jackson. "Why can't you stay here after supper?"

"I need to make contacts," he said.

"What contacts? Why?"

"To meet my colleagues, to convince other people to work for development in Manianga. To get their ideas."

"And that means more to you than I do? I have no family or old friends here. You and I only see each other late at night and early in the morning. Maybe that's normal for an African marriage, but I need a little companionship and a husband who says goodnight to his kids."

"I pick the kids up from school every day, and you're the one who's at work. You just want me to sit around here and tell you how beautiful you are."

We had the same argument over and over. I couldn't understand why he wanted to spend all his evenings away from us.

I knew it wasn't another woman. For one thing, I would have heard about it—Kinshasa kept no secrets. One day when he took his sister shopping, someone at the office said, "You know, I saw your husband downtown today with a beautiful young woman."

In Kinshasa, mistresses expected financial support and children, and Jackson hated spending money except for his projects. I knew he would never commit to another set of financial obligations. And the clincher was that Jackson's concerns about his health bordered on paranoia, and STDs were rampant in Kinshasa. He would never have taken the risk, especially after his sarcoidosis scare.

I wondered if his absences stemmed from resentment that I paid for most of the household expenses. Money is a factor in every marriage, and because I was a foreigner, I made far more as a bilingual secretary than any Zairian professional. I took in easily ten times Jackson's salary. After moving to Kinshasa, we learned that we could exchange money with Jackson's businessman friends or my colleagues at work at four times the official rate. That was what kept us afloat. The company also gave us big discounts on both of our cars—and their maintenance. INZAL soon offered me a small house at minimal rent in Limete, close to Kiame's school. I wasn't sure Jackson would want such a strong link to my company, and living there would mean that he would have a longer drive to work. To my surprise, he agreed immediately, probably because he wouldn't have to pick up Kiame from school and drive him home across town every day. Jackson showed no resentment about the income disparity, but I wondered if he just hid it well. I didn't want to believe that Jackson didn't care how I felt because he no longer loved me. That was the only other possibility I could think of. His behavior with other people should have been a clue—especially his interactions with his brothers and sister. It didn't occur to me that he could be incapable of understanding what his behavior meant, and equally incapable of changing it.

On the day of our move to Limete, I was so disabled by morning sickness that the entire move happened without me. I stayed in bed until the movers needed to load the bed into the truck and went back to bed as soon as they put it together at the new house. I knew I had an unhappy, possibly failing marriage, so it's hard to understand why I decided to have a third child. For once memory fails me. I don't know why I made that decision. I still wanted a daughter, and so did Jackson, but that doesn't explain it. Maybe I figured that if I was going to be home alone every night, I might as well have company. I only know I remained committed to the cause of improving life in Manianga—the one thing Jackson and I worked on together. Certainly I valued that commitment more than personal happiness, retaining the commitment to a moral code instilled by my religious parents. I didn't make the connection at the time, but in fact I followed the Lutheran dictum that "Faith without works is dead" and that sacrifice is necessary to achieve altruistic goals. My goals were just different from those of the Lutheran Church.

Jackson and I enabled many students to get into American colleges and helped with visas and scholarships. He wrote books and pamphlets on cultural history, and we researched ways to promote animal husbandry, reforestation, anti-erosion measures, and other projects. We knew nothing then about raising money—we had yet to even write a grant request. We were slowly learning and had a small group of like-minded friends working with us: Robert Diyabanza in Luozi, Dr. Flodin Mwimba, José Dianzungu, and others.

Just when my baby was due, in June of 1978, a political crisis hit. The year before, a rebel army had invaded the southern mining province of Shaba (previously called Katanga) and now they came back, taking Europeans and Zairians as hostages. Three hundred civilians died. Tension again gripped Kinshasa. Though Shaba was thousands of miles away, the strength of the rebels and the Zairian army's inability to dislodge them revealed the weakness of Mobutu's government and his army.

On June 18th, Jackson drove me to the Ngaliema Hospital, where our daughter was born as quickly and easily as her brothers. During the first day, I found blood oozing from her mouth, and the young pediatrician diagnosed intestinal bleeding. I didn't even know that could happen. He gave her a shot of Vitamin K, and the bleeding stopped, but the medication exacerbated the jaundice, a result of the Rh problem. She had to spend a week under UV lights. The hospital had two sets of lights, and three babies who needed them, so she had to share a crib with another baby with jaundice caused by a different blood incompatibility. She caught a respiratory infection from him and had to take antibiotics.

"We will call her Mena. It means 'germinate,'" Jackson said. "Because she is the founder of a new clan."

The Kongo people trace their ancestry through the mother. A person's immediate clan includes all the children of one mother and her sisters. The extended clan includes all the descendants of a female ancestor, usually a great- or great-great-grandmother. The new baby's clan now included Wakengo and Kiame.

While I was in the hospital with my newborn baby, the political crisis worsened, and some people prepared to flee to the countryside or to another country in case the rebels attacked Kinshasa. Jackson thought the danger was exaggerated. Then

Mobutu appealed to France and Belgium. Both sent small forces that defeated the rebels within a week. Mobutu's army of thousands proved useless, but now the world knew that the Western powers would prop up the Mobutu regime at almost any cost.

Despite its intermittent crises, I enjoyed life in Kinshasa. I liked my colleagues and my job and enjoyed the city's fabulous music and dance, its compelling visual arts, the vibrant culture full of humor and exuberance. On his frequent visits, Ronsard took Kiame on excursions that made him feel grown up and exposed him to a very different side of the city.

Baby Mena was barely a month old when I took the children to visit my parents in suburban Chicago. Because of the Rh problem, I would not be able to have any more children, so while I was there I had a sterilization done. I had asked my Belgian doctor in Kinshasa, but he refused, probably for religious reasons. I took all three children for check-ups at a new wholistic clinic near my parents' house. After listening to Wakengo's heart, the doctor said, "Of course you know this child has a heart murmur."

"No, I didn't know. No one ever detected it before."

"Does he sometimes lack energy?"

"Most of the time! I've asked at least three other doctors about it, and they all said there was nothing wrong with him."

"Well, it's almost closed now. His energy level should pick up soon." The doctor was right, and soon he was playing like other children his age.

In my hometown, I learned up close what life would be like there with three mixed-race children. Women in the grocery store would ask, "Is that your child? Is he adopted?" Kiame learned to see them coming and developed a scowling glare intended to deter them. It often did. My parents' friends, though never openly critical, clearly pitied my parents for having such a crazy daughter. Racial attitudes had changed little since 1972 when I first moved to Zaire. I clearly saw what life would be like in the States. I had a college degree, but no teaching certificate. I'd worked as a bilingual secretary, a job that wouldn't provide enough income to support three children in the States. Day care was still expensive when it was available at all. I never confided in my parents, or even my sisters, about my unhappy marriage. I couldn't bear to admit to them that it was a mistake, and I could not imagine moving in with them or asking for their support. A bad marriage, I concluded, was still better than three kids with no marriage, and my marriage wasn't my whole life in Zaire either. I went back to Zaire and my job at INZAL.

A few months later I started to have some worrying symptoms. I went back to my Belgian OB/GYN, who prescribed medication. By the time I went back to the US the following summer, the medication hadn't fixed the problem, and my doctor was on leave in Belgium. In Chicago, lab results showed "endometrial hyperplasia," a pre-cancerous condition, the doctor said, and recommended a hysterectomy. I didn't know what to do. I had no health insurance, and I would be incapacitated for at least a month. Could I take the chance of going back to Zaire without having the surgery? I could get adequate care for simple problems, but uterine cancer? I didn't know anyone in Zaire who had survived that. I decided to go ahead with the operation. It was the worst decision I ever made.

* * *

A terrible pain in my abdomen jolted me out of the anesthesia. I was in a hospital room, not the recovery room, and people in white caps and masks rushed around, murmuring to each other. One of them thrust papers at me and told me to sign.

“We need your permission to do another operation,” a woman said.

“Not now!” I shouted.

“Ma’am, we need your signature to...” I signed just to make her go away. I heard scraps of the conversation around me as a I thrashed around the bed in pain: “blood bank,” “internal bleeding,” and people repeating “O Negative, O Negative.”

“I’m going to give you some anesthesia now,” said a man’s calm voice, and above me I saw the masked face of the anesthesiologist I’d seen before the operation.

“Put me out! Put me out!” I shouted.

“OK, I can do that,” he said calmly.

I woke up in the ICU, my vision foggy and grainy. A dull ache in my abdomen had replaced the excruciating pain. Jackson and my father were standing beside my bed. As I reached for my Dad’s hand, I remembered that his mother died of complications from a similar operation when she was only forty-six. He had to be thinking about that. Jackson looked grim. I was glad to see them, but too far out of it to carry on a conversation.

After a few minutes, two nurses came in; Jackson and Dad left. I had two plastic prongs in my nose for oxygen, and the nurses came in frequently to check my temperature, the IV, and some mysterious monitors. A woman nearby screamed intermittently all night, and I wondered vaguely why they didn’t do something to help her. The tiny ICU room had glass walls, and nothing in it but the bed, the IV and the monitors. It was right in front of the nurses’ station, so I could hear all the phone conversations.

“Yeah, she’s in the ICU, but we can’t keep her here,” I heard a doctor say on the phone at the nurses’ station. “These beds aren’t for psych patients. You need to find another place for her. Right. By this afternoon.”

That explained the screaming. Sure enough, a few hours later a clutch of orderlies and nurses arrived. After they took the woman in the next room out on a gurney, the screaming stopped. I slept on and off through the first day in the ICU. On the second day the nurses changed the dressing on my abdomen, and I saw a long, curved scar extending downward from my navel. My father and Jackson visited again. I managed to ask about the children, but I couldn't talk much. On the third day I moved to a normal room and found out more about what had happened.

I had a vaginal hysterectomy, which supposedly had a lower complication rate since no incisions are made externally. It demands care and skill, though, to ensure that all the blood vessels are properly tied off, and my surgeon had missed some. Blood leaked into my abdomen. In the second operation, the doctor made an incision, located the open blood vessels, and tied them off. I don't know how long it took, but I needed six units of blood, and because I have a rare blood type (O Negative) they had to scramble to find enough.

Just when the incision healed enough for me to move around, three weeks later, nausea set in, and tests showed that I had contracted what was then called hepatitis Non-A, Non-B—now known as hepatitis C. The doctor who operated on me was an assistant to the doctor I'd seen originally. Clearly, he was incompetent, and I was furious that the hospital had used dubious sources of blood that resulted in yet another serious problem. I consulted a lawyer, but he told me that I didn't have a case. The doctor had repaired his mistake, and because blood banks didn't have a way to test for hepatitis C, the State of Illinois had prohibited personal injury lawsuits on behalf of patients who contracted the disease from blood transfusions. There was no redress.

Because of the possibility that I could transmit hepatitis to others, I had to stay in my old upstairs bedroom, seeing the children only for a few minutes a day, until my blood tests came back negative. Jackson and (mostly) my mother took care of the children. When school started, Mom enrolled Kiame and Wakengo temporarily in my old elementary school.

A month later, Jackson took Kiame back to Kinshasa—school there would start in a few days. I worried about Jackson taking care of Kiame alone, but I had no choice. It took another month for me to recover. Hepatitis C, though, can linger in the body for years and flare up at any time.

"So I'm going to have this hanging over my head for the rest of my life?" I asked.

"Unfortunately, yes," my doctor said.

When my lab results returned to normal in January, I went back to Kinshasa, with one more thing to worry about.

Kiame and Wakengo in Limete, Kinshasa, 1979.

Chapter 19
The Sharpness of Money

Money is sharper than the sword.

—Ashanti proverb

After my bout with hepatitis, I could barely stay awake long enough to put the kids to bed at night. For several weeks, Jackson stayed home more often. Then we arranged for the babysitter to stay overnight on weekdays, and he resumed his nightly wanderings.

My daily activities shrank to work, childcare, food shopping, and sleep, broken only by occasional visits to friends on Sundays. Although two-year-old Mena didn't add much to my workload, she had frequent high fevers and sore throats, so my anxiety level soared. She probably had strep, but doctors in Kinshasa never did strep tests—they just prescribed antibiotics, and I couldn't get the babysitter to give her the medication on schedule. I had to either leave it to chance, or rush home at noon to give it to her myself. I couldn't always find antibiotics in local pharmacies, so I started stocking them and other prescription medicine at home. Medicine wasn't the only shortage. Record-high oil prices meant long lines at gas pumps and unpredictable shortages of all imports, including food, car parts and appliances. These shortages could last days, weeks or months. When the bakeries ran out of yeast, they used beer to leaven the bread. I like beer well enough, but not in my bread. It tasted terrible. We all kept jerry cans of fuel in the backyard, and people who depended on kerosene or gasoline kept barrels of it in their houses. Occasionally, of course, a barrel exploded. Along the main roads at night, teenagers known as "Khadaffi" sold jerry cans of hoarded fuel at inflated prices. We bought fifty-pound bags of rice and sugar and kept them in a freezer to deter insects.

The sale of copper provided 70 percent of Zaire's foreign currency at that time, and when the price fell, the country could not fund oil and food imports in addition to the kleptocracy of Mobutu and his entourage. Inflation escalated, and everyone felt the effects. In grocery stores each item bore a colored dot with a price chart posted with corresponding colors at the end of each aisle. The chart changed daily—the price of an item could double overnight. On paydays, my co-workers immediately bought merchandise—a bag of onions, a case of powdered milk—and sold a little of it each day to stretch out their salaries. The buying power of Jackson's salary plummeted, so we existed almost entirely on the foreign currency from my job, although the crisis affected that too. Sometimes we didn't receive it for months at a time. To increase his income, Jackson rented a small shop from his brother-in-law and hired his sister as manager. He had tried and failed to raise chickens in Sundi during our first year there. The whole flock developed bird flu, and the local population just shook their heads as the chickens died off. Kept in groups, chickens always got sick. That's why the villagers only kept one or two at a time. Jackson always thought he knew better.

"How hard can it be to have a business here?" he said. "Nearly everyone in Kinshasa is selling something."

True enough, but small merchants kept their overhead low by doing almost everything themselves and hiring hand carts to transport their merchandise. When Jackson hired a truck instead, the cost of transporting merchandise ate up the profit from selling it. Most merchants had stalls in front of their houses or in the local markets, where they paid a small fee. With rent and a manager's salary to pay, the profits from Jackson's store didn't cover its expenses.

Vendors used all their ingenuity to get scarce merchandise. Everyone wanted to sell beer—it had the highest profit margin. The beer company rationed the quantity it sold to each merchant on the list, and Jackson couldn't even get on the list. In the beginning, a few merchant friends helped him out, but it wasn't enough. All his ventures lost money, and he gave them up after less than a year. I never encouraged him in these projects, and he resented my lack of support.

"You're so negative," he said.

"I'm just being realistic."

Next, he bought a used truck and hired a driver. Hundreds of trucks ply the route between Matadi or Luozi and Kinshasa, taking basic imports to the villages—salt cod, flour, oil—and bringing back cassava, beans, fruit and vegetables. Thousands of people made a living this way by keeping their overhead and risks low. Most truck drivers operated alone, with only a young apprentice to help them. They did their own mechanical repairs, often with incredible creativity. Mashed plantain, one told me, works well for patching holes in radiators. Jackson had none of these skills and depended entirely on his driver. The truck broke down constantly, and since Jackson had to pay for repairs, this venture, too, lost money.

Typical merchant truck on the road between Kinshasa and Kimpese.

Inflation climbed to the point where I had to carry a large bag of cash just to buy groceries. Then one day the government suddenly called in all paper currency. From one day to the next, the cash everyone had in their pockets was invalid, and everyone had to trade it in at a bank. Each person could exchange only Z3,000—about $500. Any additional cash became worthless. Money in a bank was safe, but hardly anyone had a bank account (we didn't) because of the horrendous inflation and cumbersome bureaucracy—cashing a check could take all morning. Now people lined up to change their paper money; banks ran out of the new currency by the end of the first day. In outlying regions of the country, banks had not yet received any of the new currency, so people started using cigarettes and barter in the absence of printed money. The government claimed they changed the currency to discourage hoarding, but we all knew that Mobutu's entourage hoarded more than anybody else. The real purpose of the change remained unclear. Probably Mobutu was pushed to this drastic step by the IMF, and other creditors, to bring the official exchange rate closer to the unofficial rate. Hyperinflation, however, continued.

For the eight years I'd lived in Zaire, I hoped that the situation of the country and our family would improve. Now I could see nothing ahead but chaos. Good people—church leaders, educators, ordinary citizens—worked hard to improve the lives of the poor. In private, they spoke of the "post-Mobutu era" when things could at last get on the right track. I could not see that happening when Mobutu had absolute power, a lock on the national security apparatus, and support from the West. Most people, like me, believed he would never leave office, and anyone who could find a job elsewhere emigrated. Even our old friends José and Suzanne Dianzungu went to work in Congo–Brazzaville after José finished his PhD in the US.

A deep depression took hold of me. Was it because of the situation in Zaire, or because my marriage was failing? I couldn't separate the two in my mind, and I knew I was sinking.

"I need to see a therapist," I told Jackson. "How can I find one?"

"You can't," Jackson said. "Not here. There's no confidentiality, and anything you say would be all over Kinshasa."

Could I have found a therapist on my own? Maybe. But depression had paralyzed me. I had no one to talk to, and I couldn't see a way out. In Jackson's attitude, I saw my mother: "You just have to snap out of it," she would have said. *My God*, I thought. *I've married my mother.*

I decided that I could put up with Jackson if I didn't have to live in Zaire. I didn't want to go the US, and I knew Jackson would never agree to move there. I didn't believe that I could support three children on my own, completely unaware that it was my depression that stood in my way, not objective reality. In any case, whenever we argued, Jackson repeatedly said, "Don't imagine you'll leave with the children. I'll never let you take them."

Had I been thinking clearly, I would have realized the emptiness of that threat. I took the children to Chicago every two years on vacation—he never objected to that. I could just stay there on my next trip—and I had considered that before my last trip turned into a disaster. Jackson wanted to control me, and I couldn't think beyond my resentment. I did not see, behind his threats, his fear of losing us.

"We need to talk," I said.

"What is it?"

I gave the speech I'd practiced so that I could deliver it with no tears and as little emotion as possible: "We need to leave Zaire. We did our best, but life here just gets more and more difficult, with no relief in sight, and I'm afraid I'll have a relapse of hepatitis. Mena is sick all the time. You need to look for a job abroad."

Jackson had talked about a "sabbatical" in another country before, so this idea wasn't completely new. During the next two years, Jackson explored many different possibilities, but none of them worked out. When I had almost given up hope that he would find anything, he found a professorship at a rural university in Liberia. The pay wasn't great, but the job included housing and benefits. We pored over the offer and learned as much as we could about living in Liberia. Finally, we agreed that Jackson should take the job.

In April 1980, while Jackson was still negotiating the details, a rebel group in Liberia staged a coup d'état, shot the president and executed thirteen other top officials on a beach in Liberia's capital before crowds of cheering onlookers. Jackson broke off negotiations immediately. If it had happened a month later, we could have been in middle of the rebellion. We felt relieved to have barely escaped the coup. Jackson began looking again. For almost a year, no serious opportunities emerged. Then one day Jackson met an old friend, Pastor Jean Massamba, visiting from Geneva where he worked for the World Council of Churches.

"There's a job open as African Secretary," Jackson said. "They are looking for someone from West or Central Africa."

"Switzerland," I said dreamily. "That would be almost too good to be true."

Weeks of correspondence ensued once again. I couldn't help hoping, even though I tried not to think about it. Finally, Jackson went to Geneva for an interview… and came back with the job.

"You understand this is a three-year contract, and I'm doing this for you," Jackson said. "I don't like living abroad, and we're coming back."

"I know."

In my desperation for a new life, I would have agreed to anything, and I knew how much could change in three years. I didn't even want to think about a future in Zaire. Within three weeks, we decided what to take (not much) and sold everything else, including our cars. We told only our closest friends and family what we were doing. Jackson's recommendation for the job came from his home church in Manianga, not Zaire's national Protestant organization. Its leadership, from a different denomination in another region, would almost certainly not have given him a recommendation. We didn't know if they would try to intervene, but we didn't want to take that chance. In September 1981, we boarded a Swissair flight to Geneva.

Chapter 20
Escape to Anonymity

Lightning flashes illuminated the sharp snowy peaks below us, and wind shook the plane. The flight from Zurich—in a snowstorm—seemed much longer than an hour, especially with cranky, feverish Mena beside me. I found medicine in my bag and gave her tablets for her fever. Her throat didn't hurt, so I didn't know what was wrong this time. We breezed through passport control and customs and went directly to the taxi line. At the hotel, Kiame and Wakengo headed eagerly to the breakfast room, thrilled with its unlimited supply of orange juice and croissants.

Right away Jackson hurried off to his new office. The hotel concierge gave me a bus map with directions to the pediatric hospital on the other side of town, and we set off with two umbrellas, but no rain jackets. Nobody used them in Kinshasa. They were too hot, and no jacket could protect you from rain that poured like water being thrown from a bucket. Like everything in Geneva, the rain there seemed polite and restrained. The concierge said that passengers bought tickets at the bus stop, but there were no ticket machines at the small stop where we boarded. It looked as though everyone rode for free because bus drivers didn't check tickets. Ticket inspectors boarded buses randomly and checked tickets, although I later found that I could ride the bus for a week without seeing an inspector. At a major hub a few stops away I spotted a ticket machine and herded the kids off the bus while I figured it out, with help from other passengers. The Swiss are kind to tourists, although I was glad I spoke French. Even so, I misunderstood their directions to the next bus.

"*Derrière l'église*," they kept saying—behind the church—but I couldn't see any bus stop there, only an archeological dig in progress. The kids were too entranced by their new environment to whine as I led them around the outside of the church. We finally found the bus stop, not at the back of the church, as I understood it, but *on the opposite side* of it. So began my education on the oddities of French as spoken in Switzerland. In Chicago, all heads turned wherever I went with my brown children, but in Geneva we attracted no attention. All races and nationalities lived in Geneva, especially around our hotel near the UN headquarters. One cold winter day a few months later, I saw a man in a dhoti, turban and bare feet on the bus, and nobody stared. In Kinshasa, I couldn't go anywhere unnoticed. In Geneva, my kids and I were just part of a crowd. I enjoyed my newfound anonymity.

The hospital reception area looked more like an upscale train station, a large open space with the reception desk in the center and large clinic rooms placed around it, all illuminated by an immense skylight. Even in the US I had never seen such a luxurious hospital. I had no idea yet what medical coverage I had, and the receptionist didn't care. Everyone here had insurance. She directed us to a door in the middle distance that led to a spacious room equipped with child-sized chairs, and toys and books.

"This is a hospital?" Kiame said, heading for the Legos.

We hardly had time to sit down before a young man in a crisply ironed white coat called us. There were no aides here. This was the doctor—young, probably a resident.

"She has an ear infection," he said. "Does she get them often?"

"She's never had one. She just has a lot of sore throats."

He scribbled a prescription and handed it to me. "You can get this at any pharmacy."

Back on the bus, I watched out the window as the bus approached our final stop, just past two tiny pharmacies. After we got off, Wakengo stood looking at the driver through the open door.

"Kiame, *viens voir,*" he said. "Come and see."

I peeked into the bus and saw nothing unusual.

"What are you looking at?"

"A woman driving the bus."

"Of course women drive buses. Stop staring." I pulled him away, wondering what other sexist notions were swirling in his little head.

While we waited for an apartment, Jackson's new employer paid for a suite at the hotel. Jackson and I had one room; the three kids slept together in a king bed in an adjoining room. Our room had a mini-fridge and a microwave. A large TV, a coffee table, sofa and chairs occupied one corner of the kids' room. Kiame eagerly turned on the TV, only to find a test pattern—Geneva had no daytime TV.

"OK, grocery shopping," I announced.

"I need to take a shower," said Wakengo, who normally had to be forced to bathe.

"You can't take a shower every time you're cold," I said. "You need to wear a sweater."

"I don't want to. They're scratchy."

In the grocery store, small by American standards, I stood transfixed before a cooler full of yogurt in every conceivable flavor: cappuccino, pink grapefruit, even hazelnut. A luxury in Kinshasa, yogurt in Geneva cost less than anything else.

Switzerland imported most of its meat, grains and fresh produce, but it upheld its reputation for dairy products and chocolate. Even in this small store, chocolate had its own large case. And the cheese! In addition to the well-known Emmenthal (what Americans call "Swiss cheese") it offered Gruyère, Tilsit, Vacherin, and at least a dozen German and French cheeses. I bought food for lunch and snacks and stored the leftovers in the mini fridge. When TV programs came on at four o'clock, the boys explored the channels while I played with Mena. Appropriately medicated, she quickly improved. We had dinner that night in a nearby restaurant since I couldn't cook a whole meal in the hotel microwave. We went to bed early, still jet lagged. We should have taken Mena into bed with us. The next day Kiame and Wakengo woke up with ear infections and fevers, and we had to repeat the entire hospital trip.

The World Council found an apartment for us in Versoix, a suburb of Geneva, and we moved in after three weeks in the hotel. We also bought a Datsun station wagon.

"Best for a big family like yours," said the salesman. I almost laughed. In Zaire a big family meant at least six kids.

We enrolled the boys in the local school and Mena in a private pre-school program, mornings only. Public pre-school started at age four, and she had just turned three. I didn't plan to work at first—after years as the main breadwinner, I needed a break. In any case, I could only work for an international organization like the UN, unless I applied for a work visa. Also, day care in Geneva was almost as problematic as in the US. The local government ran the day care centers and charged a percentage of the parents' joint gross income. No part-time job I could get would be worth the cost. Anyway, all the schools had a two-hour lunch break, and Versoix schools did not offer lunch or after-school programs, as larger schools in the city of Geneva did. Children had Thursdays off but had classes on Saturday mornings. I would not be back in the workforce any time soon.

On Thursdays, the kids and I met up with two other mothers, a Scottish World Council wife and an American who worked at a bank, and their children. We often went cross-country skiing at St. Cergue, close to Geneva, and later in the season to Annecy in France. Other days the kids played outside at the small playground and soccer field beside the apartment complex. At first, I allowed Mena to go with them… and then one day they came home without her.

"Where's Mena?"

"Oh, we thought she came home. She's not here?"

Panicked, I went out to look for her, but she was nowhere near the building. I ran to the concierge's apartment on shaking legs.

"I saw her with a little boy," said the concierge's wife. "I know where he lives." She directed me to the apartment.

"Excuse me," I said to the woman who answered the door, "have you seen a little girl?"

"Oh, I'm glad you're here. I was wondering where she came from. I'd never seen her before, and she couldn't tell me where she lives."

After that, I went with her whenever she played outside. One day when I was out with the boys, Jackson lost track of her. She'd been playing in her room while he took a nap, but when he went to check on her later, he didn't see her. After searching indoors and out, he went back to her room and found her asleep on the floor of her closet, my small collection of pendants and bead necklaces scattered around her, bangles on her wrist.

In late September, my parents and my sister Jo came to visit. They offered to stay with the kids so that Jackson and I could take a short vacation, but he decided it was too soon to take time off from his job. I was sure his boss would understand, but Jackson was adamant. A change in occupation doesn't change a workaholic's habits, and Jackson never took real vacations. So my sister Jo and I went to Venice. We took the Swiss train that wound through the picturesque vineyards of the Valais region, threading through the Alps to northern Italy, with postcard-worthy vistas all the way. I felt like a student traveler again. We stayed at the Protestant hostel and took *vaporetto* rides to the Biennale art show, attended a Vivaldi concert in the San Georgio castle, toured a Murano glass factory, and went to every museum we had time for.

Jackson traveled frequently to Africa for work, staying two or three weeks at a time. Toward the end of his longer trips, the boys tended to get a bit unruly, but otherwise, I tolerated the added complication better than I had the solitary evenings in Kinshasa. I made friends and never felt unsafe. In Zaire, I always felt as though a disaster could happen any minute, that danger lurked around every corner. In Geneva, I felt wrapped in cotton. Nothing ever happened. On the radio, broadcasters whipped through the Swiss news in three minutes and moved on to international news to fill up the time. When he wasn't traveling, Jackson took the car to work, and I took the commuter train to the local grocery store. One day I waited with some teenagers from the private boarding school up the road. I glanced at a sports bag sitting on a bench and saw a name printed in black marker—"Eketebi." I stared at it and froze.

Five years earlier, a transport minister named Eketebi had been prosecuted in one of the biggest corruption cases in Zairian history, and he took down others with him. At the time, I had just started working for INZAL, the British Leyland affiliate, and the management had several closed-door meetings about what his downfall meant, and who might replace him. INZAL needed good relations with that ministry because import permits and government orders for vehicles and parts needed the transport minister's approval.

The sight of that troublesome name disturbed me. I studied the teenagers. The tall African boy had to be Eketebi, almost certainly a relative of the disgraced minister, probably his son. Supposedly the government had confiscated Eketebi's assets. If it had, the man apparently managed to stash away enough to pay a small fortune to keep his son in a private Swiss boarding school. Suddenly I felt my imaginary cocoon fall away. I thought I'd escaped Zaire, and here it was again. Would I never get away from it?

Chapter 21

Friends and Frenemies

In the summer of 1982, the World Council of Churches offered us an apartment closer to the center of Geneva. We accepted it with gratitude. Transportation in the city would be easier, and there would be more opportunities for me and the kids. We moved to a larger, if somewhat less luxurious apartment on the thirteenth floor of a building in the same neighborhood as the hotel we stayed in when we first arrived in Geneva.

The boys changed schools without complaint, and I enrolled Wakengo and Mena in the lunch and after-school programs that their new and larger school offered. Kiame took the bus to middle school and came home for lunch. Swiss schools don't have sports teams, so I enrolled the boys in a neighborhood soccer team. Geneva had no sports teams for girls of Mena's age. They had only Rhythmics (dance gymnastics) which looked boring, so I enrolled her in a neighborhood dance class. I quickly made friends among the parents of Mena's classmates. Foreigners comprised a third of Geneva's population of 172,000. Most worked for international organizations and companies. In addition, thousands of Spanish, Portuguese and Italian-speaking immigrants had become Swiss citizens and weren't even included in the "foreign national" category. Signs in shops commonly included English and Spanish translations, a big concession for the Swiss, who expect foreign residents to learn at least one of their four national languages. We joined the English-speaking Protestant church in the center of Geneva, along with many other World Council families. The small historic church building had no classrooms, so the church held Sunday School classes at the International School fifteen minutes away. Jackson and I thought this would give the kids more practice in English. This worked well for Kiame and Mena, but Wakengo hated it and did his best to make us late every week, trying to spend as little time as possible in the class.

One night, we had a dinner guest from Kinshasa. Jackson's friend Dr. Kapita had come to Geneva for an invitation-only meeting of a World Health Organization (WHO) "consultative group" on HIV. At the WHO meeting, Dr. Kapita presented a paper that attracted international attention. Zaire had not yet acknowledged that it had cases of HIV, although Dr. Kapita and other researchers found records of a mysterious diarrheal disease dating back many years.

"My brother-in-law called me at my hotel," he said. "Apparently the government is very upset about my paper."

"That isn't surprising," Jackson said. "But what does your brother-in-law have to do with it?"

"He's in Mobutu's Security Service. He's working on getting me out of trouble. Meanwhile he told me not to give any interviews."

"Is it true that HIV has been in Zaire since the 1950s?" I asked.

"Before that. We think possibly the 1920s. Researchers are looking for old blood samples in Belgium and Zaire."

"Does your brother-in-law think you'll be arrested?" Jackson asked.

"Probably, if he doesn't intervene." Kapita gave a grim smile. "The Catholics wanted to publish a public health pamphlet about it, and the government blocked it."

"Can't you just stay here for a little while?"

"No, I have my work, and my patients," he said. "My brother-in-law will meet me at the airport. I'll be fine."

Ultimately, the Zairian Government reprimanded him, but he didn't land in jail. His revelation at that meeting in Geneva sparked a massive WHO program to contain the disease, and because of that early intervention, Zaire had only about half the infections that other African countries experienced. Later in the epidemic, he treated high-ranking government officials and their family members who contracted AIDS. For some time, he was the only physician in Kinshasa running a drug trial for AZT, the first effective medication for AIDS. He kept it quiet, though, because he had to choose patients based on the protocols of the trial, not political influence.

* * *

In the fall of our second year in Geneva, I decided to get a part-time job. Jackson's salary was just adequate to support us and send money back to Zaire. All our Zairian friends with jobs in Europe supported family back home. We had no savings. After two temporary jobs at the UN, I started to work part time with the International Labor Organization (ILO). English-speaking administrative workers were in great demand. Within international organizations, alliances and rivalries between countries played themselves out on a smaller scale, within rigid protocols. Only a candidate's nationality and professional qualifications could be considered—not race, gender or religion, and each department tried to achieve a balance of East and West, North and South. Official delegates to these organizations changed often, usually when a new head of state came to power, but permanent employees did most of the work, and stayed for decades, with comfortable incomes free from Swiss income taxes.

I liked the people I worked with at the ILO, although I found the work itself boring. Then a friend recommended me for a job with the World YWCA, editing a collection of essays by women about female empowerment. Women from all over the world formed the program staff, working on contract with the mostly Swiss permanent support staff. The whole staff had tea every afternoon in the old-fashioned *salon* of the historic building, a room with antique furniture and a view over Lake Geneva. I loved working in an organization of women, where the development officer could say, as she left early from a meeting, "I'm leaving for Fiji tomorrow, so I need to get my hair done," and all of us understood. They were all interesting women, and I learned a great deal from them about nonprofit work, about Switzerland, and about all the countries they came from. I also enjoyed the weekly farmers' market near the office, where a French merchant taught me about cheese and fed me delicious samples. The first summer, I enrolled in a jazz dance class during my lunch hour and took the water taxi across the lake twice a week. Life was good, and when Jackson's three-year contract ended, he signed up again.

"That's it though. Three more years and we're going back," he warned. I tried not to think about it.

Around this time, Jackson's secretary at the World Council went back to Hungary, and the Council assigned a British woman in her late thirties in her place. Soon I realized that Deirdre, the new secretary, had a serious crush on Jackson. I knew he didn't give her any encouragement, so I couldn't be jealous. I got to know her, although I can't say we were friends. Pity is not a basis for a genuine friendship, and sorrow enveloped her like a dark cloud. I listened to her talk about her feelings and her problems without sharing my own, since I had everything she wanted: children, a college degree, and Jackson. Deirdre emanated depression, and whenever I listened to her, I felt it infecting me. She openly shared her regret at never marrying or having children.

Jackson and our friend Pastor Massamba felt sorry for her, and in their misguided way tried to help. The pastor helped many people, most of them in much worse situations than Deirdre's. He and Jackson decided that a trip to Zaire would be good for her. They probably thought that seeing so much poverty and misfortune would help her realize how lucky she really was. I thought it was a crazy idea, especially when I learned that she would be staying with Jackson's erratic brother Benoit and his wife.

"Jackson, this trip could go very wrong," I warned. "You know you can't trust Benoit."

"She's only going for a couple of weeks. What can go wrong? His wife Elise will be there. You worry too much."

Benoit could be charming, certainly, but also unpredictable. He'd been divorced several years earlier and then married a wonderful woman who had a good job. At least she could help give Deirdre a positive experience, or so I hoped. After the trip, Deirdre reported that it went well.

"See?" Jackson gloated.

One day a few months later, at Geneva's only shopping mall, the kids were bounding through a department store when I caught sight of an African man who looked familiar. I had to look twice to be sure, but it was indeed Benoit. Jackson would certainly have told me if he knew his brother was in town. I hid behind a pillar and tried to herd the kids in the opposite direction, but before I could turn them around, Kiame spotted him.

"*Oncle Benoit!*" Kiame called in his booming voice. My quiet escape evaporated.

Benoit looked up with an embarrassed smile. I did not ask him what he was doing in Geneva, and Kiame's chatter filled the gap. I knew immediately where he was staying. Deirdre lived a few blocks away—he was having an affair with her. At home that night, Jackson barely stepped through the door before Kiame burst out, "Guess who we saw at the mall? Uncle Benoit!"

Jackson's eyebrows shot up, and his mouth dropped open. His head snapped around to me.

"Is it true?"

I nodded. "Kids, go wash your hands. It's time for dinner."

When they were out of earshot, Jackson said, "Deirdre's pregnant. It never occurred to me that Benoit was responsible."

"As if his wife didn't have enough to put up with. You still think that trip was a great idea?"

He didn't answer. I went into the kitchen and slammed the pots and pans around. Jackson appeared in the doorway.

"I never thought —"

"Too late now," I said. "You know everyone's going to think it's yours, don't you?"

He gave me an alarmed look. I was right. Nobody said anything to me directly, but at every World Council gathering from then on, people gave me sidelong glances and then looked away. I imagined them thinking, *Why is she still with him?* I told a few of my closest friends the truth about the pregnancy. Pastor Massamba's wife knew, too, but she didn't socialize much with her husband's colleagues and their wives. I don't know if my friends passed on the information, and I wasn't sure anyone would believe it anyway. I didn't speak to Jackson for a couple of weeks.

"I didn't know... I didn't realize... How could she do this?" he repeated. He was full of lame excuses but never managed to apologize or express any regret about his mistake in arranging for Deirdre to stay with Benoit. I cut off all contact with Deirdre, and Jackson had her transferred to another department. We did not tell the children what had happened. They rarely saw Deirdre, and they had little curiosity about the lives of adults.

All actions have consequences. What Deirdre did hurt Elise, a person I liked and respected. Her actions caused major problems for Jackson and me. The brothers had feuded on and off their entire lives, and after this they didn't communicate for a long time.

Chapter 22
Childhood in Geneva

Children in Geneva had an ideal life when we lived there. The State provided generous resources and paid their teachers well. Our local elementary school had small classes, a modern building, a large playground and even an indoor swimming pool with an adjustable floor. On school holidays, including every Thursday, local "Leisure Centers" took children sledding and skiing in the winter and to outdoor pools in the summer. On weekends, when the kids grew restless in the apartment, we took them to the Botanical Gardens with its peacocks, large indoor greenhouse, and room to run around, or to an immense adventure playground half an hour away, run by Switzerland's largest grocery chain. It had a spectacular view over Lake Geneva and a special area just for flying paper airplanes, right below a restaurant where parents could sip coffee while watching their children play.

Every neighborhood in Geneva had a library, a bookstore and an urgent care center, in addition to the usual retail shops. The neighborhood was so safe that children as young as four played in the parks without supervision. Each February, the State school system subsidized a week-long ski vacation at Switzerland's best ski resorts for all children attending public school. At the end of the school year, the city held a party in Geneva's biggest park, and every child received an age-appropriate gift, chosen a month earlier by parents from a catalog. Because of the many school holidays during the rest of the year, summer vacation lasted only six weeks. The Leisure Centers operated special-interest day camps: arts and crafts, water skiing and windsurfing, in addition to the ordinary day camps. Some neighborhood councils also offered week-long overnight camps in the mountains, with hiking and other outdoor activities. The Versoix scout troop, where Kiame and Wakengo belonged even after we moved to the apartment in the city, also had a week-long overnight camp every summer, staffed mostly by teenagers.

Music and dance schools abounded, and parents eagerly supported them. The city itself also organized festivals. The biggest holiday, the Escalade, combined Halloween and the Fourth of July. The whole city celebrated the victory of the Genevans over the French Savoyards in 1602. On December 7th, children dressed up in costumes and walked from door to door, receiving coins in exchange for singing at least one verse of the traditional song *Cé qué l'aino*, sung in the old Geneva dialect. In the evening, a parade of people dressed in 17th century costumes wound through the old town carrying torches, spears and muskets, accompanied by flutes and drums playing 17th century music. The pageantry evoked Geneva's Old Town in that era. The parade ended at the cathedral, where an official read the Declaration of 1602, the equivalent of our Declaration of Independence. People sampled vegetable soup from large cauldrons scattered around the Old Town to commemorate Mère Royaume (Mother Kingdom), the patriotic woman who, according to legend, dumped a cauldron of boiling vegetable soup on the enemy scaling the ramparts. Bakeries and *patisseries* sold miniature chocolate cauldrons filled with marzipan vegetables.

None of this came free, of course. The lunch program alone cost $145 a month per child for a three-course meal served family style, with volunteer monitors to ensure good table manners. Each child had a little locker for his toothbrush. Though subsidized, the Leisure Center and ski camps each cost several hundred francs. Rental for skis and poles ran about $200 a season, per person. Clothes were expensive too. Wakengo could use some of Kiame's hand-me-downs, but Kiame usually wore out his clothes. And shoes! Just as Swiss children did at home, they had to take off their "street shoes" at school and wear slippers in class. The school also required each child to keep a pair of gym shoes in their lockers. Wakengo and Kiame both had size twelve feet, and I had trouble finding shoes for them. The boys needed cleats for soccer, and Mena needed a constant supply of ballet shoes, tights and leotards.

Kiame and Wakengo obsessed over soccer; Mena's concerns centered on her friends. Sociable but reserved, she would come home several times a week in a funk because she felt left out. Her frequent strep infections made scheduling her play dates even more difficult. Fortunately, she did well in school, because I didn't have much time to work with her. Wakengo wouldn't do his homework unless I sat and coached him every night. Later, I wondered if reading would have come more easily to her if I had spent more time reading with her.

She was bored with her neighborhood dance class, so I enrolled her in a ballet school in the Old Town. Twice a week, Mena and I took the bus to her ballet lesson. She lived for her dance lessons and took them seriously. One of her teachers took me aside one day and asked, "Does Mena enjoy her classes?

She never smiles." I assured the teacher she loved her classes. She just didn't like it when other little girls disrupted the class. After every lesson, I took her to one of the small cafés in the Old Town where she ate nut tarts and drank hot chocolate, contentedly seated amongst Swiss ladies of a certain age wearing furs and diamonds while sipping their afternoon tea.

The longer we stayed in Geneva, the less Mena remembered about Zaire, and the more she absorbed Swiss culture. One day she put her hand on my arm to stop me from walking on the grass in a park. Trained in the school lunch program, she ate with her fork in her left hand, European style, and liked salad and salad dressing, which Kiame and Wakengo ate only under duress.

On dance lesson days, Wakengo had to get home from the after-school program on his own, a one-block walk. He should have been home by the time we came back, but he never was. Often I would find the door to the apartment not just unlocked, but wide open. He lost so many keys that I thought everyone in the neighborhood must have one. When he wasn't home by six o'clock, I would send Kiame out to look for him.

"He'll come home when he's ready," Kiame said.

"No, he'll come home when I want him home."

"He's the *homme du quartier*—neighborhood man," Kiame said.

Kiame thrived in Geneva. He had always done well in school, and made friends easily, but in the competitive Swiss tracking system, he excelled. He knew how much he needed to study and never needed reminding. He loved team sports and launched himself with enthusiasm into every new activity he encountered: skiing, camping, swimming, skating, karate, even Dungeons and Dragons. He had a large circle of friends, both girls and boys. He spent his pocket money on books and comics.

I felt lucky that Kiame required so little attention because Wakengo needed so much. From his infancy, I worried about that child. I took him to a pediatrician when he couldn't sit up at six months. He didn't crawl until he was a year old, and he was eighteen months before he took his first steps. Wakengo had pneumonia or bronchitis so often that it was hard to get his vaccinations done on time. He could sleep twelve hours a night and still need a nap, in contrast to Kiame, who slept like an adult when he was a year old. In Kinshasa, when I tried to put Wakengo in a neighborhood pre-school at age three, they sent him home.

"He just cries all day," the director said. "He's not ready."

At four, he enjoyed pre-school, although he didn't learn to write the alphabet despite hours of coaching. His kindergarten teacher recommended waiting a year before starting first grade. I hesitated, but his father and Heidi, the school director, wanted him to start right away, so I reluctantly agreed. Halfway through first grade in Kinshasa, though, he still didn't know his letters. I drilled him every night, to no avail. His teacher counseled patience, and since Wakengo never disrupted class, nobody paid much attention to him. Then we moved to Switzerland, and the next year was a blur as we all adjusted. Wakengo learned his letters but couldn't put them together to read or write. I read to him every night, but he fell asleep—or feigned it—whenever I tried to get him to read. In third grade, as the level of work increased, his grades fell. His young teacher had no suggestions.

"That's what he's capable of," she said with a shrug. I knew he could do better but didn't know how to motivate him. At the beginning of fourth grade, his teacher called me in.

"He needs to be tested," she said. "He's way behind in reading, and he doesn't pay attention."

It took weeks to get an appointment, weeks more to get the results. Wakengo had dyslexia, the experts told us, a learning disorder that made it difficult for him to read. The expert recommended a reading specialist and a psychiatric workup, so I took him once a week to the reading specialist the experts recommended. He didn't like it, but he improved. He still hated school, though, and getting him to do his homework was a nightly battle.

After his first appointment with the psychiatrist, the doctor said, "I need another session with him. He doesn't talk."

Finally, he had Wakengo draw pictures. Then he gave us the diagnosis. There was no pathology, but he had anxiety about going to school and feared disappointing us, especially his father.

"What can we do?" I asked.

"Madame," said the shrink in the formal language typical of Swiss officials, "It is not a pathology to dislike school."

I didn't care whether he liked school or not. He just had to get better grades. In addition to the reading specialist, I hired a tutor to work with him twice a week and worked with him myself the other days. Kiame and Mena complained that I spent more time with Wakengo than with them.

"You're always with your *chouchou,*" Kiame said. *Chouchou,* literally "little cabbage," means "favorite" in French slang. I really had no choice—Jackson had no talent or patience for homework help, and he traveled about a quarter of the year. Then, in fifth grade, Wakengo landed in the class of Mademoiselle Gaie, a powerhouse of a teacher who could see his potential and kept him after school every night to show him that he could do better. She taught him again the following year. With her help, he improved, and I was overjoyed. At last we could both feel good about his performance in school. I hated to think what would have happened to him if we hadn't come to Geneva. Now we were approaching the end of Jackson's second three-year contract. Soon we would have to leave this charmed life behind.

Chapter 23
The Nightmare

When Jackson signed his second contract with the World Council of Churches in 1984, he warned that he would not sign another. Now I had to decide whether I would go back with him. In the plan he and I presented to the children, we were all going back at the end of the summer. Children hate change, and none of them wanted to leave Switzerland. Kiame started to work on an alternative, wrangling an invitation from a Swiss friend's parents to stay with them until he graduated from high school the following year.

"No," Jackson said. "You're coming back with us."

Kiame tried to argue with him and got nowhere. He shut himself up in his room. At bedtime, Mena would cry herself to sleep. "I don't want to go there," she wailed. "I don't want to leave my friends."

Bizarre nightmares visited me every night. I've always had vivid dreams, but none before this included complete coherent stories, without jumps in logic or symbolic locations. Although they differed in detail, the story was always the same: I was at home with the kids in Kinshasa in a house very much like the one we used to live in, and Jackson was nowhere in sight. I could hear a riot getting closer and louder. Then a friend showed up to tell me that a rebellion was going on, and we needed to flee the city. I could see smoke curling up to the sky in the distance. I quickly packed a suitcase, gathered up the kids, and left, driving out of the city with the friend who brought the news. Each eerily realistic dream ended there.

If I decided to stay in Geneva, it would be mostly for Mena. We had gone back to Zaire once, for a month-long visit three years before, and she did not enjoy it. In Zaire, where everyone had a hard life, girls and women had it even harder. They suffered greater physical insecurity and limits on their activities. The harsh living conditions affected them more than the boys because of the expectation that they would do all the housework and shopping. I couldn't give Mena a pep talk when I didn't look forward to going back myself. If I stayed, I would have to get a different job. I couldn't support three children on my part-time salary, and since I didn't have a work permit, I could only work in an international organization. Even with those organizations, I would have a hard time finding a job that paid enough for us to live in one of the most expensive cities in Europe. The World Council of Churches held the lease on our apartment, so we would have to move. I didn't consider going back to the US. I didn't want to expose my children to its racism until they were old enough to have more insight into its historical roots.

Important questions kept running through my mind: Could I deprive my children of their father? Was an inadequate father better than none at all? What would happen to their sense of identity if we stayed in Switzerland? What future did they have there? It would be difficult for them to obtain Swiss citizenship.

I talked to friends, most of whom advised me to stay in Geneva. I didn't tell Jackson about my doubts although I imposed one condition. I would not go unless he bought a suitable house. He'd had almost six years, plenty of time to arrange it. An equal concern was my own sense of commitment to improving life for the people of Zaire, especially in Manianga. In Switzerland, I would be working only to survive. I had enjoyed what amounted to a lovely six-year vacation there, but I could not see a satisfying future in Geneva. I would be trapped in a kind of life I had always avoided, one in which I made no contribution to the betterment of the world—*Métro, boulot, dodo*, as the French say—commute, work, sleep.

I barely thought about permanently separating from Jackson. I stayed with him thus far for two reasons: the children and the cause. I respected him for his work, but I no longer loved him and hadn't for a long time. I still admired him, because I knew that very few people had his integrity and determination. Yet each time he hurt or betrayed me, he chipped away a bit more from what had been my attachment to him: the threat to divorce me when I was pregnant, abandoning Kiame and me in the Kimpese hospital, bullying me in Sundi, his constant absence in both Sundi and Kinshasa, and the whole business about Deirdre. He never expressed regret for any of it. I didn't trust him to make his children a priority, to care for me or even to tell me the truth about his plans and his actions. He showed no concern about the way his behavior eroded my commitment to him. And yet I pushed these thoughts to the back of my mind, because I had more important priorities: my children's future and my own commitment to an ideal. With those priorities paramount, my personal happiness could not be my major concern. Two months before we were due to leave Switzerland, a businessman friend found a house for us in our old neighborhood, Limete. I decided to go back to Zaire.

If I'd believed in omens, I had plenty to choose from. Our flight went through Brussels, and we had a surprise layover there because the plane needed repair. I soon learned why our East African friends said that SABENA stands for "Such a Bloody Experience, Never Again." We waited for an hour in the small immigration office at the airport—eight chairs and a Coke machine—so that Jackson could get a transit visa to stay overnight in the city. An airline bus took us to a large colonial-style hotel. I couldn't help thinking about the century of Belgian exploitation of Zaire that financed the hotel's original grandeur. The airline fed us supper in a strangely bare dining room, and we went to our rooms. The door from the hallway led to a small foyer, with two bedrooms and a bathroom opening off it. The boys immediately headed for the TV in their room to see what channels they could get. Jackson, Mena and I went down to the front desk to arrange transportation to the airport in the morning. When we came back, we knocked on the door, but the boys did not respond. Kiame and Wakengo had locked themselves in as instructed, but left the key in the lock, so ours wouldn't work. We banged on the door. No answer.

"They're watching TV and have the door closed," Jackson guessed.

Bang! Bang! Bang!

Still nothing.

"Should we get the front desk to call them?" I asked.

"Let's try again."

Bang! Bang! Bang!

We waited, gazing at the door. After a series of clicks, the door opened.

At the airport the next morning, airport security stopped us because the screener saw a knife in Kiame's hand baggage. An officer went through the bag twice and didn't find it, but the screener insisted. By this time, we had only thirty-five minutes before takeoff. On his third try, the officer found a sword-shaped letter opener in a plastic letter case at the bottom of the bag. We sprinted to the gate and arrived just before the flight attendant closed the door.

Chapter 24
Reluctant Return

Mena was only three when we moved to Geneva, so she had no memory of Kinshasa. In effect, Jackson and I had brought a nine-year-old Swiss girl into a strange and frightening environment. She hated it from the beginning. I didn't know which was worse, obliging Mena to come to Kinshasa, where she didn't want to go, or separating her from her father at such a critical age. What right did I have to impose my choice on this child and make her so unhappy? Did I agree to come back because I was secretly afraid I couldn't make it on my own? Now that we were in Kinshasa, there was no going back. If coming back was a mistake, it was too late to correct it. Every day I second-guessed my decision. I still felt an obligation to the work of developing Manianga and improving people's lives. At the same time I longed for a more comfortable life for myself and my children. I didn't know yet if I could achieve both. Now they knew what life outside Zaire could be like, and they knew it was a life they could have if Jackson and I would only agree to provide it for them.

The house in Kinshasa needed inside and outside renovation, so for the first few weeks, we stayed with Pastor Massamba, our old friend from Geneva, on the other side of town. Kiame enrolled in the Belgian School as a junior, which infuriated him. In Switzerland, he would have been in his last year. The following year, Kiame discovered by chance that he could have enrolled as a senior, and it was Jackson who made sure his son would spend an extra year in Zaire. Kiame didn't tell me about this until almost forty years later. I still wonder what secrets I may never discover.

In addition to Pastor Massamba's wife and two small children, several young men lived in the compound, most of them from his clan. Fortunately, the compound had an annex that housed all the young men. Most households in Kinshasa included clan members. I knew very few Zairians who lived in a nuclear family household the way we usually did. Communal living can be stressful, but it can also be reassuring. Someone is home nearly all the time, reducing the chances of a burglary, common in Kinshasa, particularly when the burglars know the house is empty. Unemployment hovered around 50 percent then, and many people would steal to survive. With a constant human presence, there is always someone available to run a quick errand, whether it was buying drinks for visitors from the corner store or babysitting for an hour. Most families took in at least one young relative, usually a sister or a niece, to help with the housework and childcare, usually in return for financing their schooling.

A week before school started, the contractor hadn't finished the renovations on our house, and we didn't want to drive across town to take Wakengo and Mena to school, so we asked the contractor to make the house minimally habitable while he continued the work. I liked the house, the biggest we'd ever lived in, with four bedrooms, two bathrooms, and a large, combined living and dining area. I would have preferred a bigger kitchen, but it was adequate, with a pantry that I could lock and a toilet and shower in the back. All the floors were tiled in circus colors, each room different: swirly green tile with a yellow border, mottled blue with a red border, black and red checkerboard. The backyard sloped gently down to the wall separating our land from the lot behind us, which turned out to be a nun's residence owned by the Catholic Church. We never saw anyone outside. In one corner at the bottom of the hill stood a banana grove, well placed to absorb runoff during the rainy season. Next door, on one side, a young woman lived with her sister and daughter. Her Italian lover visited frequently. A family with three young boys lived on the other side. I hired workers from INZAL, my former employer, who were happy to help renovate the interior of the house. They agreed to my strange request to install a hot water heater outside, instead of the usual place above the faucets, where I always worried it would someday detach and clobber someone in the bath. They welded an anti-theft cage for it, since anything not nailed down in Kinshasa tended to disappear. Avenue Cannas, the street in front of the house, dead-ended a couple of hundred feet down the hill. Beyond that, dirt paths led through a less affluent neighborhood near a small, garbage-strewn stream. When we moved in, the house had a short wall of hollow brick facing the street, which I preferred, but after a burglary attempt, we reluctantly built a higher wall of closed brick. The gardener and I did our best to cover the wall with bougainvillea.

We had barely moved in when I came down with malaria. I took the usual medications, but after two weeks I still had the odd sensation that my body was shaking inside, like the chills of malaria without the fever. Dr. Kapita, the doctor who had visited us in Geneva, ran repeated malaria tests which came back negative, so he decided it was a panic attack. Unfortunately, the symptoms of a psychosomatic illness don't change just because you know they're psychosomatic. I had no control over them. Gradually the shaking diminished, although it recurred, off and on, for months. I later learned the shaking may have been a neurological sequel to the malaria.

While we were in Geneva, Heidi Kabangu's school had outgrown her house. She bought land in a nearby neighborhood and built simple classroom buildings around a barren courtyard. During recess, boys played soccer and girls jumped rope. Heidi's niece bossed all the other girls around, and Mena did not like being bossed. Heidi's daughters, around the ages of Kiame and Wakengo, considered Mena too young to bother with, and she resented that too. Accustomed to the discreet luxury of Swiss schools, Mena had a hard time adjusting to the much simpler school in Kinshasa, with its sandy schoolyard devoid of vegetation and simple cement classrooms. She complained about it constantly. Wakengo had problems adjusting, too, although he complained less vociferously. I tried to find ways to make Kinshasa more tolerable for Mena. I found a good ballet school for her, run by a Belgian woman. Mena made friends there, and slowly she found others, including a half-Swiss, half-Zairian girl, daughter of a former missionary and friend of Heidi. Mainly because of Mena, I joined a private sports club, something I previously resisted because I found it elitist. We drove there on weekends, and it provided a welcome break from our daily life, like a bit of Europe for an afternoon. I always found beaches boring, but I was surprised that I enjoyed lounging on a beach chair under a little thatched roof, watching Mena swim while Kiame and Wakengo shot hoops. As Mena grew older, she clashed with her father more often. Now that we were back in

Zaire, he expected her to follow rules for girls, rules that didn't exist in Switzerland.

"Polite people sit with their legs together, so that nobody can see their underwear," he told her.

"Polite people don't look!" she retorted.

"You need to listen to your father!" he said. "Go to your room!"

Unlike their sister, the boys adjusted easily. Kiame maintained contact with his Swiss friends and made new ones in the neighborhood and at school, as he always had. Wakengo, more of a loner, seemed unaffected by the move. Kiame always was his best friend, and now they shared a large room. I signed them up for a Tae Kwondo class, even though I had to drive across town twice a week to take them. Jackson took them to play tennis. I hired one of Heidi's teachers to tutor Wakengo; he was already slacking off on his classwork.

Once we were halfway settled, we started to work with our non-profit, the Center for Agricultural Extension (*Centre de Vulgarization Agricole*, abbreviated to CVA.*)* The illness slowed me down at first, but I worked as much as I could. With funds gathered from various donors, Jackson bought a house a mile away from ours and converted it into an office. He hired Ernest Badia as business manager. He had been the secretary of the school at Sundi Lutete and was the most conscientious man I've ever known. Jackson also hired a driver, nephew of an old friend from Luozi, and three other staff.

Before we left Geneva, we had arranged funding for our living expenses for our first year. Jackson agreed that the Center would start to pay me a salary when the funding ended. My job would be to edit and publish books, write grant requests, handle any English correspondence, and participate in research projects as needed. I threw myself into the work. My first project was a book about AIDS written by Dr. Kapita. When he finished the manuscript, I went first to the Catholic printing house a few blocks from our house. The head monk glanced at the title page and shook his head.

"We tried to publish a public health pamphlet four years ago," he said. "The government stopped us from distributing it. *Désolé, Madame.*"

The Protestant publishing house, CEDI, agreed to publish it. They had already published nine of our books while we were in Geneva. *Le Sida en Afrique* was a huge success. It was the only publication about AIDS available to the public, and people were both alarmed by the disease and curious about it. We kept our prices low and grants subsidized our publications. But a book was still a luxury purchase for most people. We distributed books to libraries and schools free of charge and estimated that at least five people read every book we sold. The other topics included nutrition, medicinal plants, the environment, accounting, history, religion and culture.

In a nonprofit like ours, dependent on outside funding, we often had to tailor our projects to meet donors' constantly changing priorities. In the late 1980s, donors woke up to the merits of micro-financing, so CVA began a list of projects and recruited funds. Jackson arranged to rent land in a remote area west of Luozi; we raised funds to start a ranch and bought heifers. Through micro-financing, we gave heifers to others who wanted to start ranches. When their heifers calved, they would give a calf to the project. We worked with people near Luozi on a similar project with goats. We educated ourselves on reforestation and erosion control and worked with Robert Diyabanza, José Dianzungu and others to learn best practices, because we soon discovered reforestation is more complicated than planting a seed in the middle of the savannah. We had to experiment until we learned what would work, and that often took several years. The Swedish Church provided a cautionary tale. It financed a reforestation project using *leucena*, a tree that worked well in other parts of the world. The trees grew quickly and looked healthy, but they all died after two or three years. That taught us to be wary of promoting imported plants. Along with Robert Diyabanza, we decided to plant a local hardwood tree called *wenge* used for fine furniture and woodworking that was in danger of disappearing from the region. To our surprise, all the seedlings died. Then Robert learned from old villagers that *wenge* germinates only when surrounded by rich vegetation and shaded by other trees. It needs humus and shade to get started.

Jackson wanted to do more for his ancestral village, where most of his clan lived. As good activists, we knew enough to ask the people in the village what the Center could do for them. We tried to interest them in erosion control, with no success. The villagers knew what they wanted—a medical clinic. Donors rarely funded buildings or salaries, so we had to use mostly funds we generated ourselves—from books, from the ranch and from micro-financing projects. I wrote a detailed proposal that we shopped around to our donors, and we were able to get a small amount of financing for materials and salaries. Over two years, we built the clinic and then found a nurse who would run it and live in the village. The villagers were delighted, although the clinic gave us headaches. Direct health care wasn't part of our core work; supporting the clinic siphoned off money needed for true development projects. A few years later, to our great relief, the Protestant Church agreed to take over the clinic.

I started looking into alternative crops that would provide better nutrition without depleting the soil. I always enjoyed gardening and now put my pastime to practical use. The Portuguese imported manioc, also called cassava, in the 16th century, and it quickly became popular because of its resistance to pests, low labor input, and high calorie content, compared to the traditional staple of sorghum, a labor-intensive crop prone to insect infestation, but high in nutrients. Unfortunately, manioc has almost no nutritional value and depletes the soil. Local methods of cultivation also cause severe soil erosion. We looked for crops with a higher nutritional content that were less destructive to the environment. I started a vegetable garden in the backyard, with the help of our part-time gardener, and planted fruit trees and a type of bean recommended by an American-trained nutrition expert. The work kept me going through all the challenges of living in Kinshasa and the deterioration of my marriage. Jackson started to make critical remarks about me in front of other people, and I started to leave the room every time he did it. He knew I was unhappy and took it as a personal insult.

"When have you gone hungry?" he often asked when we argued about finances, as if that was all that mattered.

Jackson traveled to Luozi often, and when he was home, he once again usually went out after supper and returned around ten. I spent my evenings alone, even when he wasn't traveling, just as I had before we went to Switzerland. The kids played games together, while I depended heavily on a small but well-stocked English-language library run by a Canadian. I usually read four books a week. I couldn't safely drive alone at night, so I never visited friends or went to the films and programs put on by the embassies. When night fell, I felt like a prisoner. On Saturday nights, though, we started going to a new nightclub a couple of miles away. Like all such places in Zaire—and there were many—it had great live music and a large dance floor. When the music started, everyone danced. Just sitting and drinking in a bar had no appeal for most Zairians. If they paid to enter a club, they wanted to dance. Jackson teased me because I couldn't stay awake beyond two a.m., while everyone else danced until dawn, although he really didn't mind leaving then—he couldn't last much longer than that himself. On Sundays, if it didn't rain and there were no rumors of street demonstrations, we visited friends, including the country's best-known novelist, Zamenga Batukezanga. Other than the sports club where I took the kids on Saturday afternoon, that was the extent of our entertainment.

Chapter 25
Jaundiced

Marry for love, work for money.

—African proverb

The salary subsidy from the donors was due to end in a few months, and I reminded Jackson of our agreement that the Center would pay me when the grant ran out.

"We can't pay you," he said. "The Center doesn't have enough money yet. Maybe when the ranch becomes more profitable we can do it."

"We need money coming in now though."

"We have the money we saved in Geneva."

"That's our only savings. We shouldn't use that to pay for living expenses," I said. "I'm going to look for a paying job. I'll do the nonprofit work on the side."

He shrugged. "If that's what you think you need to do."

I started teaching English at the US Information Agency (USIA) to graduate school candidates chosen for study in the US. Before their admission could be confirmed, they had to pass the official Test of English as a Foreign Language (TOEFL). My students were all men—women comprised only a small percentage of university graduates in the 1980s. My students' proficiency varied widely, and their academic backgrounds differed too. I used one of the USIA textbooks, but the agency didn't dictate a curriculum. USIA emphasized spoken English, and a big part of the TOEFL exam also focused on that. Now I was "teaching to the exam," the opposite of what I wanted to do in Sundi, but in this exam speaking and understanding English counted more than reading and writing.

Fortunately, my class had only ten students, so I had the flexibility to teach however I wanted. I asked the students to prepare a presentation for the class related to their academic specialty, so that they would practice the vocabulary of their chosen field and practice speaking English in front of a group. The most memorable of those presentations, by a road engineer, showed why building and maintaining roads is so difficult in the tropics. I had never taught professionals—what a relief it was not to deal with classroom discipline! These students knew they had to learn fast. The diversity of the group and their ambitions made lesson planning more complicated, even with a small group of highly motivated students, to account for their varying levels in the group. These respectful, appreciative students made our class sessions a pleasure, even though I hated writing lesson plans.

Getting a scholarship to study abroad was the Holy Grail every Zairian student dreamed of. Virtually every young person I encountered wanted to leave the country, including Kiame. Jackson and I had not always envisioned college abroad for him. In the early days, we thought he would stay in Zaire for his education and expected him to work for the country after he graduated, as we were doing. For years, Jackson had inculcated

Kiame with the idea that he would study medicine. He would hold three-year-old Kiame's shoulders and say, "You're going to be doctor, aren't you?" Kiame would echo, "I'm going to be doctor," and repeated it like a little robot to anyone who would listen. Jackson repeated this indoctrination often, coupled with an admonition not to study the "useless sciences" (liberal arts) as he and I had. The Zairian university system, though, had deteriorated drastically, like everything else, and now we planned to send him overseas. Jackson wanted Kiame to study in Europe rather than in the US and made tentative arrangements with the Dutch family who had taught at Sundi Lutete in 1967. I thought asking them to provide housing for Kiame for four years was too big a favor to ask, and I knew we needed a back-up plan, so I wrote away for applications to US colleges. We had to pay rigorous attention to deadlines because the mail was so slow. I looked for people traveling to Europe or the US to mail letters there instead, something everyone else did, both expatriates and Zairians. Kiame would graduate from the Belgian School in June of 1989, so I started to prepare a year ahead, focusing on two colleges at which we had connections: Haverford College near Philadelphia, where an old friend taught anthropology; and St. Olaf College in Minnesota, where my mother had attended for two years before transferring to the University of Minnesota. My parents were planning a move from Chicago to Cottonwood, in Minnesota, to take care of my grandmother. The drive from Cottonwood to St. Olaf took three hours, but it was closer than Chicago, where my sisters lived.

In January, the Dutch family wrote that they could not house Kiame because of a family issue, so I ramped up the back-up plan. Kiame applied to Haverford, St. Olaf, Temple University and Mankato State University. He had excellent grades and

SAT scores. Since he would graduate from a French-speaking school, he took the TOEFL (Test of English as a Foreign Language) with results in the 99th percentile for all of Africa. He even had a French creative-writing prize to his credit. When his friends from the neighborhood came to visit, he would chat with them for a while, but they couldn't tempt him to cruise the neighborhood with them. Often they came to him for help with schoolwork. One day he spent more than an hour with a friend preparing for a math exam. When his friend left, Kiame said, "He's going to fail that exam. He's too far behind." A surprisingly adult assessment.

Kiame had an active social life with his friends at the Belgian school, most of them Belgians. He occasionally spent weekends at the vacation homes of his friends' families. More often, they went to one of the European-style nightclubs on a Saturday night. Kiame had a driver's license, but Jackson wouldn't let him drive alone and went to pick him up at the end of the evening. Kiame routinely ignored whatever curfew Jackson tried to impose. One night Jackson left at midnight and didn't get back until four in the morning. Like most parents, neither of us knew quite how to relate to the adult that Kiame had become.

"You could throw that kid out on the street right now, and he would do just fine," my sister Beth had told us when he was ten. We could see how capable he was, and yet we still couldn't let go of that tiny bit of illusory control we had over him. In the spring, Haverford sent an acceptance letter with a full scholarship package. It was a tremendous relief, although I still wanted to know what St. Olaf would offer. Haverford's deadline on responding to the offer approached, and we still had no package from St. Olaf. It finally arrived the week after Kiame accepted Haverford's offer. It was even more generous, but I thought Philadelphia would be better for him than Minnesota. Haverford had more Black students and a more diverse staff. It would also be easier for us to get to Haverford from Zaire. Now the envy of all his friends, Kiame had his path set for the next four years.

* * *

My job at USIA paid me in dollars, and it financed our living expenses, apart from our transportation, which was folded into the Center's budget, and the children's school fees, which we paid from our savings in Switzerland. Jackson believed that the ranch would eventually be profitable enough to support us, just as he believed in all the earlier failed business schemes. The ranch was slowly expanding, but there were always problems. Any kind of business in Zaire was risky, especially when managed long-distance. The state of the roads was the biggest issue. Even if you had cattle to sell, without a decent road you couldn't get them to market. Jackson had no control over road repairs and couldn't maintain the road himself.

By this time, I concluded we would never have even minimal financial security in Zaire. The only sensible thing we could have done would have been to buy some houses and rent them out. It would have taken all our savings, and even that was risky. Several months after we bought the house we lived in, the son of the previous owner found out that his father had sold it and threatened to sue us to get it back. It was not an idle threat. Men with political power often confiscated property, and the rightful owners had little chance of redress. Fortunately, Dr. Kapita talked him out of it.

Jackson could still have found a teaching job abroad, but he would never leave again. I had to choose: stay in Zaire, keeping afloat by working for USIA or some other US Government agency, or not come back from a future trip to the US. That year, staying in the US wasn't an option because Wakengo would stay in Kinshasa while Mena and I traveled to Haverford with Kiame. Wakengo had a small room at the Benedictine Monastery and worked in the garden, the fishponds and the piggery. He knew about the place from a school trip that Heidi organized. At Haverford, I stayed with our old friends Wyatt and Janet MacGaffey. Mena stayed across the street with another family who had a niece her age visiting for the summer. At Haverford, Kiame had two roommates. One arrived the same day we did, with ten times as much luggage. I watched his parents hang perfectly ironed button-down shirts in the closet and thought, *those shirts aren't going to look like that again until he goes home for Christmas.* Mena stayed at Haverford while I flew to Chicago to see my parents and sisters. Mom and Dad never commented on our decision to leave Switzerland, nor did they ever try to convince me to move back to the US. Only once Mom said, "I never thought about the families that my grandparents and great-grandparents left behind in Norway, how hard it must have been for them."

Mena and I flew back to Kinshasa in mid-August. Our first family dinner back in Kinshasa seemed strange without Kiame. Jackson was in a good mood, talking and joking with Mena. I realized that he was happy we were back. As I watched him laughing with her, I felt a wave of nostalgia for the time when I would have been happy to see him too. The only person I was happy to see was Wakengo. He came down with a mild case of malaria after his stay at the monastery. I always avoided leaving children in Zaire when I traveled, even after they became self-sufficient teenagers. I knew anything could happen, especially in times of political upheaval, and even a street-smart adolescent doesn't always make the right choices in an emergency, so I was pleased that Wakengo had a good experience. Monastic life suited a loner like him who didn't like to talk. He attended chapel five times a day (silent except for chanting), joined the lay brothers at communal meals (mostly silent), did manual labor, and played volleyball with the brothers for an hour before supper.

A couple of months later, we went to visit a doctor friend and his family four hours away, where he ran the hospital and clinic for employees of the sugar factory and their families. Kiame had spent a few weeks with them the previous summer to get an idea of what a doctor did in that setting. The day before we left to go home, I didn't feel good and stayed home while everyone else went out. When they returned, the doctor looked at me critically.

"You have jaundice," he said.

I looked in a mirror, and there it was, the unmistakable yellow tint of hepatitis.

"Is this a relapse? How did I get it again?" I asked Dr. Kapita the next day.

"It's hepatitis C, for sure," he said, looking at my test results. "I doubt that it's a relapse. Somehow, you contracted it again. You'll need to isolate yourself until your tests come back normal."

I thought of that old saying that there are no atheists in foxholes. I hadn't believed in a Supreme Being since I was thirteen, but now I prayed, begging God to let me live to see my children grow up. This time, I found it scarier than I had eleven years before during the first hepatitis diagnosis, after my operation. Our house fell silent as we discouraged visitors. Jackson traveled to Luozi less often and didn't go out in the evenings. He sent Wakengo and Mena to talk to me for a few minutes every day. I hardly left the bedroom. Every week or two Dr. Kapita repeated the blood tests and did an ultrasound. At first there was no change, and I began to fear I would not recover. People died from hepatitis in Zaire. I didn't tell my parents about my illness until Christmas when I had almost recovered. I didn't see the point of worrying them when they couldn't do anything about it. I didn't feel particularly sick, and I spent my time reading all the fantasy books Kiame had left behind when he left for college. Fantasy is not my favorite genre, but at least it distracted me until my lab tests returned to normal in January. I never thought I'd be so grateful for Marion Zimmer Bradley's Darkover Series.

I felt trapped in my unhappy marriage, and Jackson and I were sinking financially, even if he refused to acknowledge it.

Chapter 26
Beginning of the End

In late 1989, Zaire defaulted on loans from Belgium. The same year, the World Bank failed in a final attempt to impose financial discipline on Mobutu's government. Within a few months, Belgium and the US imposed sanctions against Mobutu, citing financial mismanagement in addition to human rights abuses and corruption that enabled Mobutu to amass a fortune outside the country. The truth was, with the Cold War in decline, the US, France and Belgium simply no longer needed Mobutu. Western governments didn't suddenly discover Mobutu's crimes—they had known about them long before and even colluded in many of them. During the Cold War, though, with an eye on Zaire's reserves of uranium and cobalt, the Western powers closed their eyes because of their fear that the Russians and Chinese would move in and grab those minerals.

Political instability increased as the economy collapsed. The army opened fire on students demonstrating against Mobutu's rcgime, killing at least eight in Kinshasa and more than twenty in Lubumbashi. The universities closed for several months. As the opposition became more vocal, repression tightened. Inflation increased, and the buying power of the population plummeted. The political opposition, led by Etienne Tshisekedi, grew stronger within the country and abroad. Tshisekedi lived only a few blocks from us, and we learned to avoid driving by his house. Traffic clustered around it, and everyone knew that Mobutu's security services watched who came and went from there.

Under pressure from Western governments, Mobutu agreed to a new multi-party system and to a National Conference that his opponents had long demanded. His announcement briefly dominated the news in April 1990, before our planned vacation in the US. Open critiques of the government and Mobutu surfaced in the press for the first time, and the people saw a glimmer of hope that they might dethrone him. But despite Mobutu's announcement, he actively undermined the opposition whenever he could. That resulted in more demonstrations, protests and strikes, all suppressed by the army, which by then had taken over most police functions in Kinshasa. That was the situation when we came back from the US in August of 1990. The slightest incident—a theft, an accident—could precipitate a riot. Stopped in traffic on the way home from the Belgian school one day, we could hear shouting and saw a cluster of people on the street a hundred yards ahead. Without a word, the driver made a U-turn and drove in the opposite direction. Suddenly such incidents happened anywhere, any time. I stopped driving myself any distance greater than a few blocks from home. The drivers knew much better than I did what to do in an emergency.

I went back to teaching at USIA and worked for the Center on the side, writing grants and publishing books. In December, a job opened at the US Agency for International Development as an office manager. The hepatitis had almost cleared up, but before I heard back from AID on my application, I came down with malaria again. As soon as I knew I had the job, I went in to negotiate my salary with the Human Resources manager, even though I still had a fever. He was also recovering from malaria, and we had a strangely desultory interview, neither of us able to muster any energy. I became Office Manager for the Development Department of USAID, which included the scholarship program—the one that sponsored my English students—and a couple of other projects, each run by a diplomat. Mike Swanson supervised all three projects. His wife worked at USIA, and we got along well. A senior Zairian employee named Makiadi ran the scholarship program, with three subordinates. His job was to assist the candidates with their tickets and other documents, take them to the Consular Office next door to get their visas, and follow up if any other documents were needed. This involved "walking" papers from one part of the Embassy to another to get them approved and submitted to the State Department for the student visa and getting various shots and medical tests, including an HIV test. No one who tested positive for HIV could get a visa.

It didn't take me long to figure out that Makiadi had to be constantly pushed by his subordinates to get his work done because he spent much of his time roaming the building, stopping to chat with other employees. He left his reading glasses in the center of his desk to show that he was in the office. Then in his fifties, Makiadi had worked for AID for years, and age garners respect among Zairians. I soon saw that he suffered from alcoholism and regularly disappeared on binges, often for days at a time, much like my old Peace Corps colleague, Maurice. Mike, my boss, said only, "Do what you can." To be fair, some of the American diplomats didn't work all that hard, either, but their deficiencies just weren't so obvious as Makiadi's.

Soon after I started work at AID, a new director arrived and took aim at Makiadi, about whom he had received complaints. Stevens, the new director, told Mike to fire Makiadi. When Mike refused ("He has eight children," Mike said), Stevens transferred Mike to Ouagadougou in Burkina Faso—an undesirable posting even before it became a target of Islamic terrorists. Mike's wife needed an eye operation, and the only safe place in Africa to get the surgery was in South Africa, so he asked for a transfer to Botswana instead. Stevens refused. These maneuvers took months, so when I left for vacation in July of 1991, Mike was still there.

That year I took Wakengo and Mena to visit my parents and stopped in Switzerland to stay with a friend. It was a tremendous relief to be away from the chaos of Kinshasa. Every few days I called Mike to find out if anything had happened. It just didn't seem possible that the place could hold together much longer. We all knew big trouble lay ahead, and I secretly hoped it would erupt while we were out of the country. If it did, I would have a good excuse not to go back. Jackson didn't know I had already decided to leave at the end of the next school year, in June of 1992. Wakengo would have finished high school, and I planned to take him to college in the US, as I had Kiame three years before, only this time I'd stay there. Jackson had often said during our many arguments, well before I had any intention of going back to the US, "If you leave, I won't let you take the kids." He never objected to our vacations in the US, though, so my plan for the following summer was to take Mena and not tell anyone in Kinshasa about my plan. I confided only in my sisters and found out much later that Mena had overheard me. She never said a word.

When we hear about political upheaval anywhere in the world, it seems inevitable in retrospect, and we wonder why people didn't get out sooner. In reality, it is not always easy to predict when or how a place like Kinshasa will explode. It can continue in chaos for months or years, and even well-connected foreigners can't just abandon their jobs and businesses because they expect the place to unravel at some unknown time in the future. Back at the USAID office, work was piling up on Makiadi's desk, and no one had seen him for a week. I gathered his subordinates together, and we went through his inbox, sharing the work that they could do, and piling up the rest for Mike to look at. When Makiadi returned the next day and saw that I had worked around him, he became flustered and upset. His subordinates hovered anxiously in the background, but I was ready for him.

"Some of those papers on your desk were there for weeks," I said. "The work has to get done, so if you're not doing it, I'll make sure someone else does."

For a while after that, Makiadi made a great show of getting his work done. A few weeks after I came back from vacation, Mike's transfer came through, and he left for Ouagadougou. The director of another department took over temporarily, and it looked like Makiadi would lose his job within days. As it turned out, Makiadi came out of the whole thing in better shape than Mike, Stevens, or me.

Chapter 27
Flight

I felt the tension in the city as never before. The Embassy issued a short-wave radio to each American employee, even local hires like me, and told us to keep it charged. What exactly led them to take this precaution nobody knew. Afterward, it seemed likely that they had some intelligence about what was going to happen. Or it could have been standard practice for the State Department when they expect a political situation to deteriorate. Outside the USAID office, on a small square of grass between the building and the street, a large army patrol appeared. Nobody could tell us whether this was a form of harassment or an attempt at protection, but we all knew that soldiers sitting around all day with nothing to do spelled trouble. The Zairian employees, especially, took care to avoid them.

One day the driver dropped Mena and Wakengo at my office while he went to run an errand for Jackson. Bored, Mena decided to walk to the European grocery store half a block away. Conscious of the idle soldiery, I told her to wait until I could find someone to walk her there.

"Mom, I can take care of myself!" she said and flounced out before I could stop her. Twenty minutes later, I decided to look for her. She came in crying, just as I reached the door.

"A soldier stopped me," she said.

"What did I tell you? Now do you see why I didn't want you to go alone? What happened?"

"He asked me my name and where I lived."

"You didn't tell him did you?"

"I was afraid. I told him."

It was September 22, 1991.

When I woke up at five thirty the next morning, I didn't hear traffic noise, a bad sign in a time of frequent demonstrations and riots. I turned on the short-wave radio and started to get dressed. Just before seven o'clock the radio sounded an "all call," signaling that an important announcement would follow. It began with the dreaded words of the Marine on duty: "Attention the American community. Attention the American community. Groups of armed military are occupying intersections throughout the city and looting in some areas. Americans are asked to stay home, or if they are already at school or work, to remain there until further notice. Keep your radio charged and inform the Marine post of anything happening in your area."

This is it, I thought. I remembered that Mena had given our address to the soldier who stopped her on the street. I hadn't told Jackson about that. He rushed next door to warn our neighbor, but the man had already left for work. He returned a few minutes later.

"A looter tried to sell me an airplane tire! What would I do with an airplane tire?" he said, incredulous. "Armed soldiers told me to turn back. They want all cars off the road by nine o'clock, or they'll take them."

Our neighbor on the other side, the single mother, knocked on our gate.

"I have a gun, if anything happens," she said. "Just call out, and I'll start shooting."

I filled a plastic barrel with water and checked our supply of kerosene, candles and matches. We had diesel fuel and gasoline in metal containers, stored in the doghouse. From then on, we stayed glued to the radio, tracking the spread of looting in different parts of the city. The downtown area reported shooting and gangs of soldiers and civilian looters in stores and warehouses. That was a shock. Until then, we considered downtown the safest place. The Marine post advised downtown apartment-dwellers to stay away from windows after reports of stray bullets coming through roofs and windows.

In our neighborhood, looting of nearby shops and warehouses went on all day and into the night. Outside the wall around our house, we heard crowds of people running on the street. Over the wall in front of our house, we could see them carrying all kinds of stolen goods on their heads: frozen chickens, powdered milk, cartons of jam, dog food, bags of potatoes. People pushed motorcycles that they didn't know how to start or drive. The son of a friend stopped by to ask if we had a bag for him to use, apparently intending to join the looting. Jackson told him to go home. Eventually we saw stoves and refrigerators floating by atop looters' heads.

Toward evening, the crowd diminished, then started up again after dark. We could hear young voices drunkenly arguing over ownership of their loot. Occasionally we heard gunfire close by when a group of soldiers confiscated loot from civilians. Another "all call" warned us to prepare one small suitcase each in case of evacuation. We started to pack. I wasn't sure what to select from the accumulated possessions of half a lifetime.

We kept the radio on all night, afraid of missing a crucial announcement. Periodically, we heard gunfire, sometimes close by. What we feared most, of course, was that the looters would start on the houses, as they already had in some areas. There would be little to stop them, and I didn't think we could count on the neighbor's gun. We put all the mattresses on the floor. I spent most of the night with Mena, who was frightened by the gunfire and the drunken disputes outside the wall. All night, we heard the rumbling sound of looters rolling fifty-five-gallon drums of kerosene, diesel and gasoline down the street.

The next morning, Tuesday, I made everyone get dressed so that we wouldn't be fleeing in bare feet and pajamas. Now we could see household furnishings going past on people's heads: chairs, tables, sofas, and even toilets, doors and window frames—a clear sign that the mob had begun to loot private houses. The Marines had a "crisis team" of armed policemen that we could summon, but they could only intervene in one place at a time, and looting had escalated.

By noon, French troops had occupied the main airport and the downtown area. Just before noon, one of the Center's employees arrived. He had walked twenty miles through the riots to help us. At his insistence, Jackson went to the office to negotiate with soldiers to protect the building. While he was gone, Jackson missed the next "all call" announcing the evacuation of all foreigners and asking Americans to drive to one of the four "safe havens" in secure areas. Now what? Drive myself, or wait for Jackson to come back? I radioed the Marine post and asked if the road between our house and the Embassy was safe.

"The road is not secure, repeat, not secure. Wait."

I could not have known that French and Belgian troops were fanning out along the road between our neighborhood and the Embassy and elsewhere in the city where foreigners lived, taking control of the major roads. Within an hour, Jackson came back.

"We need to leave now," he said.

"The Embassy said to wait."

He shook his head. "Too dangerous. The looters are close."

We gathered suitcases, some food and bedding and threw it all into the car. We took the beat-up Nissan rather than the Land Rover because it was a less tempting target for carjacking. Two soldiers squeezed in front with Jackson, one with his rifle jutting out the window. With the three of us in the back seat, we headed to Boulevard Lumumba, the main road between downtown and the airport.

Soldiers and civilians, including children, still thronged the boulevard, many carrying loot. The Nissan's horn didn't work, so whenever we couldn't get through the crowd, the armed soldier shot into the air, and everyone scattered. Looters transformed the familiar sleepy, tree-lined streets of our neighborhood into a set for a bad movie. On the other side of the broad boulevard, I could see more crowds and smoke curling up from buildings—and a French Army patrol just arriving. No other Americans lived there, but I knew French and Belgian families who did. Wrecks of cars and trucks partially blocked the road, apparently hijacked by soldiers who didn't know how to drive. Shops and warehouses stood empty, windows broken and doors ripped off their hinges. Smoke rose from a big discount store, and a crowd sifted through mounds of cardboard and paper scattered outside. On one corner, a few soldiers tried to flag us down, but our guard waved them off. The newly opened Mitsubishi agency stood empty, not only of cars but of everything else, including the building's doors and window frames. We passed three other vehicles coming from the opposite direction, one an old Mercedes driven by a clearly terrified Lebanese, the others with soldiers at the wheel, all with armed guards like ours. The soldier in our car called out in Lingala as we passed a gendarmerie.

"How's the road up ahead?"

"It's all right!" they shouted back.

This is bizarre, I thought. *We're getting advice and protection from the same people who started all this—or are we? What factions were at work here?*

Closer to downtown we passed no other vehicles, and I began to get nervous again. In one spot, two vehicles had collided head on and sailed halfway through the wall of a nearby compound. As we arrived at the edge of downtown, I could see the building that housed my office. A shirtless soldier tried to flag us down, but our guard called out, "No room!" and to Jackson, "Don't stop." We debated between the boulevard and the back road that we usually took, unsure which was safer. Our soldier guards voted for the boulevard, so we rolled down the deserted main street. The Swissair office looked like a tornado had hit it. Zairian soldiers guarded a few banks, still intact. These soldiers seemed disciplined. They ignored us. We turned onto the side street that led to the safe haven, a small American Embassy tennis club near the French Embassy and the French high school, now serving as a safe haven for French citizens. Vehicles crowded the narrow side street. At the tennis club, guards watched us closely but said nothing as we unloaded our suitcases. We were not yet safe, maybe, but we felt more secure. People looking lost and dazed wandered around the club.

"I hope I can trust these soldiers," Jackson said. "It seems strange to be doing this. What's to stop them from taking everything I have?"

"Maybe you should stay here," I said.

"I can't. I have to protect the house and the office. I'll try to come back tomorrow."

"Don't, if it looks dangerous. Will you stay in Kinshasa?"

"For a while. I'll see you before you leave."

"How can we know that?"

We couldn't know.

Wakengo and Mena said tearful goodbyes to their father. That night fifteen people slept at the club, some on cushions taken from lounge chairs around the pool, others outside on plastic recliners. More Americans arrived. One woman couldn't stop crying. Soldiers had looted her house before she and her family could get away.

"I know we're lucky they didn't kill us," she said. "It was so scary. I know it's just stuff, but I can't help it."

By morning, all the foreigners except the French and the Americans had already been ferried across the river to Brazzaville. French Army officers told us it was safer than trying to get everyone to the airport outside the city, traveling along a vulnerable road. They evacuated foreigners from small countries first, because their safe havens couldn't handle the number of people who showed up. After that, the French would go, then the Americans. A man from the American Embassy asked me to make a list of all the people awaiting evacuation, with their nationalities and destinations. It gave me something to do. One Lebanese businessman said his family would go, but he was staying in Kinshasa. I looked at him in surprise.

"I can't leave," hc said. "I have diamonds in the bank vault."

A young American couple who lived in an apartment building behind the tennis club noticed Wakengo and Mena sleeping by the pool and offered to house and feed us, so we moved into their apartment to wait. It was such a relief. Two days later, we boarded a bus that took us to the ferry dock ten minutes away. There we waited for an earlier group of West Africans to be ferried across. A shouting match between a diplomat and a port official delayed their departure. The port official probably wanted money, but the diplomat won that time. The Lebanese businessman offered me his satellite phone to call my parents. No one answered, so I had to leave a message. The Embassy distributed MREs—Meal Ready to Eat—the same as those provided to combat troops, but we had no water. The businessman made a phone call, and twenty minutes later a big black Mercedes pulled up. Its driver unloaded crates of orange Fanta and passed out bottles to everyone. We sat in the sun for another two hours before boarding the ferry.

From the top deck, we watched the familiar skyline of Kinshasa recede.

"Look at that column of smoke!" I said. "There, behind the Sozacom building. What could it be?"

"Mom," said Wakengo wearily, "you'll never know. And what can you do about it?"

At the dock in Brazzaville, we boarded a bus bound for the American Embassy. The road lined with flowering bushes wound along the Zaire River, a beautiful drive no one on the bus could appreciate that day. We had never been to Brazzaville. Wakengo and Mena just gazed at the city in silence. Behind me a small boy said, "Isn't Kinshasa pretty? Is Daddy over there? I miss Daddy." The young mother said, "Yes, Daddy is there. He'll come later." That meant her husband had been designated an "essential employee" of the Embassy. She had to be worried. Jackson could have come with us, but he chose to stay. The bus turned away from the river, and we rode through a neighborhood of old colonial-style bungalows, much like our house in Kinshasa. Here they still had the old-style low walls made of open bricks. In Kinshasa, high brick walls topped by broken glass had replaced those simple walls years before. It was a relief to escape the riots. It wasn't as though I wanted to stay in Zaire—I just didn't want to go to the US. And I wanted Zaire to be livable again. I wanted to believe once again that we could improve people's lives, the goal Jackson and I and our friends shared. But I knew that dream was dead for me now. I would never come back to Kinshasa.

Under a tent set up in the well-tended Embassy garden, evacuees picked at snacks laid out on tables, sitting on folding chairs and staring into space. The Embassy here was much smaller than the one in Kinshasa. An official called us in one by one to get a signature promising to repay the US Government the cost of our airfare. Who knew that when you heard about the US Government evacuating Americans from a faraway trouble spot, they had to pay their own way? The US Government pays only for its own diplomats, not for local hires like me. All of us non-diplomats promised to reimburse the US Treasury for the cost of our evacuation—for us, six thousand dollars, considerably more than we normally paid for a commercial flight.

The bus made several trips to the airport—there were that many of us—so while we waited we wandered over the lawn with its clipped grass, not hungry for the food laid out for us, hearing the tropical birds sing for the last time, wrapped in that peculiar tropical humidity, heavy as a warm bath.

Our group boarded the bus last, and that made me nervous. Daylight started to fade, and it would take at least half an hour to get to the airport, assuming the soldiers didn't stop us at road-blocks. Since the bus was making its fourth trip, though, the soldiers waved it through without the usual wrangling. Military aircraft painted in camouflage sat scattered around the airfield. The bus drove us so far away from the main passenger terminal that I couldn't even see it and dropped us twenty feet from a 747. Passport control consisted of an American sitting at a folding table at the bottom of a rickety mobile stairway. Inside the plane, the heat was worse than outside, and faces glistened with sweat. I realized how lucky we were to board last and felt sorry for the people who had to sit in the airless heat all afternoon. The plane started to taxi as soon as we had fastened our seat belts.

I had no chance to say goodbye to people I'd known and lived with for twenty years. I thought about the nightmares I had before we left Switzerland and how eerily they foreshadowed the riots and the evacuation. It was no surprise that Jackson chose to stay. For him, running the Center was a bigger priority than being with us. I knew him so well. The Center's work was important to me, too, but not more important than the welfare of my children. I shook off thoughts of the unfinished work I left behind. In Embassy jargon, my plan to leave at the end of the school year was OBE—Overtaken By Events. Our life with Jackson in Zaire was over.

Epilogue

A year after we left Zaire, Mike Swanson wrote me that he had retired from the Foreign Service, moved his family to his hometown in Nebraska and started a second career working for the American Refugee Service. We talked about former colleagues.

"Did Makiadi get fired?" I asked.

He laughed. "The whole office closed down, and Makiadi was there until the end. Stevens is still sitting in DC without a posting, fuming."

"So do you think God was on your side?" I asked, knowing Mike was an observant Catholic.

"It did work out better for Makiadi and me, didn't it?"

I decided to join my parents in Minnesota instead of settling in Chicago, partly because of its lower cost of living, and partly because I thought Mena and Wakengo would benefit from their grandparents' support. All that was more than thirty years ago.

Recently, Wakengo told me that before we left Kinshasa he had asked Jackson if he could stay with him.

"No, you have to take care of your mother," Jackson had said. "Anyway, your school will be closed."

Today Kiame, Wakengo and Mena are all successful adults with children of their own. Jackson still lives in Zaire. Kiame has visited him several times, once with Wakengo, but Mena has not seen her father in many years.

Family photo, Northfield, MN, 1993. Back row, left to right: Kiame, Wakengo, Mena. Front row: Jackson and me.

In August of 2021 Kiame convinced me to travel to Zaire with him and his college-age daughter Laura.

"Those people aren't going to live forever," he said. "This may be your last chance."

I won't live forever, either, so with considerable anxiety, in the middle of the Covid–19 pandemic, I flew to Kinshasa. Jackson and his wife Mama Angel graciously agreed to host the three of us in their house on the western outskirts of Kinshasa. Mama Angel is the daughter of a well-known pastor. Her brother, an ophthalmologist, was one of my brightest students in 1972. She is probably in her mid-fifties, well-educated and capable. I was happy to see that Jackson had someone to look after him, and equally glad it wasn't me.

Jackson last visited the US in 1997 when Kiame graduated from medical school. I had obtained a no-fault divorce in 2000. Wakengo went to see his father when Jackson was a visiting professor in Cameroon in 2004, and all three of the children saw him for a weekend when he made a brief trip to Canada in 2005. They met Mama Angel there for the first time. Jackson said or did something that caused Wakengo to go home early. Wakengo once said, "I'll talk to him like a son when he acts like a father." I knew what he meant. Mena talks to him when he calls. I encouraged Wakengo and Mena to stay in contact with him, because I knew that failing to reconcile with an aging parent, no matter what the cause of the dispute, can cause enormous pain. Several years ago, the three of them planned to go together to visit him, but Jackson advised them to postpone the trip for reasons of his own. Then Covid intervened.

At eighty, Jackson seemed much the same as he did thirty years before and remains in remarkably good health. The situation should have felt awkward, but somehow it didn't. It was like meeting an old acquaintance I'd somehow lost touch with. Kiame seemed less like our son than an honored guest. At meals, Jackson focused on Laura, engaging her in conversation, making sure he explained parts of the conversation that she might not understand. He was always good with young people. Only occasionally did he make a comment that made me bite my tongue, and then I recalled the daily conflicts in the last years of our marriage. I was determined not to get into arguments with him on that trip. In Kongo culture, social interactions tend to be formal, which means that people think twice before they speak and stay silent about old grievances. Jackson continues to write books about Kongo culture and Zairian history, now published through Harmattan in France. He no longer drives and uses a part-time driver on the rare occasions when he leaves his compound. The University of Luozi has been a success, and probably his greatest achievement. When I left in 1991, he had obtained permission to use the land, and with Ronsard's help, began to plant trees around the perimeter of the property. I helped write the grant proposals but had left before construction began. Created to train rural development agents, it now also trains students in environmental science, computer science and health sciences. The Lab Tech program has trained a significant number of the lab technicians now working in the Kongo Central region and even in the neighboring country of Congo–Brazzaville.

Library at the Université Libre de Luozi.

Jackson and Mama Angel formally adopted two of Mama Angel's nieces, and a third niece also lived with them, helping with cooking and errands. Two were university students and one had just graduated from high school. A young man named André also stayed there and helped with any technical issues. Running a household in Zaire, especially for older people, requires many types of expert assistance and labor. Laura and I shared a room with a window onto the back courtyard, where the nieces did some of the cooking. On the other side of the courtyard were several rooms where André and any other short-term visitors stayed. The driver stayed overnight when he was needed early the next morning, or when it was too late for him to get home by public transportation. Often we could hear songs and prayers from a nearby church service. I went to sleep with the sounds of the young people laughing and chatting as they finished their work or just socialized. I realized how much I missed that communal life, how much more natural and reassuring it felt than the isolated silence of my Boston apartment. Laura was rather reserved, but the nieces drew her into their group, and I could hear them laughing together. She spoke French well, considering that she studied it for only two years in high school. Laura last visited Congo when she was only eleven, and she laughed at how differently she saw everything on this trip. Always curious, Laura appreciated getting to know the African side of her heritage.

A few days after our arrival, Jackson and Mama Angel hosted a family party in the courtyard of their home. About a hundred people attended, including clan members, in-laws and friends. Kiame warned me I would have to make a speech, so I wrote it in Kikongo, and Jackson proofread it. Jackson made a short speech also, and then there was feasting, music and dancing. When I started to dance with Céline, people came and placed money on my head, a very old Kongo tradition of honoring a dancing old person.

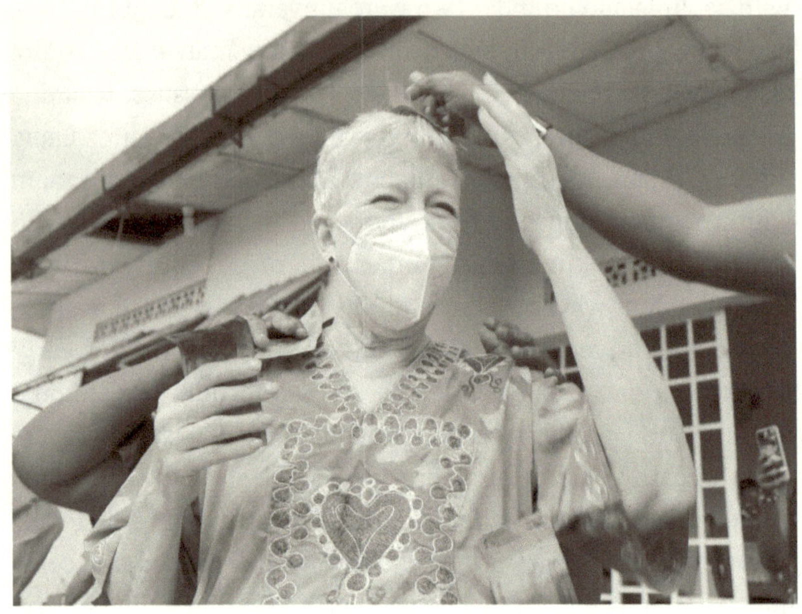

People place money on the heads of old people when they dance at a wedding or other gathering.

It was bittersweet, seeing those I knew and had not seen for thirty years, and meeting all those born into the clan since I left, especially with the knowledge that I might never see some of them again. I appreciated seeing Jackson's brother Ronsard, and his sisters Rachel, Suzanne and Céline, as well as their children, grandchildren and great-grandchildren. Ronsard's daughter, now a physician, is named after me and is married and has a toddler. Rachel and Suzanne were now in their eighties. Eli, Suzanne's son, accompanied us everywhere during our stay and served as our fixer. Of all the family members, I was closest to Ronsard, and so was Kiame, who had spent a lot of time with him before we moved to Geneva. Ronsard survived throat cancer about fifteen years ago, thanks to treatment in South Africa that Jackson paid for, but he still had residual health problems from the illness and the radiation treatment. Only one person in the family had COVID, Céline's son-in-law, and although he was in a coma for four days, he made a complete recovery. Covid–19 did not seem to be a serious problem in Kinshasa. Everyone spent most of their time outdoors, so they had less exposure. Also, half the population was under age seventeen, versus age thirty-eight in the US. The elderly live with their families, not congregated in nursing homes. There were few immuno-compromised people, because people with those conditions rarely survived early childhood even before the pandemic.

When I left in 1991, Kinshasa had 3.5 million inhabitants. Now it has 15 million, and the infrastructure has not kept pace with the needs of this vast increase, which is partly due to migration from the rural areas and partly to natural increase. The country has one of the highest birth rates in the world. An average Zairian family has 6.6 children (5.4 in Kinshasa), vs. 1.93 per family in the US. The infant mortality rate is also high, but a large majority of children reach adulthood. Traffic is so heavy that it took us twice as long to get across town as it did thirty years ago. Only the central neighborhoods of the city have somewhat reliable twenty-four-hour running water and electricity, although work is underway to expand the power station at Zongo Falls, which provides most of Kinshasa's electricity. Residents in the rest of the city must deal with unofficial rolling blackouts and low water pressure. In the area where we stayed, we usually had electricity only from about five o'clock in the evening to seven o'clock the next morning. A permanent smoky haze hangs over the city because most cooking is still done on charcoal fires.

The enormous market for charcoal has also severely depleted the little remaining forest in the regions near Kinshasa. We also saw trees that had been logged from the rain forests of Eastern and Northern Zaire, some six feet in diameter, on trucks heading for the port. The volume of the Zaire River is shrinking as deforestation advances. The deterioration of the natural environment will no doubt be the country's biggest problem in the future. I have to wonder how people will cook their food when the forests are completely gone.

The country held a presidential election in 2018, and the outgoing president remained in the country afterward, the first one to do so since Mobuto deposed President Kasavubu in a 1965 coup d'état and placed him under house arrest. The armed soldiery that constantly harassed the population during the Mobutu era has disappeared, and with it the feeling of constant tension that used to permeate the city. Gendarmes direct traffic at major intersections, most of them unarmed. We saw one beleaguered gendarme trying to unsnarl traffic using a toy light saber. Gasoline and diesel are now easily available, unlike during the Mobutu years, when periodic shortages of foreign exchange resulted in long lines at fuel stations. Nearly everyone has a cell phone. I paid my cell phone carrier a minimal amount to get unlimited data through a French affiliate while I was there, and I had good reception even when we traveled to Kimpese, because cell phone signals bounce off satellites, not cell towers. After thirty years of cranking out university graduates, the country at last has enough trained professionals to staff schools, clinics and hospitals. We visited our old friend Dr. Kapita, now in his eighties, who still runs a clinic, now with his daughter. She has a busy obstetrics practice. Dr. Kapita also built a clinic in his village near Luozi and finances its operations. He is the President of the University of Luozi's Board of Directors.

We visited Zongo Falls, partly to give Laura a break from the meetings with relatives and friends that she might find tedious. The falls are a local tourist attraction as well as the site of an important hydroelectric station. The road into the Kongo Central region, now a toll road, is well-maintained. We passed several road crews shoring it up against the ever-present threat of erosion. The smaller local roads were not as well maintained, so getting to Zongo is a challenge, but worth the effort. The falls are spectacular and still pristine. Our hotel supplied guides to take us there, and after they discovered that I spoke Kikongo, they refused to accept any gratuity.

The towns and cities along the main road to Kimpese have grown so that there is now little open country between them. I hardly recognized Kimpese. The airfield of the Missionary Aviation Fellowship no longer exists, and construction now crowds the space that used to separate it from the entrance to the hospital. We stayed overnight at the hospital's Guest House which has expanded since I left. It now has a large dining area, kitchen, offices and several rooms and suites. Laura and I stayed in a comfortable suite with two bedrooms and a lounge with a mini fridge and a television. We had a peek at the older, original rooms, where Kiame and I stayed when we had malaria in 1973, and where Wakengo was born in 1974. Those rooms seemed so luxurious then, but now they seem small and ordinary. We visited Dr. Mahema, Mama Angel's brother, whose house overlooks the countryside beyond the hospital grounds. That area used to be covered with trees. The woods have all disappeared, leaving only bare savannah dotted with fields and a few palm trees. The hospital grounds look much the same. There are a few new buildings around the edges of the property, mostly built with foreign aid, but the central buildings housing the operating rooms, clinics, laboratories and wards were built in the 1950s and 1960s and are showing their age.

Kiame met with the doctors there while Laura and I visited two of my old friends who live in Kimpese: Suzanne, José Dianzungu's widow; and Christine, Jean Balekita's widow, who so kindly befriended me when we lived in Sundi Lutete. José died in 2020, and it has been hard for Suzanne. I was glad that I was able to see José and Suzanne in the US when they came for a grandchild's high school graduation a few years before. Three of their children live in the States; one lives in Belgium, and all of them visit regularly. Christine's oldest son is also in the States; the younger son is an orthodontist in Kinshasa. Christine spent most of her life in the countryside of Manianga as principal of several primary schools. Both women moved to Kimpese in recent years, and both occupy well-built, comfortable houses.

Me, Suzanne Dianzungu and Christine Muniangu, Kimpese 2021.

Unlike Luozi and the villages in Manianga, Kimpese has twenty-four-hour water and electricity, and has sprawled across the landscape like other smaller cities. As in many other areas of the world, more and more people have left the countryside to live in these cities. Even if making a living is difficult, and the unemployment rate high, the proximity of schools, hospitals and markets make the city a logical choice. At least in the city, young people can hope to find work other than tilling the fields with hand tools.

On the way back to Kinshasa on the main road, we stopped at a toll station. We waited on the side of the road while Eli, our fixer, went to pay the toll. A soldier approached the car. He was alone, unlike the old days when groups of armed soldiers manned roadblocks all along the main road, stopping cars and shaking down drivers to let them pass. All of that had disappeared, but now here was this soldier asking for our papers.

Our unflappable driver asked with contempt, "Why do you want to see their papers? That's not your job."

That could have earned him a beating in the old days. When the soldier insisted, the driver said, "Those two are Zairian. She's the only foreigner."

Strictly speaking, that was true, but Kiame and Laura were not traveling with Congolese papers.

"Passport," said the soldier.

I handed it to the driver, who slowly handed it to the soldier with a hostile glare.

Meanwhile a small crowd began to gather behind the soldier, and when he took the passport, they began to murmur and edged closer, nearly surrounding him. The soldier began to get visibly nervous. Naturally, he wanted money, but he couldn't very well get aggressive in the middle of a hostile crowd. He handed the passport back and said, "Can't you give me just a small tip?"

I'd never seen a soldier beg for a bribe.
"No," said the driver.
Just then Eli came back, and we drove off.

* * *

Through all the changes Zaire has seen since 1991, what most impressed me was the continued strength of the clan system and the degree of sacrifice people are willing to make for the benefit of the clan. Jackson and Mama Angel pay the school fees of at least four young people. Jackson's sister Céline allows a developmentally disabled niece to live rent-free in a house she could easily rent for additional income.

Kimpianga Mahaniah (Jackson) at his 84th birthday party, July 2025.

Every expatriate Zairian I know sends money to family members back home. Kiame, Wakengo and Mena have all contributed to school fees for family members and other projects. Kiame is working with other Zairian expatriates to create a non-profit organization devoted to ensuring the future of the University of Luozi. Time and money could not be better spent.

Kiame's son Kieto, on the south bank of the Congo River, 2022.

I fell in love with Jackson in part because of his ideals and sense of mission. In the year before our marriage, I thought only about our love and hope for our future in Zaire, ignoring obvious warning signs. In 1968, I did not acknowledge, even to myself, how much my disillusionment with my own country influenced my decision. At first the beauty of Kongo culture reinforced my conviction that I had made the right choice, and my attraction to other cultures and languages made my adjustment easier, but I adjusted only partially and reluctantly to African marriage. It would have been difficult to sustain a Western-style marriage even if Jackson had been committed to it, and he was not. Clan pressures pushed everyone toward a different model, where birth family was all-important, and companionship in marriage was either secondary or completely absent. That time-tested model worked well for women who grew up in it. They could rely on their birth family and clan connections for emotional support, but my socialization was different, and I had no such connections. Even as our marriage steadily eroded, Zaire in those decades proved in many ways to be a pretty good place to raise children, but by the time we left Geneva in 1987, all that remained between Jackson and me was that early idealism and sense of mission.

A Brief History of the Democratic Republic of Congo

The Democratic Republic of Congo has been inhabited for an estimated fifty thousand years, originally by Mbuti and Twa forest people. The forest people lived in small bands of hunters and gatherers and left little if any material culture behind. Later, the Bantu savannah people migrated from further north. They remain the principal population today. When the Portuguese arrived at the mouth of the Zaire River in 1493, the Kingdom of Kongo was already a large, centralized state, with a significant trade network dealing in metals, raffia, ivory, pottery and slaves. At its height, it covered parts of what is now the Republic of Congo, the Democratic Republic of Congo, Cabinda and Angola. Though weakened, the Kingdom of Kongo survived until the late 19th century.

At the Conference of Berlin in 1885, the European nations led by King Leopold of Belgium divided Africa amongst themselves and split the Kongo Kingdom into three parts, ruled by Belgium, France and Portugal. King Leopold of Belgium took over what is now the Democratic Republic of Congo to create the Congo Free State. Leopold's brutal exploitation of the population in extracting rubber and ivory is well known. Atrocities and disease brought by Europeans caused the deaths of an estimated ten million people. The resulting international scandal forced the Belgian Government to take over the country as a colonial state in 1908.

Belgium continued to exploit Congo's resources, especially mining. Congo has significant reserves of copper, gold, tin, diamonds, cobalt and other minerals. Responding to criticism of Leopold's abuses, Belgium invited the Catholic Church to help establish schools, hospitals, and clinics. The colonial State built roads and railroads. Even with strong military intervention, though, Belgium never entirely subdued the eastern part of the country. Under pressure from the rest of the world, Belgium granted political independence to Congo in 1960 with no planning or preparation. The result was years of political upheaval and rebellions, culminating in Lumumba's murder in 1961 and a coup d'état in 1965 that propelled Mobutu to power. Western powers encouraged Mobutu, believing him to be their bulwark against communism in Central Africa. They also expected him to bring the fractious regions into line while preserving Western dominance over the Congo's vast resources. Education, especially for women, advanced significantly during Mobutu's reign. Some writers have deemed the national identity as Mobutu's principal accomplishment. Overall, though, this was a period of corruption and decay. The West, particularly the US, supported Mobutu for many years, despite early indications of Mobutu's incompetence and corruption. They feared Russia and China would move in if the country broke apart. With the decline of the Cold War, though, the Western powers no longer needed Mobutu. Western powers did not intervene when Laurent Kabila's troops took over Kinshasa in 1997, forcing Mobutu to flee the country. Rwanda and Uganda invaded Eastern Congo, and the ensuing war took an estimated 2.5 million lives. Peace treaties were signed in 1999, and rebel leaders were included in an interim government. Joseph Kabila took over the presidency in 2001, when his father was assassinated by a bodyguard. He won the 2006 election, but fighting resumed and the UN authorized additional peacekeeping troops in 2008 and again in 2013 in another unsuccessful attempt to disarm rebels in the East.

The government postponed the 2016 elections after government troops killed dozens of people protesting new electoral laws, claiming they were intended to keep Kabila in power. Elections finally took place in 2018, under a deal negotiated between Kabila and his political opponents. Felix Tshisekedi, son of long-time opposition leader Etienne Tshisekedi, won the election. Kabila still lives in Kinshasa, the first president to oversee a peaceful transition of power. As of March 2026, UN peacekeeping troops remain in eastern Congo as fighting and displacement of civilians continue.

Acknowledgements

Most of all I want to thank my children Kiame, Wakengo and Mena for their support and encouragement. Thanks also to my cousin Tobe for inspiring me with his experience as a writer, and to my cousin Kaye, who told me an important family secret.

For several years, only Ian Graham Leask believed I could write. His classes motivated me to keep writing. His expert advice as Editor of Calumet Editions has been indispensable. I owe thanks to Lissa Franz, whose Memoir Class first inspired me to write a memoir. Calumet Editions' publishing team offered valuable and patient guidance. Many thanks to Penny, Simona, Dawny, Joyce C, Joyce R, Scott and others, who provided valuable critiques on parts of this memoir. The members of the Write for Your Life group, too, have offered help and encouragement for almost ten years, including Cathy, Karen, Judy, Barbara D, Barbara P., Phyllis, Elli, and Margaret.

Thanks also to Chuck Adams for his advice, and to Janet Cooke, who gave me insightful comments in the last stages of editing.

About the Author

Sandra Chambers Mahaniah left her Chicago home at eighteen and has been a nomad ever since. With a lifelong passion for writing she has so far published articles in local newspapers and journals, but was inspired by writing classes in Minneapolis and Boston to reflect on her turbulent and constantly changing life. Raising three children within a tumultuous marriage amid the chaos of Zaire (now Democratic Republic of Congo), she persevered as editor and grant writer for a nonprofit publishing house, as an office manager for USAID and as an ESL teacher. Since returning to the US, she has worked in health care administration, most recently as a project manager. Unable to sit still, she is currently emerging from her third retirement.

www.ingramcontent.com/pod-product-compliance
Lightning Source LLC
LaVergne TN
LVHW041112080826
845145LV00007B/1785

* 9 7 8 1 9 6 2 8 3 4 7 5 9 *